The Great Athanasius

The Great Athanasius

An Introduction to His Life and Work

John R. Tyson

CASCADE *Books* · Eugene, Oregon

THE GREAT ATHANASIUS
An Introduction to His Life and Work

Cascade Books
An Imprint of Wipf and Stock Publishers
199 W. 8th Ave., Suite 3
Eugene, OR 97401

www.wipfandstock.com

PAPERBACK ISBN: 978-1-62564-752-8
HARDCOVER ISBN: 978-1-4982-8866-8
EBOOK ISBN: 978-1-5326-1403-3

Cataloguing-in-Publication data:

Names: Tyson, John R.

Title: The great Athanasius : an introduction to his life and work / John R. Tyson.

Description: Eugene, OR : Cascade Books, 2017 | Includes bibliographical references and index.

Identifiers: ISBN 978-1-62564-752-8 (paperback) | ISBN 978-1-4982-8866-8 (hardcover) | ISBN 978-1-5326-1403-3 (ebook)

Subjects: LSCH: Athanasius, Saint, Patriarch of Alexandria, –373. | Christian saints—Egypt—Alexandria—Biography. | Theology, Doctrinal—History —Early church, ca. 30–600.

Classification: BR1720.A7 T97 2017 (print) | BR1720.A7 T97 (ebook)

Manufactured in the U.S.A.   04/05/17

Contents

Preface

I first embarked upon this project because Athanasius was a historical figure I had long studied, taught about and admired over several decades of professional work. Since I was first introduced to the life and work of Athanasius by Dr. James H. Pain, of the Graduate School at Drew University, I have found him to be a fascinating and formative figure. It was my opinion that Athanasius is not as well known among contemporary Christians as he deserves to be known. Nor was I, at that time, satisfied that I knew very much about him myself. So the present project had its inception in my desire to know more about Athanasius for myself and for others, so that his huge contributions to Christian faith and theology might be better known, appreciated, and understood.

It is my opinion that this fourth-century African bishop, pastor, and theologian remains an important partner in dialogue for contemporary Christians as we struggle to understand and articulate important theological questions: how shall we speak of the relationship between God the Father and God the Son? What bearing does the Incarnation of the Word of God have upon our understanding of salvation? What is the true nature of the Person of Jesus Christ? These are perennial questions with which modern Christians must concern themselves, and Athanasius points a constructive way forward in these matters and many others.

There are always quite a lot of people to thank when a project like this comes to a close. First on my list is my family, who had to put up with my absence from their lives more often than was desirable for all of us. I also want to thank Mr. Ted Lewis of Wipf and Stock Publishers for first suggesting this project. My gratitude extends also to Mr. Charlie Collier, and to Wipf and Stock Publishers, for their great patience in waiting for me to complete this manuscript. It took a lot longer than I originally planned. I would also like to thank my friends and academic colleagues Dr. Melanie Duguid-May, John Price Crozer Professor of Theology at Colgate Rochester Crozer Divinity School, in Rochester, New York, and Dr. David Kim, Arthur J. Gosnell Associate Professor of Christian Social Ethics (also at CRCDS), for their kind willingness to read this manuscript in its embryonic form. I am deeply indebted to them, and to my former student Mr. Charles Meeks, PhD candidate at Wycliffe College, University of Toronto, for their willingness to supply me with helpful suggestions for improvement. Obviously, the fault for any shortcomings in this work belongs to me alone. I also want to thank Ms. Marge Nead, Librarian at CRCDS, for her kind help in locating many of the resources used to produce this volume.

This book is gratefully dedicated to Dr. James H. Pain, who first got me started on this inquiry so many years ago.

Introduction

"The great Athanasius" was a title first applied to Athanasius of Alexandria (296–373) by the Cappadocian bishop Gregory Nazianzen (330–90) in a funeral oration given in 380, seven years after the Alexandrian's death.[1] By the time the Christian chronicler Theodoret (393–458?) was writing his *Ecclesiastical History* (between 441 and 449), "holy," "divine," and "great" had become standard descriptions of Athanasius.[2] For both men Athanasius was a hero of the faith and profound shaper of the Christian tradition. In Gregory's mind, Athanasius was a great and holy man, "a pillar of the church," who had withstood the onslaught of theological enemies in church and state in order to ensure the success of the theology enshrined in the Nicene Creed.[3] Most especially, Athanasius was a champion of the full divinity and true humanity of Jesus Christ at a time when both of those affirmations were open questions for the Christian church. In the first half of the fourth century, Christian theology was still quite fluid, even with respect to the main doctrines; Athanasius was one of the chief architects and most persistent defenders of what would come to be accepted as the standard and orthodox understanding of the relationship of God the Father and God the Son. His writings on the Holy Spirit also helped pave the way for a truly full Trinitarian theology, and his use of and passion for Holy Scripture contributed significantly to the closing of the New Testament canon. Athanasius is a theologian to be acknowledged and

---

1. Gregory Nazianzen, *Oration* 21, in *A Select Library of Nicene and Post-Nicene Fathers of the Christian Church*, second series, vol. VII, *Cyril of Jerusalem and Gregory Nazianzen* (reprint, Grand Rapids: Eerdmans, 1970) 269–80. Hereafter this series will be cited as *NPNF*.

2. Theodoret, *Ecclesiastial History*, *NPNF*, vol. III, 33–159.

3. Gregory Nazianzen, *Oration* 21.26, *NPNF*, vol. VII, 276.

admired every time the Christian church affirms the Nicene Creed, and he deserves to be known and remembered everywhere and every time that the Nicene Creed is esteemed as an apt summary of the Christian faith.

The twenty-first-century reader, for whom Athanasius may be an unfamiliar figure from the ancient Christian past, owes him a deep debt. Writing at a time when Christian theology was still in its infancy and foundational questions like the relationship of God the Father and God the Son were still openly disputed, Athanasius was one person who pointed a solid and consistent way forward that has provided a lasting and spiritually satisfying solution to that problem. In the days before the great Christian creeds were developed and while Christianity was still a minority religion in the Roman Empire, Athanasius laid many of the theological foundations that would become Christian orthodoxy. As we shall see, his insistence upon the full divinity and equality of God the Father and God the Son would become a cornerstone of Trinitarian theology. His reflections upon the importance of the Incarnation of the Word of God, as well as Christ's true humanity and full deity, would become standards of Christian discourse for nearly two millennia. His solution to the dilemma posed by human sin and God's economy of salvation would become one of the standard formulations of the Christian faith. His insights about the canon of Holy Scripture as well as the Person and Work of the Holy Spirit are equally substantial and epoch-making. Wherever these theological verities are affirmed or explored—even today—the long shadow of Athanasius falls silently across our path.

Gregory of Nazianzus probably knew Athanasius during his own student days in Alexandria (ca. 350),[4] and in his mind Athanasius was a bishop and theologian who epitomized all the great Christian virtues. "In praising Athanasius," he declared, "I shall be praising virtue. To speak of him and to praise virtue are identical, because he had, or, to speak more truly, has embraced virtue in its entirety."[5] There was no question in the Cappadocian's mind that Athanasius was a hero and a treasure to the church whose memory deserved to be cherished and celebrated and whose example should be emulated. He was lavish in his praise of Athanasius's character: "gentle, free from anger, sympathetic, sweet in words, sweeter in disposition; angelic in appearance; more angelic in mind . . ."[6] So extravagant are Gregory's praises

4. Arnold, *Early Episcopal Career*, 93, and Ruether, *Gregory of Nazianzus*, 19–20.

5. Gregory Nazianzen, *Oration* 21.1, *NPNF*, vol. VII, 269.

6. Ibid., 21.9, 271–72.

of Athanasius that R. C. P. Hanson discounts them as reliable sources for his character, describing them instead as an "unrealistic eulogy."[7]

The contemporary, scholarly picture of Athanasius is not as glowingly appreciative as the aforementioned ancient one. There has been a growing awareness that he was a controversial figure in his own day who left a complicated legacy. He was a stalwart defender of the Nicene theology—of that there can be no doubt. Athanasius also was a prolific theological writer and courageous polemicist—in support of that same cause—even under difficult circumstances. He also was archbishop, or patriarch, of Alexandria for forty-six years; of those years, seventeen were spent in exile, suffering for what he considered to be the truth. His courage was never in question. Athanasius was consistently willing to speak truth to power; even as a young and relatively untried bishop, he directly disobeyed Emperor Constantine when he believed that a crucial point of Christian faith and practice was at stake. He routinely withstood the direct orders and plans of Emperor Constantius when he believed him to be motivated by heretical theological concerns. He opposed tyranny and falsehood—even when that prophetic posture put him in great personal peril. And those who sought theological compromises from Athanasius, even in the spirit of political harmony or ecclesiastical unity, generally went away disappointed.

But Athanasius was also among the most polarizing people in the fourth century. He forced everyone within earshot to take sides either for him or against him. If a person was "for" him and the Nicene theology, that person was to be considered "orthodox." But if a person was "against" Athanasius, or his theology, then Athanasius was apt to decry them as an "Arian maniac." Indeed, a close look at those theological controversies of the fourth century, which have come to be known as "the Arian controversy," indicates that the dominating figure throughout that period was not Arius but Athanasius himself.[8] It was he who drew up the battle lines and it was he who often determined the theological terrain upon which that conflict would be fought.

None of Athanasius's fourth-century opponents ever charged him with heresy, but there were plenty of complaints and formal charges about the forceful way he administered his episcopal office. His opponents viewed Athanasius as being tyrannical and ruthless, to the point of using physical intimidation and violence to enforce compliance from theological or

---

7. Hanson, *Christian Doctrine of God*, 241.

8. Behr, *Formation of Christian Theology*, vol. 2, pt. 1, 163.

ecclesiastical dissidents in Alexandria. These formal charges, and the imperial exiles that stemmed from them, have cast a dark cloud over the contemporary assessment of Athanasius's character and legacy. Hence, Maurice Wiles described him as "brutal and unscrupulous,"[9] and Timothy Barnes went so far as to portray the bishop as "a gangster"[10] who was apt to (as it might be said of the Godfather) "make you an offer you couldn't refuse." The ecclesiastical charges against him, including abuse of power and authority, along with sorcery, were so well known in the fourth century that they are even reported by the secular Roman historian Ammianus Marcellinus.[11]

For his part, Athanasius viewed and presented these charges as thinly veiled schemes, on the part of his theological opponents—the Arians and Meletians—to attack him because of his defense of the Nicene theology. Hence, Timothy Barnes reminded his readers, "an impartial historian cannot simply pin his faith on the utter veracity of Athanasius or dismiss the testimony of his enemies without due consideration."[12] Athanasius was vehement in his defense of what became orthodox theology, and fiercely loyal to his friends; he was equally vehement in his polemics against his theological and ecclesiastical opponents, and his forceful approach was more apt to cause conflict than to resolve it. Yet, he was also a profoundly charismatic and spiritual leader capable of inspiring deep loyalty and long-lasting respect; otherwise, as Frances Young pointed out, "his legend could never have developed."[13] Hanson expressed some of this same contemporary ambivalence when he described Athanasius as "an unscrupulous politician" as well as a "genuine theologian" who wrote with "passion and conviction."[14]

Before we delve more deeply into the life and work of "the great Athanasius," a few words must be said about the ancient sources at our disposal. The most obvious place to begin learning about Athanasius is through reading his own writings—of which there are many. The closest one can come to a "critical edition" of Athanasius's works is the incomplete German edition prepared by H. G. Opitz in the mid-1930s. This multivolume set is very difficult to find, and it offers the Greek text, so it is doubly inaccessible

9. Young and Teal, *From Nicaea to Chalcedon*, 71.

10. Barnes, *Athanasius and Constantius*, 230.

11. Ammianus Marcellinus, *Later Roman Empire*, 80.

12. Barnes, *Athanasius and Constantius*, 2.

13 Young and Teal, *From Nicaea to Chalcedon*, 69.

14. Hanson, *Christian Doctrine of God*, 422.

to most contemporary readers.[15] For the current study, I have used the most common English-language collection of Athanasius's writings, *Select Writings and Letters of Athanasius, Bishop of Alexandria*, edited by Archibald Robertson. First published in London in 1892, in the series *Nicene and Post-Nicene Fathers* (NPNF), this work has been reprinted many times and is still available as a reprint edition.[16] This edition contains eighteen major treatises by Athanasius, as well as a robust selection of his letters, including many of the important *Festal Letters*.[17] While the translation is rough and the language archaic at some points, the Robertson edition remains a usable resource that is readily available to the contemporary reader. This collection has been supplemented by several single volumes of Athanasius's sundry works that are currently available. Since one of my goals in offering this introduction is to encourage the reader to encounter "the great Athanasius" in his own writings, I have worked from English-language sources that are readily available. I will also use English-language translations of the titles of his treatises, along with the familiar Latin titles used by scholars.

The writings of Athanasius fall into three general types: treatises, polemics, and letters. These categories are helpful to some degree, but they cannot be viewed as hard-and-fast distinctions. For example, *Against the Gentiles* (*Adversus Gentes*) and *On the Incarnation* (*De incarnatione verbi Dei*) are clearly theological treatises, and they do not attack Arianism, at least directly. But the *History of Arianism* (*Historia Arianorum*), which purports to be a historical treatise, is really a polemic. In a similar way, Athanasius's *Festal Letters*, which appear to be pastoral correspondence for his churches, are often loaded with theological reflection. His *Letters to Serapion* are really treatises on the Holy Spirit, and Athanasius's *Letter to Marcellinus* reads very much like a treatise on biblical interpretation. Hence, there is significant overlap in any facile attempt to categorize his writings.

So strident is our hero in his defense of the Nicene theology, and so vehement are his attacks upon Arianism, that contemporary scholars urge us to view Athanasius's reconstructions of his opponents' theology, as well

15. The Opitz project, taken up by the University of Erlangen in 1996, is gradually moving towards completion. Cf. http://www.fourthcentury.com/index.php/athanasius-werke-contents. ⁺

16. *NPNF*, vol. IV (reprint, Grand Rapids: Eerdmans, 1978).

17. The *Festal Letters* were composed as encyclicals announcing the proper date for the celebration of Easter, which were issued each year Athanasius was patriarch or archbishop of Alexandria. These letters are full of spiritual and theological reflection and give us some indication of the pastoral mind of their author

as the conclusions he draws based on them, with a critical eye. Athanasius often wrote under extreme ecclesiastical and political pressure, defending both his faith and his person from attack; under these circumstances he probably did not present a very objective portrait of his opponents. His "for me or against me" mentality caused him to see conspiracies and Arians where there might have been none, and it allowed for no middle ground between Arianism (as Athanasius defined it) and his own brand of orthodoxy. Many bishops and pastors in the early fourth century found themselves located in precisely that sort of middle ground, and Athanasius's polarizing approach may have forced significant controversies where conversation and compromises sometimes might have been more appropriate. With this in mind, then, we will try to corroborate Athanasius's assessments by consulting other ancient sources—when they are available.

While we have a wealth of writings upon which to draw in order to reconstruct the views and actions of Athanasius, the same cannot be said of his opponent, Arius. The paucity of authentic Arian sources is most certainly due to the fact that his writings were condemned and proscribed at the Council of Nicaea in 325. Sozomen, an early church historian, reported Emperor Constantine as saying, "Whoever should be found secreting his [Arius's] writings and who should not burn them immediately on the accusation, should undergo the penalty of death, and suffer capital punishment."[18] Hence, possessing Arius's writings was extremely dangerous, and most of them were destroyed. Fortunately, several of Arius's letters have been preserved in the writings of early church historians (Theodoret and Socrates). Among the most important of these materials are the *Creed* and *Letter* that Arius sent to his bishop, Alexander of Alexandria, in 320–21; his *Letter to Eusebius of Nicomedia*, from 321–22; and the creed he sent to Emperor Constantine in his attempt to be reconciled to the Church in 333.[19]

Athanasius, who frequently makes point-for-point rebuttals of his opponents' propositions, also unwittingly preserved large blocks of Arius's work. But the use of Athanasius's materials on Arianism creates the additional critical problem of trying to ascertain how fair and accurate Athanasius's presentation of his opponents really was. In fact, the case may be that, as David Gwynn explains it, "Athanasius' definition of 'Arianism' derives from the imposition of his own interpretations upon those he wishes to

---

18. Sozomen, *Church History* I.21, *NPNF*, vol. II, 255.

19. Gwynn, *The Eusebians*, 187. Cf. Williams, *Arius*, ch. 3, "The Nicene Crisis: Documents and Dating."

condemn."[20] At the very least, however, this dilemma makes one cautious about trying to draw a picture of Arius's views solely from the descriptions given by Athanasius. This matter is further complicated by the fact that Athanasius is not entirely consistent in the way he presents Arius's writings. The composition of Arius's main work, the *Thalia*, is a case in point. This important poem and theological manifesto is preserved only in two separate documents of Athanasius, and those two sources present divergent renditions of the text.[21] This has caused Frances Young to conclude, "Reconstruction of the work has proved virtually impossible."[22] David Gwynn, after making a painstaking study of the text and contents of those two treatises, decided in favor of the text of the *Thalia* of *De Synodis* (*On the Synod*).[23] But even this version of the *Thalia* is fragmentary and must be used with caution. The full scope of letters and documents to, from, and about Arius that have survived from antiquity numbers thirty-four; but most of these are fragmentary and are reproduced in writings penned by Arius's opponents.[24]

Six ancient church historians offer us important documents, commentary, and corroborating evidence about Athanasius's life and times. Most of these men wrote after Athanasius and were dependent (to greater or lesser degrees) upon his writings. Three exceptions to this pattern exist; the first, Eusebius, managed to tell the story of Nicaea without even mentioning Athanasius, and Philostorgius—who was an "extreme Arian"—took a contrary point of view.[25] And the secular Roman historian of the period, Ammianus Marcellinus, also mentions Athanasius in a brief but important passage.[26]

Eusebius, bishop of Caesarea (ca. 260–ca. 339), who is also known as Eusebius Pamphilus, was the first major historian of the Christian church. He was personally involved in the "Arian controversy," and he was present at the Council of Nicaea where the Arian option was discussed

20. Gwynn, *Eusebians*, 169.

21. *De Synodis* (*On the Synod*) and *Orationes contra Arianos* (*Orations Against the Arians*).

22. Young and Teal, *From Nicaea to Chalcedon*, 44.

23. Gwynn, *Eusebians*, 189. Cf. Stead, "The Thalia of Arius and the Testimony of Athanasius," 20–38.

24. See the helpful chart and collection of documents at http://www.fourthcentury.com/index.php/urkunde-chart-opitz/.

25. Hanson, *Christian Doctrine of God*, 289.

26. Ammianus Marcellinus, *Later Roman Empire*, 80.

and condemned. His *Ecclesiastial History* traces the development of the church from its inception, through the centuries of horrible persecution, to its arrival at most-favored-religion status under the guidance of the first Christian Roman emperor, Constantine. Eusebius's own role in the events surrounding Arius was somewhat suspect, however, since initially he seemed to have supported Arius, and then he—apparently with some reluctance—signed the Nicene solution against him. His church history is remarkably silent about these events and does not even mention the name of his erstwhile theological opponent, Athanasius. These silences speak nearly as loudly as firsthand information from Eusebius might have, since they show us his theological intent as an author. His *Life of Constantine* provides an interesting window into the opening of the Council of Nicaea, and it also preserved Constantine's opening address to the Council.[27] It must also be said, however, that Eusebius wrote always in support of Constantine and his government. He was thoroughly convinced that God was acting through the first Christianized Roman emperor, and implicitly, perhaps, that the kingdom of God was coming to fruition through him. Eusebius was also equally careful to protect his own historical legacy, and if one were to read his own writings alone, one would never know he equivocated on the Arian question.

Socrates Scholasticus (ca. 380–450) composed the next *Church History* sometime between 438 and 443. A native and resident of the new imperial capital, Constantinople, he was not a member of the clergy. He held no church office. It is generally believed he was a lawyer. He knew of Eusebius's earlier work and wrote consciously to complete it and bring it up to date; hence, Socrates's *Church History* begins with the year 309 and draws to a close at 439. The overlap between his work and that of Eusebius was easily explained by the fact that Socrates found Eusebius's treatment of the Arian controversy woefully inadequate. Socrates's work is very valuable for assessing the period under consideration because of the many primary sources he edited into his own composition; in this he was following the method that Eusebius had used before him. Unlike Eusebius, however, he did not paper over the disputes and schisms within the church, and in fact these controversies became the grist for his writing of church history. Socrates relied heavily upon Athanasius's account of what transpired, and thereby evidenced himself to be an implicit supporter of the Nicene theology.[28] He

27. See *NPNF*, vol. I (reprint, Grand Rapids: Eerdmans, 1976) for these documents.
28. See *NPNF*, vol. II, 1–179, for Socrates's *Church History*.

was also a huge fan of the theology of Origen of Alexandria and might have written, in part, to rehabilitate his hero's tarnished image.[29]

Sozomen was likewise a resident of Constantinople, but unlike Socrates, he was not a native son of the city; he had been born in Bethelia, near Gaza, in Palestine. He arrived in the capital city sometime after 424, and completed his *Church History* in 443. Like Socrates he was not a cleric and was probably a lawyer. His work is clearly dependent upon that of Socrates and draws heavily upon it. In his preface Sozomen tells his reader that he was drawn to write his church history because of the miraculous and positive change that Christianity was having upon the Roman Empire. His history covers the period 325–425 and is another important completion of Eusebius's narrative. Unlike Socrates, who gave large sections of primary source documents, Sozomen often preferred to summarize events and to interject anecdotes, which he claimed came from oral tradition. As compared to Socrates's more documentary and factual account, Sozomen's *Church History*, as Frances Young described it, "gives the impression of being a gossip column rather than a serious history. It is full of anecdotes and biographical details."[30]

Philostorgius (ca. 368–439) was born in Borissus, in Cappadocia (in modern-day Turkey). His church history, which treats the years circa 300–430, was probably composed between 425 and 433. It concerns itself largely with the Arian controversy. Unfortunately, the work survived only in fragmentary form. It must be extracted from two subsequent works that quote it at length: the *Passion of Artemius*, the story of an Arian martyr, and the epitome of Photius (d. 376). Even in this fragmentary form, Philostorgius's work is important for our inquiry because it was written from an Arian perspective and offers a drastically different point of view from the more mainstream reports of Socrates and Sozomen. But the reliability of what he wrote was in question, and Photius considered him to be "a liar, quite capable of writing sheer fantasy."[31] Hence, Philostorgius's work, however interesting, must also be read with a critical eye.

Theodoret of Cyrus (393–ca. 460) was a contemporary of both Socrates and Sozomen. But unlike them, he was both a bishop and a theologian. He wrote many theological works and was a staunch defender of

---

29. Chesnut, *First Christian Histories*, 177–78.

30. Young and Teal, *From Nicaea to Chalcedon*, 33. Cf. *NPNF*, vol. II, 179–427, for Sozomen's *Church History*.

31. Philostorgius, *Church History*, 2.

the Nicene theology. His *Church History*, which was composed sometime between 441 and 449, treats the years 323–428 and was also intended as a deliberate continuation of Eusebius's earlier work. In his *Church History*, as in his other theological writings, Theodoret continued to defend the fully God and fully human Christology of the Council of Nicaea, and his various writings played a significant role in the ultimate definition and victory of the posture at the Council of Chalcedon in 451.[32] Like Socrates before him, Theodoret introduced many important primary source documents into his text, and this gives his work lasting value. But his distaste for Arianism was so acute that his *Church History* sometimes reads more like a theological polemic than objective history.[33]

Rufinus of Aquileia (ca. 345–410) is most famous as a translator of the treasures of Greek Christian antiquity into Latin for an eager Western audience. He was born near Aquileia and educated in Rome; in Rome he met St. Jerome, from whom he learned a passion for the monastic life. After spending the years 373–80 in the deserts of Egypt, Rufinus founded a double monastery (for men and women) in Jerusalem, on the Mount of Olives, in 381. He spent the balance of his life there, translating the Greek language works of Origen and others into Latin. Upon translating Eusebius's *Ecclesiastical History*, sometime after 395, he added two additional books of his own composition to bring the historical narrative up to date; his own *Church History* concludes with the death of Theodosius I (395). Rufinus's work preserved some important Eastern traditions and stories that were ignored or unavailable to the other church historians, and therein lay the chief value of his work.[34]

Epiphanius of Salamis (ca. 315–403), while not considered a church historian, also contributed a work that is important for our consideration. It was entitled *Panarion* ("medicine chest"), since it was written as an antidote to heresy and schism in the church. Epiphanius made his career as a heresy-hunter and a polemicist. *Panarion* describes the inception and teaching of each of the major heresies its author faced in the fourth century; it provides us with important information about the Arians and Meletians, in particular.[35]

32. Chesnut, *First Christian Histories*, 208.
33. Theodoret's *Church History* can be found in *NPNF*, vol. III, 33–160.
34. Cf. Rufinus, *Church History of Rufinus of Aquileia*.
35. Cf. Epiphanius, *The Panarion of St. Epiphanius: Select Passages*.

In developing the following narrative about Athanasius and his works, attention will be paid to references in other contemporary Christian writers of the period who shed light upon our understanding of events in his life. Among these are Hilary of Poitiers (ca. 315–ca. 367), who was a Latin, Western ally and supporter of Athanasius, and an advocate for the Nicene theology. Gregory Nazianzen (ca. 329–90), whose *Oration* 21 we have already mentioned, will also be consulted. And finally, a manuscript titled LP-1914 also bears mentioning here; the nomenclature stands for a "London papyrus," which was discovered and translated in 1914. It is thought to be a Meletian letter, written in 335, which reports the violence and abuses of power used against them by Athanasius.[36] Since this manuscript is fragmentary, it is difficult to assess its full value and authenticity; R. C. P. Hanson placed significant weight upon it in his assessment of Athanasius's character,[37] whereas Duane Arnold opined that it "poses more questions than it answers with any degree of certainty."[38]

It is with these preliminary considerations in mind, then, that we delve into our introductory survey of the life and work of "the great Athanasius."

36. Bell, *Jews and Christians in Egypt.*
37. Hanson, *Christian Doctrine of God*, 252.
38. Arnold, *Early Episcopal Career*, 181.

An Approximate Chronology of the Life of Athanasius of Alexandria

296?   Athanasius born among the lower classes of Alexandria, of Coptic ethnic background, perhaps to Christian parents

303–11   The "great persecution" of the Christian church by Diocletian

311   Arius ordained presbyter by Achillas, bishop of Alexandria

313?   Athanasius meets Alexander, the bishop (patriarch) of the city, while playing on the beach. Alexander becomes his mentor; Athanasius becomes Alexander's assistant.

318–20   Arius begins teaching his novel doctrines in Alexandria, which leads to controversy with Bishop Alexander

319   Arius's *Letter to Eusebius of Nicomedia*

320   Arius's *Letter to Alexander of Alexandria*

320–24   Alexander publishes his encyclical letter announcing the deposition of Arius (which may have been penned by Athanasius)

320–28?   Athanasius publishes his *Against the Gentiles* and *On the Incarnation of the Word of God*

325   The First Ecumenical Council at Nicaea; Arianism is condemned and the Nicene Creed is developed as the theological standard of the Christian church. Athanasius, a deacon at the time, attends as an assistant to his bishop (Alexander).

328   Patriarch (Bishop) Alexander dies (Apr. 17)

          Athanasius elevated as bishop of Alexandria (June 8)

Constantine recalls Arius from exile

332	Athanasius called to the court of Constantine to answer charges against him associated with the Meletian schism
335	The Council of Tyre called, and Athanasius exiled (Feb.) to Trier in Gaul
336	Arius dies suddenly, at Constantinople, just before the formal ceremony to reinstate him as a cleric
337	Emperor Constantine dies; Athanasius returns to his see
338	Council of Antioch deposes Athanasius and exiles him to the West (Rome)
339	Athanasius flees Alexandria; replaced by Gregory
339–40	*Encyclical Letter*
340	Synod of Rome, called by Pope Julius I, clears Athanasius of all charges
339–46	*Orations Against the Arians*
341	The Dedication Council of Antioch condemns Athanasius
343	The Council of Serdica defends Athanasius
345	Bishop Gregory dies in Alexandria
346	Athanasius returns to his see
346–56	The "Golden Decade" of Athanasius's work in Alexandria
350–56?	*On the Council of Nicaea*
353	Constantius becomes sole emperor
353–57?	*Defense before Constantius*
356	(Feb.) Beginning of Athanasius's third exile, in the Egyptian desert
356	*Encyclical Letter to the Bishops of Egypt and Libya*
356–62?	*Life of Antony*
356–60?	*Letter to Serapion on the Death of Arius*
357	*Defense Against the Arians*

1

Athanasius of Alexandria

The Egyptian metropolis Alexandria was laid out and named by Alexander the Great sometime in 332 BC. Plutarch reports that the idea of Alexander's new capital city came to him in a dream one night.[1] He probably chose its location because, situated on the Nile Delta, it had access to the Mediterranean, the Nile River, and the Red Sea. It had two natural harbors, one on the eastern and one on the western side of the city. A third harbor, fed by a man-made canal on the landward side of the city, linked Alexandria to Lake Mariout and gave access to the Nile from the Mediterranean Sea, and hence also to upper Egypt and north central Africa. The harbor's famous Pharos Lighthouse, which was built circa 280 BC, was esteemed as one of the seven wonders of the ancient world. It served as a guiding light for travelers and sailors, just as the city itself became a beacon for merchants, travelers, religious pilgrims, and the finest intellectual minds of the ancient world.

Alexandria was a wealthy and bustling mercantile city when Athanasius was born there around AD 296. It was the heart of the empire's grain trade. Corn and grain, vital to the empire's well-being, were grown up and down central Egypt because of the annual flooding and irrigation of the Nile River; Egyptian grain was the lifeblood of distant cities like Rome and Constantinople. And indeed, the political stability of those distant capitals often depended upon the arrival of the Alexandrian grain fleet. It is estimated that between four and a half million bushels of grain (a poor year) and eight and a half million bushels (a bounty year) flowed through Alexandria annually.[2] Western merchants also found that going through

---

1. Plutarch, *Age of Alexander*, 281.

2. Vaggione, *Eunomius of Cyzicus*, 33.

Alexandria, down the Nile, and across the imperial roads that linked the Nile with the Egyptian ports on the southeastern coast gave them rapid access to the Red Sea, the Indian Ocean, and important trading centers in the East—without going through the arduous overland route and expensive Arab middlemen.

The city of Alexandria was divided into five wards, which were populated by various ethnic groups. One, called *Rakotis*, was made up predominantly of native Egyptians; another was almost exclusively Jewish; others were diversely populated by Egyptians, merchants, foreigners and dignitaries. Hence, Alexandria had a rich heritage of religious, cultural, and ethnic diversity. It was, in the finest sense of its Hellenistic founder's ideal, a *cosmopolitian* place, which both represented and embraced the entire world.[3]

The city had a rich intellectual and religious history, reaching back to the pre-Christian era, when the expansive library of more than five hundred thousand volumes and legendary museum—where the muses disseminated learning through the efforts of poets, philosophers, and scientists—were the crown jewels of the ancient intellectual world. These were ultimately destroyed by fire in AD 31, but were symbols of the city's proud and diverse intellectual history. Alexandria was also the undisputed religious center of Egypt during this same period. It was a haven of Hellenism, as well as of native Egyptian religion. Shrines to many pagan cults were located there, as were Jewish and Christian places of worship. Christianity was said (by Eusebius) to have come to Alexandria early, through the efforts of St. Mark, the evangelist.[4] If so, that influence almost certainly was based in the thriving Jewish community there, which boasted the work of Philo (ca. 20 BC–AD 50), a famous Jewish philosopher and biblical scholar of the Hebrew Scriptures. A Christian school was soon established in Alexandria under the direction of Pantaenus (about whom almost nothing is known). He was succeeded first by Clement (ca. 160–215) and then by the most famous of the Alexandrian theologians, Origen (ca. 185–ca. 251).[5] The work of Clement and Origen, in particular, was richly textured by their appreciation for the Greek philosophy known as Platonism, which brought with it

3. The word *cosmopolitan* is made up of the Greek words for "world" and "city." It describes a city or a person that is worldly, and embraces the diversity that both represents and makes up the larger world.

4. Eusebius, *Church History* II.16, *NPNF*, vol. I, 116.

5. Eusebius, *Church History* VI.6, *NPNF*, vol. I, 253.

a spirit-body dualism and offered a predominantly spiritual understanding of the world as emanating directly from God.

Alexandrian Christian theology was christocentric (Christ-centered) and focused largely on the role of Jesus Christ as the *Logos* (Word) of God. It drew upon aesthetic and philosophical impulses, as well as Scripture—which was often interpreted symbolically through the means of allegory. Knowledge or *gnosis* was also an important feature of Alexandrian theology; God-given knowledge came through Christ, who both taught and empowered one to imitate the life of God. The holy life of believers was thought (as in much of Eastern Orthodox theology) to enable persons to become "partakers of the divine nature" (2 Pet 1:4). This process, called *theosis* (deification), focused upon the goal of Christian life as transformation, holiness, and sanctification; it longed for restoration of the Divine nature within humans (Gen 1:26) and not merely forgiveness or pardon.

But what was most typical of Alexandrian religion, perhaps, was the religious synthesis that occurred there. In a synthesis between the Egyptian gods Osiris and Apis, along with Greek Hellenistic influence, Emperor Ptolemy I (367–283 BC) invented a new god named Serapis. He was depicted as a bearded king upon a regal throne and called "the source of all things." In a similar way, during the beginnings of Christianity, apostolic Christianity merged with Greek and Egyptian mystery religions to form various Gnostic-Christian sects, like those led by Valentinus and Basilides. These eclectic faiths included Jesus Christ in their pantheon but viewed him through the lens of the Greek spirit-body dualism. The spirit was seen as good and the body as evil. This meant that the Incarnation of Christ, when "the Word became flesh and dwelt among us" (John 1:14), came to be reinterpreted in ways that deviated from traditional Christology. Two Gnostic christological options emerged: the one, called Docetism (from the Greek word for "appear"), held that Christ only appeared to have a physical, human body—really he was a being comprised entirely of spirit; the other, called Adoptionism, suggested that Jesus and Christ were actually two separate beings, Jesus having been a devout human who was taken over and possessed by a Divine Spirit named Christ. Noncanonical documents like the *Gospel of the Egyptians* and the *Gospel of the Hebrews* are thought to have stemmed from these Egyptian Gnostic communities.

The Christian church was well established in Alexandria by the time Athanasius was born there in the late third century AD. The city was the citadel of Christian Egypt, and the bishop of Alexandria was more like an archbishop or metropolitan who had responsibility for more than one hundred other bishops in Egypt, Libya, the Thebaid, and surrounding regions.[6] The bishop of the city was called *papa* or "pope" some fifty years before that title of respect and authority was applied in the church of Rome.[7]

The Roman Empire was in the able hands of Diocletian, who had reorganized the administration and brought renewed economic and political stability to the empire. He put the government in the hands of a tetrarchy—a leadership team of four rulers, each of whom was responsible for a particular region. The empire was divided into East (Greek-speaking) and West (Latin-speaking) regions. Each region had a supreme ruler called Augustus, as well as a lieutenant-emperor called Caesar. Diocletian himself was Augustus of the East, with Galerius under him; Maximian was Augustus of the West, with Constantius Chlorus ruling as his Caesar. The genius of this division of labor was, in part, that it provided for a stable line of succession to the leadership role; each Caesar was, in fact, an Augustus in training.

Diocletian's wife, Prisca, and their daughter, Valeria, were both Christians, and this development seemed as though it would provide the Christian church with a modicum of protection and peaceful development under his rule. But this was not to be the case. As Christians refused to serve in the Roman army, and soldiers who became Christians mutinied in the field (ca. 295), a series of significant tensions arose between the Christian church and Diocletian's government. As these tensions escalated, Diocletian became convinced that the Christians were conspiring against him and his government. In retaliation, he decreed that church leaders should be arrested, and subsequently he demanded that all Christians must offer sacrifice to the traditional Roman gods. Following the strict monotheism (worshiping only one God) of the Judaic-Christian heritage, many Christians refused. This resulted in the government unleashing the most severe persecution the Christian church had ever experienced. Cruel punishments and tortures were used as inducements to try to force Christians to give up their scriptures, renounce their faith, and embrace the gods of Rome.

The Christian chronicler Eusebius described the suffering of the Egyptian Christians in this manner:

> Thousands of men, women, and children, despising the present life for the sake of the teaching of our Savior, endured various deaths. Some of them, after scrapings and rackings and severest

6. Theodoret, *Church History* I.1, *NPNF*, vol. III, 34.

7. Gwynn, *Athanasius of Alexanria*, 22.

scourgings, and numberless other kinds of tortures, terrible even to hear of, were committed to the flames; some were drowned in the sea; some offered their heads bravely to those who cut them off; some died under their tortures, and others perished with hunger. And yet others were crucified; some according to the method commonly employed for malefactors; others yet more cruelly, being nailed to the cross with their heads downward, and being kept alive until they perished on the cross with hunger.[8]

The Great Persecution finally came to an end in 311 when Galerius—who was mortally ill—came to believe that his persecution of the Christians brought God's judgment (in the form of his illness) upon him and that the prayers of the Christians would heal him.[9]

Athanasius was born during the dangerous days of the Great Persecution. No reliable record survives of his early years. A tenth-century Arabic account, entitled *History of the Patriarchs of Alexandria* and written long after these events, reports that his parents were not Christians and that he was "the son of an eminent woman who was a worshipper of idols and very rich."[10] The same source related that Athanasius was converted to Christianity and baptized as a youngster; he soon had a father-son-like relationship with Alexander, the Christian bishop of the city, who eventually ordained him as a deacon and made him his scribe and secretary.[11] Information about Athanasius's nationality comes entirely from circumstantial evidence; Athanasius spoke both Coptic and Greek, he was revered by the common people of Alexandria and by the monks of the Egyptian desert, and he was reviled by his theological opponents as "a black dwarf."[12] From these hints, it may be suggested that he was from the native Egyptian Coptic population, as opposed to the Greek upper class that made up the aristocracy of the city.

Rufinus related a story, which some consider a legend,[13] of how Athanasius first came to the attention of Bishop Alexander. One day, the eminent bishop was gazing out of his window and observed a group of young

8. Eusebius, *Church History* VIII.1, *NPNF*, vol. I, 329.

9. Cf. González, *Story of Christianity*, 1:118–26.

10. Anatolios, *Athanasius*, 3.

11. Ibid.

12. González, *Story of Christianity*, 1:200. González wrote, "Though mocked as 'the black dwarf,' Athanasius was a theological giant."

13. Duane Arnold considers this story "apocryphal." See Arnold, *Early Episcopal Career*, 29.

boys playing on the beach at some distance away.[14] After watching them absent-mindedly for a short time, Alexander became aware that the boys were playing church: "mimicking a bishop and things which were customarily done in the church."[15] After watching for some time, the bishop sent for the boys and had them ushered into his presence. He discovered that many of the boys had been playing the part of catechumens, who were being instructed for church membership and prepared for baptism. One of the boys, young Athanasius, was playing the role of the bishop who taught, examined, and baptized the others. After a lengthy interview, Alexander told the boys that they need not be baptized again. He sent for their parents and put them under an oath to raise the children in the church. "A short time later, after Athanasius had been thoroughly educated by a scribe and received adequate instruction from a teacher of literature, he was at once given back to the priest [Bishop Alexander] by his parents, like a deposit from the Lord kept faithfully, and like another Samuel[16] was brought up in the Lord's temple."[17] Rufinus implied that the bishop became like a father in the faith to young Athanasius, serving as mentor and teacher until the time came for Athanasius to replace him. Sozomen, recalling a report by Apolinarius the Syrian, mentioned that at this time Athanasius was at Alexander's side as "an assistant, and behaved as a son would to his father."[18]

Gregory Nazianzen, in his oration "On the Great Athanasius," corroborated some of the assertions of Rufinus when he reported, "He [Athanasius] was brought up, from the first, in religious habits and practices, after a brief study of literature and philosophy, so that he might not be utterly unskilled in such subjects, or ignorant of matters which he had determined to despise."[19] That Athanasius was well educated in ancient literature and philosophy is clear from his written works, which occasionally quote Plato and Aristotle. Gregory's eulogy, however, seems to contradict the Arabic report that Athanasius was born to non-Christian parents. Gregory also indicated that Athanasius came to despise the study of literature and philosophy, because he spent the rest of his life "meditating on every book of

14. The same report is, however, corroborated by Sozomen in his *Church History* II.17, *NPNF*, vol. II, 269.

15. Rufinus, *Church History* X.15, 26.

16. Cf. 1 Sam 2.

17. Rufinus, *Church History* X.15, 27.

18. Sozomen, *Church History* II.17, *NPNF*, vol. II, 269.

19. Gregory Nazianzen, *Oration* 21.6, *NPNF*, vol. VII, 270.

the Old and New Testament, with a depth such as none else has applied even to one of them . . ."[20]

Meanwhile, the tetrarchy, which Diocletian had invented to provide stable leadership and a line of succession to power, proved to be rather unstable; the Caesars soon vied for power among themselves, and against the Augusti. In the West, Constantius had died, and his legions chose his popular son, Constantine, to succeed him. After a brief period of political stability, Constantine began to march on Rome, in an attempt to unify the empire under his sole rule. As he marched upon Rome, Eusebius reported, Constantine paused to pray, and while he prayed he saw a vision of the letters *chi* and *rho* (the first two letters of the word "Christ" in Greek) emblazoned upon the sun; he was told "by this sign you shall conquer." So the soon-to-be emperor had these letters (called the *labarum*) emblazoned upon the shields of his troops. They did indeed conquer, winning a crushing victory over their opposition at the Battle of the Milvian Bridge. Constantine received religious instruction and became a Christian, though the depth of his personal faith is frequently questioned because of the many inconsistencies harbored within it.[21]

The Edict of Milan, which was issued by Constantine in 313, marked the end of persecution (in the West), and religious toleration for the Christian church. Constantine continued to extend his power and the scope of his rule, and by 324 the entire eastern half of the Roman Empire was in his sole possession as well. With the extension of his rule, Constantine also extended his growing favoritism towards Christianity. Where former Roman emperors had claimed to be divine, in order to demand allegiance from their subjects, Constantine was to be viewed as godly but not divine. He decided to use Christian faith as the glue to hold Roman society and his vast empire together. In this way, and to this end, Christianity gradually became established as the official religion in the new Christian Roman Empire.

There was at this same time a serious schism underway in the Alexandrian church. It reached back into the late third and early fourth century, when Peter the Martyr was bishop in that city, during the Great Persecution. The issue under debate had to do with the problem of the "lapsed" (those who had renounced Christian faith under threat of torture). Those who had faced torture and seen loved ones endure martyrdom advocated for the

20. Ibid.

21. Eusebius, *Life of Constantine* I.28–32, *NPNF*, vol. I, 490–91. Cf. González, *Story of Christianity*, 1:124–26.

church to take a hard line with those who had renounced their Christian faith and offered sacrifice to idols in order to save their lives. In his *Panarion*, Epiphanius explained, "This caused a great commotion and disturbance among the martyrs, with some saying that those who had once lapsed, denied the faith, and not persevered in courage and in the contest ought not to be granted a chance to repent, lest those still left, having less concern about punishment on account of the swift permission to return given to the others, be turned aside to the denial of God and pagan worship."[22] This approach was advocated for by Alexandrian priests Meletius, Peleus, and others.[23]

The saintly bishop of Alexandria, Peter, took a more conciliatory approach. He "begged and beseeched them, saying: Let us accept them who repent and assign them a period of repentance that they may hold fast by the church, and let us not reject them even from the clergy . . ."[24] It was an honest disagreement and a genuine dilemma for the Alexandrian church, because there were merits to both sides of the argument. Epiphanius recalled, "Peter's words were on the side of mercy and kindness, and those of Melitius and his party on that of truth and zeal."[25] Soon the two parties had separated from one another, holding separate worship services and prayers. Both parties were severely persecuted for their Christian faith, and yet they kept separate prayer services even in prison. Peter, the Alexandrian bishop, was martyred for his faith. Meletius and many others were exiled to the mines of Phaeno. When persecution of the Christians ended in the east, following AD 311, the two separate factions each established separate churches. Peter's faction called itself the "Catholic Church," while the Meletians called themselves the "Martyrs' Church." Alexander succeeded the martyred bishop, Peter, to the episcopal office and tried unsuccessfully to reconcile the two feuding groups in the Alexandrian church.[26]

---

22. Epiphanius, *Panarion* 68.2, 248.

23. The question of what to do about the "lapsed" was a burning issue in the church at this time. In the West it was at the heart of the schism brought about by Novatian (ca. 200–258) during the persecution of Decius (249–50). Novatian viewed Pope Cornelius's policy towards reconciling the lapsed to the church as being too lenient and rejected it. In North Africa, a similar scenario was played out during the Donatist controversy (ca. 311–12 and thereafter) in Carthage.

24. Epiphanius, *Panarion* 68.3.1, 248.

25. Epiphanius, *Panarion* 68.3.2, 248.

26. Cf. Socrates, *Church History* I.6, *NPNF*, vol. II, 5, and Theodoret, *Church History* I.8, *NPNF*, vol. III, 46–47. See also "Documents Concerning the Meletian Schism," at www.fourthcentury.com.

2

Athanasius's Early Works

Scholars disagree significantly as to when Athanasius began his literary career. His first two works, *Against the Heathen* (*Contra Gentes*) and *On the Incarnation of the Word of God* (*De incarnatione verbi Dei*), are probably best understood as twin books or two halves of the same major treatise. Older scholarship has placed these theological treatises in the early years of Athanasius's ministry in Alexandria, before the so-called Arian controversy that erupted there in circa 320. Archibald Robertson, the editor of Athanasius's works in *NPNF*, is an apt example of this approach.[1] He dates *Against the Heathen* and *On the Incarnation* circa 318, when Athanasius was between eighteen and twenty-one years of age. The reason for this early dating of these two treatises is the fact that they make absolutely no reference (direct or indirect) to the Arian controversy. It is assumed that this theological crisis was of such major proportions that it would have had to have been mentioned in a far-reaching, two-volume defense of the Christian faith.

More recent scholarship has taken a different approach that locates the writing of these twin treatises in the period after Athanasius became bishop of Alexandria, in 328. Some scholars date them as late as his first exile in 337, because in *Against the Heathen* (§ 1) the writer mentioned that he did not have his books at hand. Others point to phraseology in *On the Incarnation* (§ 24) that is paralleled in Athanasius's *Festal Letter* of 337.[2] Hence, Timothy Barnes dates these treatises between 325 and 335,[3] and Hanson locates them in Athanasius's first exile to Trier (in Gaul), in 335 or

1. Robertson, introduction to *Contra Gentes*, *NPNF*, vol. IV, 1. Johannes Quasten, *Patrology*, 3:25, follows the same approach.

2. Anatolios, *Athanasius*, 26.

3. Barnes, *Athanasius and Constantius*, 13.

9

336.[4] John Behr acknowledges the difficulties in dating these two treatises and opts for a time frame in the early years of Athanasius's episcopacy in Alexandria, which would place them in 328 or soon thereafter.[5] This rich diversity of opinion about the dating of these works makes it very difficult for us to reconstruct a historical context for them.

The current study follows the older dating scheme, which places these treatises prior to the dispute over Arianism in the Alexandrian church (ca. 318), for the reasons that Robertson and others have suggested; it is difficult for me to imagine that our author would have written two major apologetic works on the nature of the Christian faith, after or during the Arian crisis, without mentioning a single word about it. This approach assumes that *Against the Heathen* and *On the Incarnation* were written by a young but also extremely talented and energetic theological intellect—and this does not seem antithetical to what we know about Athanasius from his various other writings.

The title of *Against the Heathen* may be a bit off-putting for modern readers. *Contra Gentes* is also sometimes translated *Against the Pagans*; today, the Christian apologist would probably say "To the Non-Christians," for that is certainly the readership Athanasius had in mind. It is an ambitious and far-reaching work that seeks to demolish some of the main religious claims of non-Christians, in order to clear the floor (so to speak) for the acceptance of the Christian faith. *Against the Heathen* looks beyond the church to her lively religious opposition, an opposition that was both spirited and somewhat troublesome—particularly in Alexandria. In reaching beyond the readership of Christianity, and hoping to reach non-Christians, Athanasius stood in a long tradition of Christian apologists who sought to win a fair hearing and religious toleration for the Christian faith by giving "reason for the hope that was within them" (1 Pet 3:15).

In his apologetic approach Athanasius seems to have read and known the approaches used by both Justin Martyr (ca. 100–165) and Irenaeus of Lyon (ca. 130–202) before him. From Justin Martyr, Athanasius inherited the attack upon pagan idols and idol worship. Like Irenaeus, he stressed the deep inner connection between God's two great acts in creation and redemption. But there is no textual indication of his direct borrowing from these earlier Christian apologists, so perhaps Athanasius's creative and

---

4. Hanson, *Christian Doctrine of God*, 418.

5. Behr, *Formation of Christian Theology*, vol. 2, pt. 1, 168.

retentive mind developed his apologetic approach without direct recourse to these earlier Christian writers.

Against the Heathen is the first offering in this pair of early works. It is addressed to Macarius, whose name means "blessed one," who desires to hear about "our religion." Whether this "Macarius" is a real person or a literary device remains a matter of conjecture. The introduction, however, makes clear the purpose Athanasius had in mind in writing the treatise: "The purpose of the book [is] a vindication of Christian doctrine, and especially of the Cross, against the scoffing objection of the Gentiles."[6] It is comprised of forty-seven short sections, which are grouped into three main parts: (1) "The Refutation of Heathenism"; (2) "The Knowledge of God Possible (The Soul)"; and (3) "Nature a Revelation of God." The broad outline provided by the titles of the three sections offers a helpful window into the development and approach of this work.

The first section is quite polemical. Athanasius went on the attack, seeking to demolish the credibility of the non-Christian faiths around him by showing that they cannot properly describe the origin of evil in the world, that their idolatry is sheer folly, and that pantheism (the identification of God with nature and natural forces) is an utter dead end. Athanasius argued that evil had no real part in God's original creation, nor in the original constitution of human nature; hence, like other Eastern Orthodox theologians before and after him, he started his defense from a foundation of "original righteousness" instead of "original sin." Evil was described as a human development through the misuse of human freedom. The human soul "fell into lust of themselves, preferring what was their own to the contemplation of what belonged to God."[7] The heading of section 5 summarized well the nature of evil, as Athanasius viewed it: "Evil, then, consists essentially in the choice of what is lower in preference to what is higher."[8] After attacking certain non-Christian approaches to the nature of evil—that is, that evil is a substance, and that evil resides in matter (dualism)—Athanasius turned his polemic attack upon idolatry.

Athanasius stressed that idolatry is a prime example of the fall of the human soul into evil, because it seeks to find God while engrossed in earthly things (§ 8). In a similar way idolatry led to the worship of celestial bodies, animals, and fabled creatures (§ 9), and even mortals—like the supposed

6. *Against the Heathen* I, NPNF, vol. IV, 4.
7. *Against the Heathen* III.2, NPNF, vol. IV, 5.
8. *Against the Heathen* IV, NPNF, vol. IV, 6.

Greek gods (§§ 10–11)—became deified. The "shameful actions ascribed to heathen deities all prove that they are but men of former times, and not even good men."[9] In worshipping images, not only are people submitting to great evil (as evil was defined above) but they are also dishonoring art by misusing the skill of mere humans (§ 13). Furthermore, the Scriptures are clearly against the making and use of idols, because idolatry deceives the human heart, and "none can deliver his soul."[10] Hence, Athanasius argued that "the gods conveyed in the representations of them by poets and artists show that they are without life, and that they are not gods, nor even decent men and women."[11]

After attacking and laying aside several of the arguments in support of idolatry (§ 16), Athanasius concluded, "The truth probably is, that the scandalous tales [about the gods] are true, while the divine attributes ascribed to them are due to the flattery of the poets" (§ 17).[12] He then went on the attack again, arguing against the idea that "the gods [should be] worshipped for inventing the Arts of Life" (§ 18).[13] This is completely wrong: "For men having a natural capacity for knowledge according to the definition laid down concerning them, there is nothing to surprise us if by human intelligence, and by looking of themselves at their own nature and coming to know it, they have hit upon the arts."[14] The variety and diversity of idolatrous cults prove that they are false (§ 23), and the fact that "the so-called gods of one place are used as victims [for sacrifice] in another" shows that there is no unified truth to be found in idolatry (§ 24).[15] The height of this absurdity is seen in human sacrifice, which produces calamitous results in society, "for nearly every city is full of licentiousness of all kinds, the result of the savage character of its gods . . ." (§ 25).[16] In fact, "the moral corruptions of Paganism all admittedly originated with the gods" (§ 26).[17]

Having demolished the credibility of idolatry, the most popular form of non-Christian worship, Athanasius turned his attention towards

9. *Against the Heathen* XII, *NPNF*, vol. IV, 10.

10. *Against the Heathen* XIV.1, *NPNF*, vol. IV, 12.

11. *Against the Heathen* XV, *NPNF*, vol. IV, 12.

12. *Against the Heathen* XVII, *NPNF*, vol. IV, 13.

13. *Against the Heathen* XVIII, *NPNF*, vol. IV, 13.

14. *Against the Heathen* XVIII.3, *NPNF*, vol. IV, 13.

15. *Against the Heathen* XXIV, *NPNF*, vol. IV, 16.

16. *Against the Heathen* XXV.4, *NPNF*, vol. IV, 17.

17. *Against the Heathen* XXVI, *NPNF*, vol. IV, 17.

nature-worship (pantheism). He argued that "Nature witnesses to God by the mutual dependence of all her parts, which forbid us to think of any one of them as the supreme God" (§ 27).[18] Hence, the order, design, and unity of the various parts of creation do not show us that they are divine, but rather remind us that they had and have a Divine Creator, the God and Father of our Lord Jesus Christ, "Whom the would-be philosophers turn from to worship and deify the Creation which proceeded from Him, which yet itself worships and confesses the Lord Whom they deny on its account."[19] God cannot be diffused into the various and dissimilar aspects of nature, for God is incapable of dissolution (§ 28). And "the balance of powers in Nature shows that it is not God, either collectively, or in [its] parts" (§ 29).[20]

The second section of *Against the Heathen* focused attention upon the human soul. Drawing upon Platonic philosophy and Scripture—in which humans are said to be created in the image of God (Gen 1:26)—Athanasius argued that all humans have an immortal soul and that in their soul they have a reflection or mirror of the Divine nature. Hence, he wrote, "The soul of man, being intellectual, can know God of itself, if it be true to its own nature" (§ 30). This soul is both rational and immortal (à la Plato); it is what distinguishes humans from other creatures (§ 31). The role of the soul is seen in its ability to overrule the instincts of "the bodily organs" (§ 32). The fact that the soul is immortal is proved by (1) "its being distinct from the body, (2) its being the source of motion, [and] (3) its power to go beyond the body in imagination and thought" (§ 33).[21] Because of its heavenly origin, the human soul is capable of knowing God and God's revelation through the *Logos* (Word, Logic, Mind) of God. The human predicament, therefore, is not one of the finitude of human nature but of corruption of the human soul; "the soul, then, if only it get rid of the stains of sin is able to know God directly, its own rational nature imaging back the Word of God, after whose image it was created. But even if it cannot pierce the cloud which sin draws over its vision, it is confronted by the witness of creation to God" (§ 34).

In Part III, the created world is viewed as a proper revelation of certain aspects of God; these include God's existence, God's unity, as well as God's role as Designer and Sustainer of nature. Athanasius wrote, "Creation [is]

18. *Against the Heathen* XXVII, NPNF, vol. IV, 18.
19. *Against the Heathen* XXVII.3, NPNF, vol. IV, 18.
20. *Against the Heathen* XXIX, NPNF, vol. IV, 19.
21. *Against the Heathen* XXXIII, NPNF, vol. IV, 21.

a revelation of God; especially in the order and harmony pervading the whole" (§ 35).[22] The argument from "design" (§§ 36–37) leads to the assertion of the unity of the Godhead: "The Unity of God [is] shown by the Harmony of the order of Nature" (§ 38).[23] This unity points to the "impossibility of a plurality of Gods" (§ 39).[24] Athanasius, following but not quoting John 1:1–4, introduced the *Logos* as the Agent of God's creative act and the ongoing power of God at work in revealing God in the world and to human souls. He wrote, for example, "The rationality and order of the Universe proves that it is the work of the Reason or Word of God" (§ 40).[25] The *Logos* is not only Creator of the world but also its Sustainer, as Athanasius wrote: "The presence of the Word in nature [is] necessary, not only for its original Creation, but also for its permanence" (§ 41).[26] After discussing the "function of the Word [*Logos*] at length" (§ 42), he offered three analogies (§§ 43–44) that were designed to illustrate this profound relationship between Creator and creation.

The brief conclusion (§§ 45–47) recapped the theology of Part I, and Part III, from the standpoint of the scriptural witness. It also provided a rationale and a point of departure for the second treatise, *On the Incarnation of the Word of God*. It provided a rationale by pointing out the inadequacy of the non-Christian approaches to knowing God, and by doing so cleared the way for the options offered by Christian faith. Secondly, it provided a point of departure by introducing the theme of God as the *Logos*—Who will be the One incarnated in human flesh—as the reconciling revelation of God in the second book.

On the Incarnation of the Word of God, the second of the twin treatises under consideration here, is arguably Athanasius's most famous and most widely read work today. Like its predecessor, it is divided into three main parts: (1) "The Incarnation of the Word," (2) "The Death and Resurrection of Christ," and (3) "The Refutation of Contemporary Unbelief," which are followed by a brief conclusion. The book is comprised of fifty-seven short sections and is—like its predecessor—addressed to "Macarius." Also like the previous work, *On the Incarnation* draws upon Platonic philosophy and the Christian Scriptures to explain and to prove Christian doctrine.

22. *Against the Heathen* XXXV, *NPNF*, vol. IV, 22.

23. *Against the Heathen* XXXVIII, *NPNF*, vol. IV, 24.

24. *Against the Heathen* XXXIX, *NPNF*, vol. IV, 24.

25. *Against the Heathen* XL, *NPNF*, vol. IV, 25.

26. *Against the Heathen* XLI, *NPNF*, vol. IV, 26.

Bridging back to *Against the Heathen*, Athanasius presupposed the doctrine of Creation by the Word of God, and that God Who had made the world through the *Logos* had determined to save the world by Him through Whom it was first made. Once again, the idolatry of the non-Christian world is the subject of his polemic, as well as the occasion for the demonstration of the Word's divinity: "He by His own power demonstrates to be divine, subduing the pretensions of idols by His supposed humiliation—by the Cross—and those who mock and disbelieve invisibly winning over to recognize His divinity and power."[27] The same Word of the Father, by Whom the Universe was made, appeared and was made manifest in human form for our salvation. As Athanasius wrote, "He has yet of the loving-kindness and goodness of His own Father been manifested to us in a human body for our salvation."[28]

Once again stressing the interconnection between creation and redemption as the re-creation of humanity, Athanasius proceeded to explain, critique, and reject several erroneous views of creation, including those of Epicureanism, Platonism, and Gnosticism (§ 2). In the next section (3) he introduced "the true doctrine" of creation, which stressed creation out of nothing, by God, and the creation of humans "in the image of God." Because of the dignity of their created nature, humans are capable of participating in the blessedness of God. He explained that God "made them after His own image, giving them a portion even of the power of His own Word; so that having as it were a kind of reflection of the Word, and being made rational, they might be able to abide ever in blessedness, living the true life which belongs to the saints in paradise."[29] But also knowing that humans possessed a free will that "could sway to either side," God also gave the first humans the grace of a commandment, which was to prepare their way towards blessedness. This commandment (or "law") stated, "'Of every tree that is in the garden, eating thou shalt eat: but of the tree of the knowledge of good and evil, ye shall not eat of it, but on the day that ye eat, dying ye shall die.' But by 'dying ye shall die,' what else could be meant than not dying merely, but also abiding even in the corruption of death?"[30]

Through the violation of this commandment or "law," humanity fell into corruption and death, hence providing both the need and the necessity

27. *On the Incarnation of the Word* I.2, NPNF, vol. IV, 36.

28. *On the Incarnation of the Word* I.3, NPNF, vol. IV, 36.

29. *On the Incarnation of the Word* III.3, NPNF, vol. IV, 37.

30. *On the Incarnation of the Word* III.5, NPNF, vol. IV, 38.

for the Word becoming flesh: "For in speaking of the appearance of the Savior amongst us, we must needs speak also of the origin of men, that you may know that the reason of His coming down was because of us, and that our transgression called forth the loving-kindness of the Word, that the Lord should both make haste to help us and appear among men."[31]

The plight of humans caused a "divine dilemma" (§ 6). God, Who created us in God's image for incorruption and blessedness, also laid down a law for us. The willful violation of God's good law made humanity subject to corruption and death. The crux of the dilemma, as Athanasius draws it, is between Divine Goodness (in creating and redeeming humans) and Divine Justice (in requiring death of those who transgress God's holy law). Hence, he wrote, "It was, then, out of the question to leave men to the current of corruption; because this would be unseemly, and unworthy of God's goodness."[32] So a means of redemption needed to be devised that would allow God to "appear true to the law He had laid down concerning death. For it were monstrous for God, the Father of Truth, to appear a liar for our profit and preservation."[33] Here then is the dilemma caused by the human predicament; if humans are allowed to live in corruption and death, God's goodness seems to be violated. If humans are reconciled to God through mere repentance, without fulfilling the law of death, then God's justice and veracity seem to be violated.

After examining the various options offered by this dilemma, Athanasius concluded that the only One who could justly renew all humanity was the *Logos* through Whom and by Whom humanity was originally created; only He could re-create all, suffer for all, and represent all to the Father by way of intercession (§ 7). Athanasius explained, "For His it was once more both to bring the incorruptible to incorruption, and to maintain intact the just claim of the Father upon all. For being Word of the Father, and above all, He alone of natural fitness was both able to recreate everything, and worthy to suffer on behalf of all and to be ambassador for all with the Father."[34] His solution to the dilemma addresses both aspects of the problem—namely, the debt of humanity in sin and a solution that is worthy of the goodness of God. Athanasius's solution addressed both horns of the

---

31. *On the Incarnation of the Word* IV.2, NPNF, vol. IV, 38.

32. *On the Incarnation of the Word* VI.10, NPNF, vol. IV, 39.

33. *On the Incarnation of the Word* VII, NPNF, vol. IV, 38.

34. *On the Incarnation of the Word* VII.5, NPNF, vol. IV, 40.

dilemma, in that it both covered the debt that humanity owed and restored the image of God within humanity.

This "dilemma" then is the rationale behind the Incarnation of the Word of God, in which—borrowing the language of the Fourth Gospel (John 1:14)—"the Word became flesh and dwelt among us." As Athanasius put it, "He took pity on our race, and had mercy on our infirmity, and condescended to our corruption, and, unable to bear that death should have the mastery—lest the creature should perish, and His Father's handiwork in men be spent for nought—He takes unto Himself a body, and that of no different sort from ours."[35] His body, however, was born of a Virgin, so as not to be under the penalty of our corruption. Hence, our Divine Maker took a body like ours in order to banish death and corruption from us, "like straw from the fire."[36] Since only His death could stop the plague that infested the human race, the Word took a body that was mortal, like ours, so that it could avail redemption for all; hence, by becoming mortal, He clothed us with immortality (§ 9). This is the basis of the famous dictum that is used to summarize Athanasius's theology of redemption: "He became what we are, to make us what He is."[37]

After developing an extended "simile" or parable with which to illustrate the interconnection between the Incarnation of the Word and reconciliation with God (§ 10), Athanasius turned to the second reason for the Incarnation of the Word of God (§ 11). The second fundamental reason for the Incarnation was so that humans, who were made in the image of God, might be able to know God the Father through the ministrations of the Word—God's Son. In their perversity, however, humans turned to idolatry rather than to God. God sent humanity the Law and Prophets (§ 12), in order that God might be known and received by them, but they continued to live according to their own desires rather than seeking after God where He might be found. When these messages and messengers failed, God resolved not to keep silence but instead came to humanity in person, in the person of God's Son, the Word; hence, "the Word of God came in His own person, that, as He was the Image of the Father, He might be able to create afresh the man after the image. But, again, it could not else have taken place had not death and corruption been done away. Whence He took, in natural fitness,

---

35. *On the Incarnation of the Word* VIII.2, NPNF, vol. IV, 40.

36. *On the Incarnation of the Word* VIII.4, NPNF, vol. IV, 40.

37. *On the Incarnation of the Word* LIV.3, NPNF, vol. IV, 65.

a mortal body, that while death might in it be once for all done away, men made after His Image might once more be renewed."[38]

Even while *in* the body, the Word was not limited *to* the body; while in the body, the Word continued working in the universe, working through Providence, and was not absent from creation (§ 17). The divinity of the Word was not diminished by the incarnation. In fact, the divinity of the Word was seen in and attested through His human actions, like casting out demons, performing miracles, and being born of a Virgin (§ 18). The chief of the Word's works, however, and the one by which His deity was most clearly confessed was His death and resurrection (§ 19).

With this mention of Christ's death and resurrection, Athanasius moved into the second major section of his treatise, in which he examined the death and resurrection of the Word. In order to pay the debt of death, He "offered up" the Temple of His body (§ 20). Athanasius explained, "He offered up His sacrifice . . . on behalf of all, yielding His Temple to death in the stead of all, in order firstly to make men quit and free of their old trespass, and further to show Himself more powerful even than death, displaying His own body incorruptible, as first-fruits of the resurrection of all."[39] Having first stressed the importance of the Word's death as a substitute for that of humanity, he emphasized the Word's resurrection as the first-fruits of humanity. Athanasius went on to explain why it was necessary that God's Son, who lived a life of obedience to God, would die an unnatural, public death at the hands of others (§§ 21–24). Death upon a cross was necessary so that the Word could bear "the curse" (Deut 21:23) of corruption and death under which humanity dwelt (§ 25). After considering why it was necessary that the Word be raised on the third day, and not sooner (§ 26), Athanasius reported that Christians no longer fear death, because of the cross and resurrection of Christ, "but by the sign of the Cross and by faith in Christ [they] tread it down as dead."[40] No longer living in bondage, terror, and dread, Christians scoff at death, "jesting at him and saying what has been written against him of old, 'O death, where is thy victory? O grave, where is thy sting?'"[41] This truth has been proven over and over again by practical experience; let those who doubt it become Christians and

38. *On the Incarnation of the Word* XIII.7–9, *NPNF*, vol. IV, 43.

39. *On the Incarnation of the Word* XX.2, *NPNF*, vol. IV, 47. Note here the "all" of a universal application of the atonement of Christ, for all humans.

40. *On the Incarnation of the Word* XXVII, *NPNF*, vol. IV, 50–51.

41. *On the Incarnation of the Word* XXVII.4, *NPNF*, vol. IV, 51.

see for themselves (§ 28). Like someone or something encased in asbestos "knows that fire has no burning power over it, and as he who would see the tyrant bound goes over to the empire of his conqueror, so too let him who is incredulous about the victory over death receive the faith of Christ, and pass over to His teaching, and he shall see the weakness of death, and the triumph over it."[42]

The reality of the resurrection is proved by various facts, including the victory over death, the wonders of grace at work in the lives of those in whom the Savior lives, and the fact that the Living Christ is able to break the power of (allegedly) alive pagan gods (§ 30). If power is a sign of life—and it certainly is—then the power of Christ's death and resurrection testify to His divinity and eternal life (§ 31). "For it is plain," Athanasius wrote, "that if Christ be dead, He could not be expelling demons and spoiling idols; for a dead man the spirits would not have obeyed."[43]

In the third part of this treatise, "The Refutation of Contemporary Unbelief," Athanasius returned to his polemic against Judaism and Greek religion. Both of these were live options and competitors with Christianity for the hearts and minds of people in Alexandria when he wrote this treatise; hence, they are not hypothetical arguments for him. While these polemic sections are not "live" issues (perhaps) for modern readers, they do continue to flesh out the basic argument of *On the Incarnation of the Word of God* and are worth reading for that reason.

Athanasius's apologetic towards Jews largely amounts to an argument from fulfilled prophecy, since both Christians and Jews esteem the Old Testament as Scripture. This assumption forms the basis of his approach. After surveying the prophecies from the Hebrew Scriptures that predicted the coming of One who was both God and Man (§ 33), those that predicted the circumstances of Christ's suffering and death (§ 34), those that predicted His death on the cross (§ 35), and those that predicted His Sovereignty and flight into Egypt (§ 36), he pointed to the cessation of prophecy and the destruction of Jerusalem as indications that God had taken the promises first offered to the Jews and given them to the Gentiles (§ 40). "What more remains for the Messiah to do, that Christ has not done?"[44] Athanasius asked.

His "answer to the Greeks" (§§ 41–54) used Greek philosophy to show the credibility of the Christian message of the incarnation, death, and

---

42. *On the Incarnation of the Word* XXVIII.5, *NPNF*, vol. IV, 51.

43. *On the Incarnation of the Word* XXXII.4, *NPNF*, vol. IV, 53.

44. *On the Incarnation of the Word* XL, *NPNF*, vol. IV, 57.

resurrection of Christ. His point of contact with his non-Christian readers in this section is the concept of the *Logos* (Word), which plays a major role in Greek (Platonic) philosophy, as well as in Christian theology. The relationship of the *Logos* to creation at large shows us how it is that the *Logos* can also be manifested in a human body (§ 42). The very same works that the Greeks see the *Logos* perform in the natural universe were also performed by the *Logos* incarnate as Man (§ 43). Since God made the universe and humanity by the Word, it was fitting that God should also restore humanity by way of God's Word. Hence, "He put on a body, that He might find death in the body, and blot it out."[45] Nature itself testifies to the reality of the Incarnation by the miracles it yields (§ 45). Where there is incredible diversity in non-Christian worship, the worship of Christ is catholic (universal) and uniform (§ 46). Pagan oracles and idols are further attacked and offer evidence of human evil since they are dispelled by the sign of the cross (§ 47). The courage and constancy of martyrs and virgins points to the power of their message, and the power of Christ is to be distinguished from the power of magic and magicians (§ 48). Christ's birth and miracles exceed that of the Greek gods, who are viewed as divine because of their inferior works (§ 49). Christ's resurrection is completely without parallel in Greek thought (§ 50). The impact of Christian faith upon society as a force for revolutionary change, for peace and purity, also shows its truthfulness (§ 51). Wars that are aroused by demons, and the hatred they breed among people, are lulled by Christianity (§ 52). The conversion and transformation of large portions of the pagan world by Christian faith also points to its truthfulness (§ 53): "For whom they used to worship, them they are deserting, and Whom they used to mock as one crucified, Him they worship as Christ, confessing Him to be God."[46]

That the Word of God incarnate was fully divine was evidenced from His works: "If a man should wish to see God, Who is invisible by nature and not seen at all, he may know and apprehend Him from His works: so let him who fails to see Christ with his understanding, at least apprehend Him by the works of His body, and test whether they be human works or God's works."[47] This divinity in Christ is most aptly seen in his "deifying mission" so that in coming to faith in Christ, humans may live a purer and more honorable life than they did before. As Athanasius wrote, "For He

---

45. *On the Incarnation of the Word* XLIV.6, *NPNF*, vol. IV, 60.

46. *On the Incarnation of the Word* LIII.2, *NPNF*, vol. IV, 65.

47. *On the Incarnation of the Word* LIV, *NPNF*, vol. IV, 65.

was made man that we might be made God; and He manifested Himself by a body that we might receive the idea of the unseen Father; and He endured the insolence of men that we might inherit immortality."[48] These two features of Christ's mission—the deification of humans through redemption and revelation of the unseen God—were then the twin reasons for the Incarnation of the Word of God.

In summary of the foregoing argument to Greeks, he pointed to the cessation of pagan miracles, the propagation of the Christian faith, and the transformation of lives and society as indicators that "the True King has come forth and silenced all usurpers."[49] Readers are asked to search the Scriptures in order to flesh out what has been said in this treatise, and urged to prepare themselves for the second coming of Christ and the Last Judgment (§ 56). This was all written, said Athanasius, so that the reader might have knowledge of God in Christ, and possess an honorable life and a pure mind (§ 57). The treatise closed with a Doxology: "'Eye hath not seen, nor ear heard, neither have entered into the heart of man,' whatsoever things are prepared for them that live a virtuous life, and love the God and Father, in Christ Jesus our Lord: through Whom and with Whom be to the Father Himself, with the Son Himself, in the Holy Spirit, honor and might and glory forever and ever. Amen."[50]

Athanasius's presentation of the Christian gospel was well established in these two early treatises, and most especially in *On the Incarnation of the Word of God*. In these treatises the goodness of creation was stressed, as well as the continuity of creation and redemption as twin acts of the *Logos* of God. Humans were viewed from the standpoint of their God-given identity as ones created in the "image of God." This meant, among other things, that they were given an immortal soul and rationality; that high and blessed station also held within it the potential of their own undoing. Through the misuse of their will and rationality, humanity fell into corruption and evil. Evil was powerfully described as having its locus in the human will and in a willingness to exchange devotion to God, the Creator, for the worship of this world and the desires thereof. Idolatry, then, is symptomatic of humanity's fall and fundamental problem. Hence fear, death, and corruption reigned in humans through the breaking of God's primordial law; the penalty for breaking God's law was decreed to be death.

---

48. *On the Incarnation of the Word* LIV.3, *NPNF*, vol. IV, 65.

49. *On the Incarnation of the Word* LV, *NPNF*, vol. IV, 66.

50. *On the Incarnation of the Word* LVII.3, *NPNF*, vol. IV, 67.

This dire situation posed a dilemma for God and for humans; it meant that death and corruption ruled in those whom God had blessed with God's own image and love. It was a dilemma involving the consistency of a just and loving God, Who had created humanity for fellowship with God and life in God's image, and yet also laid down a law of obedience for them to follow; hence "it were monstrous" that humans, who had been made in God's image, should live and perish in fear, corruption, and death. And yet, a just God must also redeem humanity in a manner that was consistent with God's own nature and law. The Incarnation of the *Logos* is the answer to the divine dilemma—of what to do about the plight of humans in a way that both vindicates God's goodness and validates God justice. The incarnate One "took a body like our own" which was capable of death and corruption. He lived a pure life and died a public death at the hands of His enemies. The *Logos*, as the God-Man, satisfied the requirement of God's justice through dying as a substitute for humanity, and He vindicated the goodness and love of God's nature by dying on behalf of others. Thus, the Incarnation of the *Logos* finds its inner logic and rationale in the Christian theology of redemption, whereby God was in Christ reconciling the world to Himself. Hence, the death of the incarnate One both reconciles humanity to God and reveals the true nature of God. Christ's redemption of humanity not only reconciles God and humanity, it brings about the sanctification or deification (*theosis*) of those who believe and live by faith in Christ. This was stressed through Athanasius's famous dictum: "He became what we are to make us what He is."

If this rendition of the Christian gospel sounds at all familiar—if it sounds like faithful and traditional Christianity—that is because Athanasius said it first here, in these two treatises, in the early fourth century. While others had written on many of these same themes, few have drawn them all together with the scope, power, and perception evident in these two works of "the great Athanasius."

3

Enter Arius

Few figures in ancient church history have had more written about them, especially in the last twenty years, than Arius (ca. 256–336). This development is singularly ironic, since so little definitive information has survived from the fourth century about him. The research path back to Arius is further complicated (as we noted above) by the fact that most of what we do know of him stems from the writings of his theological and ecclesiastical opponents. One can only conjecture how much their opposition to his views has distorted the picture presented by his loyal and highly spirited opposition. Hence, Hanson observed, "Directly Arian sources untainted by pro-Nicene prejudice are rare."[1] The surviving paper trail of genuine, unadulterated Arian materials is, as Frances Young described it, "limited."[2]

Of Arius himself information is equally meager. According to Epiphanius he was born in Libya, "in the time of Constantine, the great and blessed emperor."[3] Not surprisingly, when Arius developed his theological posture, he was able to draw considerable support from the Libyan bishops (who were linked institutionally with Alexandria). Both Epiphanius and Sozomen implicated Arius in the Meletian schism that was ripping apart the Alexandrian church in the late third and early fourth century.[4] Arius was ordained a deacon (ca. 311) by Bishop Peter, and when he supported the Meletian "church of the martyrs" against the "Catholic Church" of Peter, Arius was anathematized and excommunicated from the Catholic Church. He subsequently repented of his schismatic tendencies and was restored to

1. Hanson, *Christian Doctrine of God*, 99.

2. Young and Teal, *From Nicaea to Chalcedon*, 44.

3. Epiphanius, *Panarion* 69.1.1, 255.

4. Ibid.; Sozomen, *Church History* I.15, *NPNF*, vol. II, 251. Cf. Theodoret, *Church History* I.2, *NPNF*, vol. III, 34.

fellowship and office by the martyred Peter's successor, Achillas, who also ordained Arius as presbyter (priest) by AD 313.[5] From Sozomen's report one should conclude that Arius was a priest in good standing in the Alexandrian church when the controversy that carries his name broke out. Bishop Alexander, who succeeded Achillas, held him in high regard and described Arius as "a most expert logician . . . [who] was not lacking in such knowledge."[6] If we ask what being a "logician" meant in this context, it seems to reflect the idea that he was skilled in Platonic philosophy and critical thinking.[7] Subsequent commentators, like Theodoret, who supported the Nicene theology, impugned his motives and depicted Arius as being motivated by envy and a lust for power.[8] Epiphanius, the heresy-hunter, simply described him as a tool of the devil.[9]

The actual outbreak of the theological controversy in Alexandria is shrouded in conflicting testimonies. Socrates suggested that Arius reacted negatively to a sermon on the Holy Trinity preached by Bishop Alexander. He thought it sounded too much like a popular second- and third-century heresy called Sabellianism (which had the tendency to reduce the Trinity into one singular entity). In Socrates's mind, Alexander tried to explain too much about the mystery of the unity of the Holy Trinity, in his "too philosophical" discourse. Arius responded to Alexander by saying, "If . . . the Father begat the Son, he that was begotten had a beginning of existence: and from this it is evident, that there was a time when the Son was not. It therefore necessarily follows, that He had His subsistence from nothing."[10] Epiphanius reported that a complaint had been lodged with Alexander about Arius's teaching and that was what prompted his inquiry into Arius's theology.[11] Sozomen blamed Arius's love for logical speculation and theological novelty for the eruption of controversy, and doing so "under the pretext of piety, and of seeking the more perfect discovery of God . . ."[12] Hence, Arius developed a doctrine that "no one before him had ever suggested; namely, that the Son of God was made out of that which had no

---

5. Sozomen, *Church History* I.15, *NPNF*, vol. II, 251.

6. Ibid.

7. Wiles, *Archetypical Heresy*, 24.

8. Theodoret, *Church History* I.2, *NPNF*, vol. III, 34.

9. Epiphanius, *Panarion* 69.1.1., 255.

10. Socrates, *Church History* I.5, *NPNF*, vol. II, 3.

11. Epiphanius, *Panarion* 69.3, 256.

12. Sozomen, *Church History* I.15, *NPNF*, vol. II, 251.

prior existence, that there was a period of time in which he existed not; that, as possessing free will, he was capable of vice and virtue, and that he was created and made."[13] Theodoret also impugned Arius's motives, suggesting that after he had "been enrolled in the list of the presbytery, and entrusted with the exposition of the Holy Scriptures, [Arius] fell a prey to the assaults of jealousy, when he saw that the helm of the high priesthood was committed to Alexander. Stung by this passion, he sought opportunities for dispute and contention."[14] In a similar way, Rufinus reported, "A presbyter of Alexandria named Arius, a man religious in appearance and aspect rather than in virtue, but shamefully desirous of glory, praise, and novelties, began to propose certain impious doctrines regarding the faith of Christ, things which had never before been talked about. He tried to sever and divide the Son from the eternal and ineffable substance or nature of God the Father, something which upset very many in the church."[15] Whatever one concludes about Arius's motives, and they might simply have been to make an honest theological inquiry, it is clear that his reshaping of Trinitarian doctrine was the spark that ignited an explosion that nearly blew the fourth-century church apart.

If we inquire into the roots and antecedents of Arius's theological posture, several popular suggestions are forthcoming. In a letter to Eusebius of Nicomedia, written in the midst of this controversy, Arius describes the recipient as "a fellow Lucianist."[16] This implies that both men studied with the fabled Bishop Lucian of Antioch, who was martyred for his faith in 312. The Arian historian Philostorgius listed some of the disciples of Lucian and gave credence to a theological school emerging under his tutelage, but Arius was not mentioned among them.[17] Adolf von Harnack represents an older scholarly consensus that concluded "this school is the nursery of Arian doctrine, and Lucian, its head, is the Arius before Arius."[18] From this assertion is deduced that Lucian (like Arius) professed a Christology that was centered in the conception of Christ as the *Logos* (John 1:1–17), or Word of God; said Christology was assumed to have been subordinationist in its emphasis; subordinationism suggested that Jesus Christ is subordinate

13. Ibid.
14. Theodoret, *Church History* I.1, *NPNF*, vol. III, 34.
15. Rufinus, *Church History* X.1, 9.
16. Theodoret, *Church History* I.4, *NPNF*, vol. III, 41.
17. Philostorgius, *Church History* II.14, 30.
18. Harnack, *History of Dogma*, Kindle loc. 22501.

to (or less than) God the Father and served under the Father's authority and direction (cf. John 5:19). More recent scholarship, like that of Frances Young, Rowan Williams, and John Behr, suggests that since almost nothing is known about Lucius of Antioch, it is not particularly helpful to look to him as the "Arius before Arius."[19] Yet, if there were theological kinship between Arius and his "fellow Lucianists," this association would amply explain the wide reception of Arius's theology in Syria and Asia Minor. In this sense, Arius was probably more a participant in an older theological tradition than a founder of a new one.

It seems that we are on much firmer ground if we look for the roots of Arius's theological innovations within the eclectic theological traditions and diverse trajectories within Alexandria and the Alexandrian church itself. For example, Arius's theological predecessor in Alexandria, by about fifty years, was the creative and eclectic theologian Origen. A Platonist and a Christian theologian, Origen also taught what appeared to be a mild subordinationism.[20] The conflict between Alexander and Arius may be understood as an inter-family squabble among the theological descendants of Origen. If that were the case, then Arius belongs on the progressive side of the Origenist camp, and Alexander represents the more conservative aspect of it. The subordination of the Son to the Father was much more commonplace in the early fourth century than it was thereafter; hence, Hanson observed, "With the exception of Athanasius, virtually every theologian, East and West, accepted some form of subordinationism at least up to the year 355."[21]

This debate is frequently couched as a struggle over biblical hermeneutics: how do you interpret the Bible? The particular exegesis of Proverbs 8:22–25 figures largely in the connection between the Alexandrians and Origen. In his *On First Principles* (*De Principiis*) Origen looks upon this passage as a description of the pre-incarnate *Logos'* (Word's) relationship with God the Father, and in this sense the Wisdom passage is brought alongside John 1:1–17 as an explanation of the birth of the *Logos* (or Wisdom) of God.[22] John 1:14, in most English versions, reads "the only Son of

19. Young and Teal, *From Nicaea to Chalcedon*, 47; Williams, *Arius*, 167; and Behr, *Formation of Christian Theology*, vol. 2, pt. 1, 51.

20. Writing in the third century, Origen used theological terminology that was subsequently unsettling to fourth-century Christian theologians and their successors, most notably Jerome.

21. Hanson, *Christian Doctrine of God*, xix.

22. Origen, *On First Principles* I.2, *ANF*, vol. IV, 246.

the Father"; however, in New Testament Greek the phrase is more literally rendered, "the *only begotten* Son of the Father." The "only begotten" section is represented by the Greek word *monogenas,* which means "only one born out of." Proverbs 8:22, in which the voice of Wisdom is speaking, is taken by the Origenists as a statement by the pre-incarnate *Logos* of God: "The LORD created me at the beginning of his work, the first of his acts of old." A synthesis of these two passages gives the impression that the *Logos* (Wisdom, Second Person of the Trinity) was "born" (John 1:14) or "created" (Prov 8:22) by God the Father as the first act of creation. It would be on the basis of this exegesis that the Arians would eventually conclude that (1) the Son, created by God the Father, is a creature Who is superior to all other creatures; and (2) there was a time when the Father existed and the Son did not exist. Hence, Jaroslav Pelikan reports, "in his account of Arian doctrine, Hilary [of Poitiers] said that 'they maintain that [Christ] is a creature, because of what is written in Prov. 8:22.'"[23] Epiphanius echoed this same textual connection in his *Panarion*: "Arius took his cue from Origen."[24] And more specifically, later in the same work:

> Now therefore, Arius, inspired by a diabolical energy, and knowing no restraint of tongue or shame, raised his voice against his own Master. His starting point was his attempt to interpret the words of Solomon in Proverbs: "the Lord created me the beginning of his ways. Before the world he established me in the beginning, before making the earth and before making the abysses, before all the hills he produced me." This became the introduction to his error; he and his disciples were not ashamed to call a creature him who created everything, the Word begotten from the Father outside time and without beginning. From that point on, from that one passage, driving his malignant doctrine into many evil paths [he] and his successors attempted countless blasphemies against the Son of God and the Holy Spirit.[25]

When Emperor Constantine subsequently reported that the disagreement in the Alexandrian church had to do with the exegesis of "a certain passage of divine Scripture," perhaps he too was referencing this discussion over the meaning of Proverbs 8:22–25.[26]

23. Pelikan, *Christian Tradition,* 1:193.
24. Epiphanius, *Panarion of Epiphanius of Salamis,* 137.
25. Epiphanius, *Panarion* 69.12, 264.
26. Eusebius, *Life of Constantine* II.69, *NPNF,* vol. I, 516.

Hence, Sozomen reported that Arius "fell into absurd discourses, so that he had the audacity to preach in the church what no one before him had ever suggested; namely, that the Son of God was made out of that which had no prior existence, that there was a period of time in which he existed not; that, as possessing free will, he was capable of vice and virtue, and that he was created and made; to these, many other similar assertions were added as he went forward into the arguments and the details of inquiry."[27] Both Sozomen and Epiphanius report that Bishop Alexander drew together the presbytery of priests and bishops to hear Arius's doctrine and to judge its veracity.[28] But some of the other clergy blamed Bishop Alexander for being too lenient, in "not opposing the innovations at variance with doctrine."[29] Determined to use persuasion instead of force or excommunication, Alexander "sat down as a judge with some of his clergy, and led both sides into a discussion."[30] Sozomen reported, "Arius defended his assertions, but the others contended that the Son is consubstantial and co-eternal with the Father."[31] When the debate had concluded both sides claimed victory, and the net result was an awkward theological standoff. Hence, "the council was convened a second time, and the same points contested, but they came to no agreement amongst themselves."[32] Sozomen asserts that the debate was further complicated by the fact that Alexander, as judge, seemed to incline first towards the teaching of one party and then the other.[33] If that unsupported allegation is true, it may have been a feature of the bishop's fact-finding approach, for his own written assertions show no equivocation regarding what would become orthodox doctrine. Socrates indicates that it was at this time that the Meletians joined with the Arians in opposing Bishop Alexander;[34] whether this was a strategic alliance ("the enemy of my enemy is my friend") or one based on theological doctrine is unclear.

At the end of the second council meeting, Alexander demanded that Arius receive the doctrine that Christ is consubstantial (of the same substance) and co-eternal with the God the Father, and reject his former

27. Sozomen, *Church History* I.15, *NPNF*, vol. II, 251.
28. Ibid.; Epiphanius, *Panarion* 69.3, 256.
29. Sozomen, *Church History* I.15, *NPNF*, vol. II, 251.
30. Ibid.
31. Ibid.
32. Ibid.
33. Ibid.
34. Socrates, *Church History* I.6, *NPNF*, vol. II, 5.

statements to the contrary.[35] Arius "could not be persuaded to compliance, and many of the bishops and clergy considered his statement of doctrine to be correct. Alexander, therefore, ejected him and the clergy who concurred with him in sentiment from the church."[36] Sozomen included a list of ten clergy (bishops, presbyters, and deacons) who were excommunicated that day. "Many of the people, likewise, sided with them; some, because they imagined their doctrines to be of God; others, as frequently happens in similar cases, because they believed them to have been ill-treated and un-justly excommunicated."[37] The Arians, as we might now appropriately call them, began to ardently seek support for their point of view, both within and beyond Alexandria. Socrates's metaphor is an apt one: "From a little spark a large fire was kindled: for the evil which began in the church at Alexandria, ran throughout all Egypt, Libya, and the upper Thebes; and at length diffused itself over the rest of the provinces and cities."[38]

Alexander, for his part, began a letter-writing campaign and sent an encyclical letter to "the ministers of the Catholic Church." This letter is preserved in Socrates's *Church History*. It not only named and denounced Arius and those who followed him (the list was getting longer!) but also gave a lengthy summation of "the dogmas which they have invented." The gist of his long summary amounts to three main points against the Arians: (1) they deny that God has always existed as a consubstantial Trinity; (2) they assert that the *Logos*, or Son of God, was created before time and is not of the same substance as the Father; and (3) they hold that the Word or Son is a creature and is therefore susceptible to change. Theodoret, in his *Church History*, preserves a letter that Alexander, bishop of Alexandria, wrote to his counterpart and namesake in Constantinople during this same period. It, too, is a lengthy letter that lists the excommunicated and apostates, and is full of denunciations and doctrinal summaries of what the Arians affirmed. Alexander's letter stated, "I have stirred myself up to inform you of the unbelief of certain persons who say that 'there was a time when the Son of God was not'; and 'He who previously had no existence subsequently came into existence; and when at some time He came into existence He became such as every other man is' . . . 'We are also able,' say these accursed wretches, 'to become like Him, the sons of God; for it is

---

35. Sozomen, *Church History* I.15, *NPNF*, vol. II, 251.

36. Ibid.

37. Ibid., 251–52.

38. Socrates, *Church History* I.6, *NPNF*, vol. II, 3.

written—*I have nourished and brought up children* [Isa 1:2]."[39] These and many other assertions are registered in the letter to Constantinople, and they parallel the same points registered in the earlier encyclical letter of Alexander. In this later letter, however, we begin to glimpse some of the slogans or catch phrases of Arius's doctrine.

If we ask what Athanasius was doing during these early phases of the "Arian controversy," the historical record greets us with a disturbing silence. He had been ordained as a deacon in the church of his native city, and as such was very likely employing his considerable intellectual and literary abilities in the service of his father in the faith, Alexander, who was also his bishop. Athanasius had a passion for theological truth, as he was given to see the truth, and a willingness to debate theological doctrine when he believed truth was being assailed—these characteristics are amply documented in his subsequent anti-Arian writings—hence, it is difficult to imagine that he sat on the sidelines when Alexander called two separate theological councils in his diocese. It seems more likely that as Alexander's assistant, young Athanasius was in the thick of things and played a lively part in the theological debates that were raging in Alexandria. Furthermore, it is very likely that, functioning as Alexander's secretary, he penned the theological epistles that the bishop issued to the church as a result of these debates. Contemporary scholars claim to see the hand of Athanasius at work in both of these letters sent out under Alexander's signature.[40]

The *Deposition of Arius* (*Depositio Arii*), which was probably written in 322, is an encyclical letter issued by Alexander that was probably penned by Athanasius, who was serving as his scribe and assistant. The letter names the Arians who were anathematized and excommunicated in Alexandria and explains their theological innovations.[41] In a tightly worded paragraph, the writer enumerated the Arians' heresies:

> The novelties they have invented and put forth contrary to the Scriptures are these following:—God was not always a Father, but there was a time when God was not a Father. The Word of God was

39. Theodoret, *Church History* I.3, *NPNF*, vol. III, 35–36.

40. Cf. Barnes, *Athanasius and Constantius*, 16, and Gwynn, *Eusebians*, 66.

41. Among those named here: "Arius, Achilles, Aeithales, Carpones, another Arius, and Sarmates, sometime Presbyters: Euzoïus, Lucius, Julius, Menas, Helladius, and Gaius, sometime Deasons: and with them Secundus and Theonas, sometime called Bishops." *Depositio Arii* 2, *NPNF*, vol. IV, 70.

not always, but originated from things that were not; for God that is, has made him that was not, of that which was not; wherefore there was a time when He was not; for the Son is a creature and a work. Neither is He like in essence to the Father; neither is He the true and natural Word of the Father; neither is He His true Wisdom; but He is one of the things made and created, and is called the Word and Wisdom by an abuse of terms, since He Himself originated by the proper Word of God, and by the Wisdom that is in God, by which God has made not only all other things but Him also. Wherefore He is by nature subject to change and variation, as are all rational creatures. And the Word is foreign from the essence of the Father, and is alien and separated therefrom.[42]

Central to this characterization of Arian theology are the twin assertions that the Son of God has a beginning and is a rational creature. The same epistle attacked Eusebius of Nicomedia for interjecting himself into this affair and for writing various churches urging the acceptance of Arius and his doctrinal innovations.

During this period, Epiphanius reports, "Arius spent a long time in the city [of Alexandria] . . . So Arius worked schisms and ruined many people by stealing them away one by one. Later when he had been caught, brought to judgment in the city, and excommunicated, he fled from Alexandria and made his way to Palestine. Upon his arrival, he approached each of the bishops with flattery and wheedling in order to acquire many collaborators for himself. Some received him while others rejected him."[43] At this point, Arius began to receive support from some of the leading bishops in that region, including two men both named Eusebius: the one the bishop of Nicomedia, who would become a lifelong supporter; the other the bishop of Caesarea and famous church historian (sometimes called Eusebius Pamphilus), who would subsequently change sides at the Council of Nicaea.

Before his forced departure for Palestine, Arius composed a letter to Eusebius of Nicomedia. This letter has been preserved for us in the *Church History* of Theodoret. In this correspondence Arius sought to establish contacts with his "fellow Lucianist" and to complain about the persecution that had fallen upon him in Alexandria. He outlined his own position in this way: "We say and believe, and have taught, and do teach, that the Son was not unbegotten, nor in any way part of the unbegotten; and that He does not derive His subsistence from any matter; but that by His own will and

42. Ibid.

43. Epiphanius, *Panarion* 69.4.1–2, 257.

31

counsel He has subsisted before time, and before ages, as perfect God, only begotten and unchangeable, and that before He was begotten, or created, or purposed, or established, He was not. For He was not unbegotten."[44] This passage affirms that the Son is and has been created by the Father, in consort with the Son's own will; and that the Son is not a creature like any other creature (because He is before time). Yet, the Son has a beginning, and hence is not eternal, and is not of the same "substance" as the Father (the Unbegotten). "We are persecuted," Arius complained, "because we say that the Son has a beginning, but that God is without beginning. This is the cause of our persecution, and likewise, because we say that He [the Son] is of the non-existent. And this we say, because He is neither part of God, nor of any essential being [with God]. For this we are persecuted."[45] During this same period of time (ca. 318–20), Arius composed and propagated his famous theological song-poem known as the *Thalia*.[46]

When the reports of Socrates, Sozomen, and Theodoret are taken together, a consensus about the main themes of the theology of Arius emerges. These might be summarized as follows: (1) Arius taught that the Son was begotten and therefore had a beginning; (2) that since God (the Father) is unbegotten, the Son is not of the same substance as the Father; and (3) that the Son is a creature—albeit a special creature—who enables Christians to become children of God. Based on this general consensus it seems possible to speak of Arius's views as having three significant trajectories that resonated with various themes of fourth-century theology. And "Arianism" (including the thought of Arius and subsequent developments) has been treated from each of these points of view. The first of these is that Arianism was a kind of radical monotheism, which seeks to protect and honor the mystery of the Godhead as inexpressible and unknowable. Secondly, Arianism has been presented and understood as a new way of understanding the complex relationship of the Father and the Son, which was developed (following Origen) at a time when that matter was still an open and unanswered question in Christian theology. And finally, Arianism has

44. Theodoret, *Church History* I.4, *NPNF*, vol. III, 41.

45. Ibid.

46. Since the text of the *Thalia* is available only in Athanasius's reconstruction of it in two separate polemics, it will be treated in the sections dealing with his response to Arius, rather than here. For a reconstructed text of the *Thalia* see Hanson, *Christian Doctrine of God*, 12–15; Williams, *Arius*, 98–116; or http://www.fourthcentury.com/arius-thalia-intro/.

been understood from the standpoint of the implications of its approach to Christian salvation (soteriology).[47]

Exploring and developing each of these alternatives gives us important insight into the inner workings of Arius's views, such as we understand them, but this task also involves equally large amounts of generalization and the acceptance of various aspects of the picture that Arius's subsequent commentators (ancient and modern) have given about his position. Taking the "radical monotheism" tack first, Arius seems to be concerned to safeguard the nature and identity of the Unbegotten and ineffable God. Yet, since Christianity affirms a suffering Savior, how is the holy nature of God to be maintained in the face of the suffering and death of God's Son? Working with passages like John 1:1–17 and Proverbs 8:22–23, as we saw above, Arius postulated a demigod, One who was created by God, as a creature (though far above other creatures) and was therefore capable of suffering. The Son had a free will, therefore His voluntary suffering could be considered meritorious before God. This approach, while not without some problems (which Arius's critics pointed out), sufficiently protected the nature of God in a way that was somewhat palatable to Christian Platonists and Judeo-Christian monotheists, and embraced the suffering of Christ as a central message of the Christian gospel. For example, as Hanson writes, "We can now perceive the rationale of Arianism. At the heart of the Arian Gospel was a God who suffered. Their elaborate theology of the relation of the Son to the Father which so much preoccupied their opponents was devised in order to find a way of envisaging a Christian doctrine of God which would make it possible to be faithful to the Biblical witness to a God who suffers. This was to be achieved by conceiving of a lesser God as a reduced divinity, who would be ontologically capable, as the High God was not, of enduring human experiences, including suffering and death."[48] This approach was particularly attractive to fourth-century pastors and theologians who were upset by the earlier heresy of Sabellius (in which the monotheism of the Trinity was preserved by urging that the One God went through three separate phases of being).

This first approach also suggests why Arius and the Arians were cautious not to affirm that the Son and the Father had the same substance

47. While it is difficult to completely delineate between these themes and scholars who have used them, it does seem to be fair to say that Hanson, *Christian Doctrine of God*, takes the first approach, while Williams, *Arius: Heresy and Tradition*, takes the second, and Gregg and Groh, *Early Arianism: A View of Salvation*, follow the third.

48. Hanson, *Christian Doctrine of God*, 121.

(*homoousia*), because the Son was capable of human suffering and the Father was not. Furthermore, as Socrates quotes Arius as saying, "if the Father begat the Son, he that was begotten had a beginning of existence; and from this it is evident that there was a time when the Son was not. It therefore necessarily follows, that he [the Son] had his substance from nothing."[49] It was for this reason, and others, that Arius and a few cohorts would subsequently refuse to affirm the creed produced at the Council of Nicaea in 325.

The second approach to understanding and characterizing Arius's views is no less complex than the first. The theological heritage of Origen of Alexandria is an important background of this approach; that means, in part, that a mild subordination of the Son to the Father and the Father's will was not untenable or theologically unacceptable. Williams offers "three basic theological points" that characterize the thought of Arius and his followers: "(i) The Son is a creature, that is, a product of God's will; (ii) 'Son' is therefore a *metaphor* for the second hypostasis ["person"], and must be understood in the light of comparable metaphorical usage in Scripture; and (iii) the Son's status, like his very existence, depends upon God's will."[50] This picture of a God-dependent, "begotten Son" of the Unbegotten Father squares well with some of the Scriptures that were under discussion in this controversy, and explains the relationship between Father and Son in a manner that fits well with the common use of those terms. Because of this linguistic connection, Arius's "solution" to the problem posed by Alexander's sermon on the Trinity also had some significant traction in the early fourth-century church.

Third, Arianism could be viewed from the standpoint of the theology of salvation (soteriology). Building from passages like Philippians 2:5–11 and 2 Corinthians 2:9, as well as many gospel passages that evidence the human characteristics of Christ the Redeemer, Arius may have postulated an approach to salvation that stressed the importance of conformity of one's will with that of the Father and a willingness to live one's life as a servant. This approach would have fit well with the developing Eastern Orthodox theology of deification (*theosis*), which stressed that through abandonment of one's own will and dedication to God, through grace, believers could become "partakers of the divine nature" (2 Pet 1:4). It was through His obedient and selfless ministry and dedication that Jesus as the Son of God

49. Socrates, *Church History* I.5, *NPNF*, vol. III, 3.

50. Williams, *Arius*, 109. See 131–32 for three syllogisms that comprise Arius's argument.

34

became a "partaker of the divine nature." Alexander quoted an Arian slogan in his letter, which—following Isaiah 1:2—affirmed "we are also able . . . to become like Him, the Sons of God; for it is written—*I have nourished and brought up children.*"[51] This path, which Jesus trod before us, has been laid open to us by Him and His revelation. This approach resonated well with the spirituality of *apatheia* (the cultivation of a selfless will), which was embraced by Eastern monks, ascetics, and clergy.[52]

The role of Eusebius of Nicomedia (d. AD 341) in the so-called Arian controversy has been undergoing (like most aspects of this topic) recent review and revision. David Gwynn, for example, challenges Athanasius's assertion that there were those "around Eusebius" (the "Eusebians") who embraced the Arian cause and schemed against him by using both church and state to silence his defense of the Nicene theology. In his rendition of this group and its teaching, Gwynn asserts that they "were in fact neither a 'party' nor 'Arian.'"[53] Gwynn mounts an interesting argument, indicating that the "Eusebians" were more a feature of Athanasius's polemical writings than a fact of history.

It is clear, however, that Eusebius interjected himself in the dispute that was raging in the Alexandrian church in several ways. He wrote to Alexander and urged him to reinstate Arius (ca. 320). In the same year he wrote to Paulinus of Tyre explaining the new theology to him in very positive tones. Eusebius also urged Paulinus—if he were of like mind—to write at once to Alexander.[54] What motives are to be ascribed to Eusebius in these matters is unclear. Charles Kannengiesser views this as an example of the *willezurmacht* ("will-to-power") on the part of Eusebius,[55] but it is also clear that he had both sympathy and a theological kinship with Arius, his "fellow Lucianist."

A regional synod was held in Bithynia. The leaders there "wrote to all the bishops, desiring them to hold communion with the Arians, as with those making a true confession, and to require Alexander to hold communion with them likewise." When that injunction failed to gain compliance, a commission comprised of Paulinus of Tyre, Eusebius of Caesarea, and

51. Theodoret, *Church History* I.3, NPNF, vol. III, 36.

52. Cf. Gregg and Groh, "The Arian Christ," in *Early Arianism*, 1–43.

53. Gwynn, *Eusebians*, vii.

54. Theodoret, *Church History* I.5, NPNF, vol. III, 42–43. Sozomen mentions this as well (*Church History* I.16, NPNF, vol. II, 252).

55. Kannengiesser, *Arius and Athanasius*, 2.

Patrophilus, bishop of Scythopolis, was sent to Alexander to urge him to allow the Arians to form a separate church for themselves in Alexandria. This also failed to gain compliance; hence those three bishops granted Arius's petition and allowed him to establish a church in Palestine.[56] Alexander had become a lightning rod for controversy, as Sozomen reported: "Some [bishops] wrote to Alexander, entreating him not to receive the partisans of Arius into communion unless they repudiated their opinions; while others wrote to urge a contrary line of conduct."[57]

Socrates reported that news of the debate that was now raging in the Eastern church soon reached the ears of Emperor Constantine. "When the emperor was made acquainted with these disorders, he was very deeply grieved," he wrote, "and regarding the matter as a personal misfortune, immediately exerted himself to extinguish the conflagration which had been kindled, and sent a letter to Alexander and Arius by a trustworthy person named Hosius, who was bishop of Cordova, in Spain."[58] The historian's account includes a digest of the letter (the full text of which is carried in the *Life of Constantine*). Constantine's letter urges both men to silence and reconciliation, without attempting to resolve the doctrinal issues that separated them. The emperor urged them, "Listen to the counsel of your fellow servant. And what counsel does he offer? It was neither prudent at first to agitate such a question, nor to reply to such a question when proposed: for the claim of no law demands the investigation of such subjects, but the idle useless talk of leisure occasions them. And even if they should exist for the sake of exercising our natural faculties, yet we ought to confine them to our own consideration, and not incautiously bring them forth in public assemblies, nor thoughtlessly confide them to the ears of everybody."[59] A second reason for urging them to lay aside the doctrinal debate was that it was dividing "the people of God"—which was in Constantine's mind both "unbecoming" and "altogether unlawful."[60] Sozomen characterized Constantine's epistle in this way: "The Emperor openly charged Arius and Alexander with having originated the disturbance, and wrote to rebuke them for having made a controversy public which it was in their power to have concealed, and for having contentiously agitated a question which

56. Sozomen, *Church History* I.15, *NPNF*, vol. II, 252.
57. Ibid.
58. Socrates, *Church History* I.7, *NPNF*, vol. II, 6.
59. Ibid.
60. Ibid., 6–7.

ought never to have been invoked, or upon which at least their opinion ought to have been given quietly. He told them that they ought not to have separated from others on account of difference of sentiment concerning certain points of doctrine."[61] Constantine's letter, while written with considerable piety, seemed more concerned with unity in the church—which fit well his own political agenda—than with the doctrine of the Trinity. Hosius of Cordova, however, seemed to have clearly grasped the significance of the theological debate that was wracking the Eastern church; he soon became an ally of Alexander of Alexandria.

61. Sozomen, *Church History* I.16, *NPNF*, vol. II, 252.

4

The Council of Nicaea

As Emperor Constantine consolidated his rule in the West, the "Arian controversy" in Alexandria and in the East seemed to have been either halted or stalled by Licinius's decree against allowing the Christian bishops to meet in councils.[1] When Constantine emerged as sole emperor in the East, in 324, controversy erupted again. The new "Christian emperor" soon interjected himself into the theological tumult because he intended Christianity to be the unifying force for his far-flung empire. Imagine his surprise and irritation when he found out that the Christians could not be depended upon for supplying social and ecclesiastical unity!

The first step in this imperial intervention came in the form of a lengthy letter to Alexander, bishop of Alexandria, and Arius, urging both of them to peace and harmony. Constantine seemed to have his own opinion about how the controversy arose: "When you, Alexander, inquired of your presbyters what each thought on a certain inexplicable passage of the written Word, rather on a subject improper for discussion; and you, Arius, rashly gave expression to a view of the matter such as ought either never to have been conceived, or when suggested to your mind, it became you to bury it in silence."[2] He blamed both parties for speculating about a difficult passage of Scripture, probably Proverbs 8:22, about which they both should have kept silent. The emperor urged them to listen conscientiously to each other and to avoid "useless talk" so that harmony and communion among them might be restored. For "who can grapple with the subtleties of such investigations without danger of lapsing into error?"[3] Constantine wrote

---

1. Eusebius, *Life of Constantine* I.15, *NPNF*, vol. I, 486.
2. Socrates, *Church History* I.7, *NPNF*, vol. II, 6.
3. Ibid.

not so much as an emperor giving commands, but as "a fellow-servant" offering Christian exhortation; yet the shadow of imperial power hung over his request. In view of the division and disharmony being caused, the theological matters about which they were contending were, Constantine wrote, "of small or scarcely the least importance." Since both parties strive to worship the same God and Christ, should they not stress those things that lead to harmony? Because they are both charged with the leadership of the people of God, their divisive contention with one another "not only is unbecoming, but it is also believed to be altogether unlawful."[4] Without broaching the theological issue that divided the Alexandrians, Constantine urged them, "The great God and Savior of us all has extended to all the common light. Under his providence, allow me, his servant, to bring this effort of mine to a successful issue; that by my exhortation, ministry, and earnest admonition, I may lead you, his people, back to unity of communion. For since, as I have said, there is but one faith among you, and one sentiment respecting religion, and since the precept of the law, in all its parts, combines all in one purpose of soul, let not this diversity of opinion, which has excited dissension among you, by any means cause discord and schism . . ."[5]

The letter to the Alexandrians was hand-delivered by one of Constantine's leading religious advisors, Hosius, bishop of Cordova. Socrates told his readers, "The Emperor greatly loved this man and held him in the highest estimation."[6] As it turns out, Hosius was a good choice, from the standpoint of Alexander and Athanasius, because he clearly understood the theological ramifications of the controversy, in a way that Constantine could not—or did not care to. Upon his arrival in Alexandria, Hosius called a church council, which debated the issues causing dispute. A circular letter was drafted by the council that stressed the importance of the theological matters under consideration and indicated that a reconciliation had not been achieved. The gravity of the questions under debate was readily apparent to the bishop from Cordova, and Hosius soon became a champion of what would become the Nicene solution. He also became an important ally of Alexander and Athanasius against Arius at the Council of Nicaea. After the local synod, Hosius left Alexandria and began his return trip to the seat of the emperor at Nicomedia.

4. Ibid., 6–7.
5. Ibid., 7.
6. Ibid., 6.

On his way east, Hosius stopped in Antioch of Syria, where the church was in chaos following the death of their bishop. Soon after Hosius arrived, a new bishop was elected. Hosius presided over a council of fifty bishops that met to adjudicate several doctrinal and ecclesiastical matters that were troubling that church, among which seemed to have been the Arian question. A creed was drawn up by the Synod of Antioch, in early 325, that affirmed that the Son was "not as made but as properly an offspring, but begotten in an ineffable, indescribable manner, because only the Father Who begot and the Son Who was begotten know . . . Who exists everlastingly and did not at one time not exist. For we have learned from the Holy Scriptures that He alone is the express image [Gk. *Eikon*], not (plainly) as if He might have remained unbegotten from the Father, nor by adoption . . . ; but the Scriptures describe Him as validly and truly begotten as Son, so that we believe Him to be immutable and unchangeable."[7] This creed strongly reflects the position of Alexander and Athanasius over and against the views of Arius. And in case even the casual reader did not "get" the anti-Arian slant of the Creed of Antioch, its anathemas (condemnations) made its posture completely clear: "we anathematize those who say or think or preach that the Son of God is a creature or has come into being or has been made and is not truly begotten, or that there was a time when He was not."[8] Philostorgius, the Arian church historian, complained that Hosius and Alexander met prior to the Council of Nicaea and plotted to develop an anti-Arian creed that would include the phrase *homoousia* ("consubstantial"), and that in collusion they agreed to anathematize Arius.[9] This meeting, which Philostorgius located in Nicomedia, could have taken place either in Alexandria or at the Council of Antioch.[10]

Constantine continued to be "deeply grieved at the diversity of opinion that prevailed" in the church, both concerning the date of Passover (and hence Easter celebrations) and subsequently—upon hearing the report of Hosius—about the divisions over doctrine.[11] Hence the emperor, either at the urging of the bishop of Cordova or the prompting of Alexander of Alexandria, decided to call an ecumenical church council.[12] Socrates reported

---

7. Kelly, *Early Christian Creeds*, 209.

8. Ibid., 210.

9. Philostorgius, *Church History* I.7, 9.

10. Ibid.

11. Socrates, *Church History* I.16, *NPNF*, vol. II, 252.

12. Epiphanius attributes the calling of the Council of Nicaea to Alexander of

this event as follows: "When it was found that the event did not answer the expectations of the emperor, but that on the contrary, the contention was too great for reconciliation, so that he who had been sent to make peace returned without having accomplished his mission, Constantine convened a synod at Nicaea, in Bithynia, and wrote to the most eminent men of the churches in every country, directing them to be there on an appointed day."[13]

Bishops and their entourages began arriving by mid-May 325. Constantine himself did not arrive at Nicaea till after July 3, and the council began to meet in earnest after that, finally adjourning on August 25, 325.[14] Philostorgius reported, "Seeing that the bishops had many different views at the time, the emperor Constantine decided to summon a council of all the bishops to Nicaea and to put an end to their mutual bickering."[15]

It was a distinguished gathering of church leaders, with the Eastern bishops outnumbering those who made the long trip from the Latin West. It is symptomatic of the confusing and sometimes contradictory path laid out by our various sources that our early church historians cannot agree on exactly how many bishops attended. Eusebuis and Athanasius—both of whom were at the Council of Nicaea—report "more than 250" and "more than 300," respectively.[16] Sozomen stated that "about three hundred and twenty bishops were present, accompanied by a multitude of presbyters and deacons. There were likewise men present who were skilled in dialectics, and ready to assist in the discussions."[17] In a later writing, Athanasius fixed the number at precisely 318—a total that may have been suggested to him by the text of Genesis 14:14, and the size of the holy posse that rode out with Abraham to rescue Lot.[18] The meager paper trail that has been left to us and the fact that even eyewitnesses like Eusebius and Athanasius cannot agree on the exact number of participants does not give the contemporary reader much confidence that she can know the details of the deliberations

---

Alexandria (*Panarion* 68.4, 249). Hanson finds this to be "unlikely" (*Christian Doctrine of God*, 154).

13. Socrates, *Church History* I.17, NPNF, vol. II, 253.

14. Kidd, *History of the Church*, 2:22.

15. Philistorgius, *Church History* I.7, 10.

16. Eusebius, *Life of Constantine* III.8, NPNF, vol. I, 522; Athanasius, *History of the Arians* 66, NPNF, vol. IV, 294.

17. Sozomen, *Church History* I.17, NPNF, vol. II, 253.

18. Kidd, *History of the Church*, 2:23.

at the Council of Nicaea. In fact, Eusebius's eyewitness account is notable for its glorification of Constantine and for its utter silence about the "Arian controversy."

It is generally agreed that the official opening of the Council of Nicaea corresponded to the arrival of Emperor Constantine and his "Opening Address," reported by Eusebius in his *Life of Constantine*. Other "opening addresses" were attributed to Eusebius[19] and to Eustathius of Antioch.[20] These and other important speeches were probably delivered prior to the emperor's arrival. Eusebius probably introduced the Emperor Constantine, and Eustathius's important address on the meaning of Proverbs 8:22 was also probably part of the deliberations.[21] But there can be no doubt that the presence of Emperor Constantine was the galvanizing force of the Council and the focus of attention of the bishops present. It is further suggested, by Athanasius, that Hosius was the presiding chairman of the council.[22]

When Constantine entered the room of their deliberations a silence fell upon the place. The emperor stood in the midst of the bishops, who rose and bowed to him and thereby "intimated their desire that he should be seated."[23] Taking his place among them, the emperor addressed the bishops "[in] words of exhortation to harmony and unity, and entreated each to lay aside all private pique."[24] He told them that as soon as he heard "news of your dissension," he judged this to be a matter of the utmost importance and resolved to "remedy this evil."[25] Constantine spoke to them, in Latin, which was also translated into Greek by an interpreter: "Delay not, then, dear friends: delay not, ye ministers of God, and faithful servants of Him who is our common Lord and Savior: begin from this moment to discard the causes of that disunion which has existed among you, and remove the perplexities of controversy by embracing the principles of peace. For by such conduct you will at the same time be acting in a manner most pleasing to the supreme God, and you will confer an exceeding favor on me who am

19. Sozomen, *Church History* I.19, *NPNF*, vol. II, 254.

20. Theodoret, *Church History* I.7, *NPNF*, vol. III, 24.

21. Sozomen, *Church History* I.19, *NPNF*, vol. II, 254 n. 4.

22. Hanson, *Christian Doctrine of God*, 154. Hanson points to a reference in Athanasius's *Apology to Secunda*, which referred to Nicaea as "the General Council of Ossius."

23. Socrates, *Church History* I.8, *NPNF*, vol. II, 9.

24. Ibid.

25. Eusebius, *Life of Constantine* III.12, *NPNF*, vol. I, 523.

your fellow-servant."[26] Constantine's first action among them was to show the assembly a bundle of petitions and complaints that he had received from them against one another. He ordered a brazier to be brought out, and he burned these in the presence of all, saying, "'Christ enjoins him who is anxious to obtain forgiveness, to forgive his brother.' When therefore he had strongly insisted on the maintenance of harmony and peace, he sanctioned again their purpose of more closely investigating the questions at issue."[27]

After the Council had dispensed with several other issues—including the date and celebration of the Christian Passover, Easter—"the emperor himself being present, leading all into unanimity, established unity of judgment, and agreement of opinion among them."[28] The debate over the Arian theology proceeded through the presentation of creeds, sermons, and discussions. It began when Arius, who was present by the emperor's command, set forth his case "in painstaking detail." "Finally," Rufinus noted, "after long and detailed discussion it was decided by all, and decreed as though by the mouth and heart of all, that the word *homoousios* [consubstantial] should be written, that is that the Son should be acknowledged to be of the same substance as the Father, and this was most firmly declared by the vote of them all."[29] This vote was preceded by a discussion led by Eusebius of Nicomedia, about squaring the Nicene formula with the terms used in Holy Scripture, seeking to show that the phrase *homoousia* was an innovation and not consistent with the biblical witness. Athanasius recalled that they buzzed about the actual definition like a swarm of gnats, either because it caused them to "stumble out of ignorance" or because it served as "an accurate declaration and full in the face of their heresy."[30] When those in favor of the *homoousian* terminology drew upon scriptural phrases and analogies to explain their usage, the Arian party disputed that it was not strictly speaking a biblical word and was thus an innovation.[31] Since this process seemed to be going nowhere, Eusebius of Nicomedia put forth a formulation of his own composition, which was viewed by Eustathius of

26. Ibid.

27. Socrates, *Church History* VIII.8, *NPNF*, vol. II, 9.

28. Ibid., 9–10.

29. Rufinius, *Church History* X.5, 13.

30. Athanasius, *To the Bishops of Africa* 5, *NPNF*, vol. IV, 491.

31. Theodoret, *Church History* I.7, *NPNF*, vol. III, 44.

Antioch (among others) as being so heretical that it was snatched from his hands and torn to pieces before the entire assembly.[32]

In his self-congratulatory letter to his home church about the Council of Nicaea, Eusebius Pamphilus (Eusebius of Caesarea) claimed that at this point he presented their own creed before the emperor and the Council, as a working draft from which to develop a conciliar document.[33] Hence, the Nicene Creed was developed out of this earlier creed, with the emperor himself insisting upon the insertion of the words "one in essence" (*homoousia*) to describe the consubstantial nature of the God the Father and God the Son.[34] Those who refused to subscribe to the "one essence" phraseology, or who insisted upon saying that the Son had a beginning, or that the Son was created, were anathematized.[35] As Sozomen explained, "The next debate by the priests turned upon doctrine. The Emperor gave patient attention to the speeches of both parties; he applauded those who spoke well, rebuked those who displayed a tendency to altercation, and according to this apprehension of what he heard, for he was not wholly unpracticed in the Greek tongue, he addressed himself with kindness to each one. Finally all the priests agreed with one another and considered that the Son is consubstantial with the Father."[36]

In this *Defense of the Nicene Definition* (*De Decretis*) Athanasius subsequently described the heterodoxy of Eusebius of Nicomedia and his cohorts that was evidenced at Nicaea: "While they stood out in their irreligion, and attempted their fight against God, the terms they used were replete with irreligion; but the assembled Bishops who were three hundred more or less, mildly and charitably required of them to explain and defend themselves on religious grounds. Scarcely, however, did they begin to speak, when they were condemned; and one differed from another; then perceiving the straits in that their heresy lay, they remained dumb, and by their silence confessed the disgrace that came upon their heterodoxy."[37] In the process of debate, and after one day's delay, Eusebius of Caesarea, who had originally opposed the "same substance" phraseology, changed sides and found a way to accept the Council's decision in favor of consubstantial,

---

32. Ibid.

33. Eusebius, *Council of Nicaea* 1, *NPNF*, vol. IV, 74.

34. Eusebius, *Council of Nicaea* 4, *NPNF*, vol. IV, 75.

35. Eusebius, *Council of Nicaea* 8–9, *NPNF*, vol. IV, 76.

36. Sozomen, *Church History* I.20, *NPNF*, vol. II, 255.

37. Athanasius, *Defense of the Nicene Definition* II.3, *NPNF*, vol. IV, 152.

"one essence" language to describe the relationship of the Father and the Son. Hence, as Athanasius reported, "And what is strange indeed, Eusebius of Caesarea in Palestine, who had denied the day before, but afterwards subscribed, sent to his Church a letter, saying that this was the Church's faith, and the tradition of the Fathers; and made a public profession that they were before in error, and were rashly contending against the truth."[38]

Thus, the majority of the Arians, perhaps for fear of reprisals, were gradually won over to the Nicene theology of "one essence" shared between the Father and Son. "At the commencement of the conference," Sozomen noted, "there were but seventeen who prized the opinion of Arius, but eventually the majority of these yielded assent to the general view. To this judgment the emperor deferred, for he regarded the unanimity of the conference to be a divine approbation; and he ordained that any one who should be rebellious thereto, should forthwith be sent into banishment, as guilty of endeavoring to overthrow the Divine definitions."[39] In the end, only six—Arius, as well as bishops Secundus, Theonas, Eusebius of Nicomedia, Theognis, and Maris—stood by their aberrant opinions. These were anathematized by the Council of Nicaea and banished by the emperor into exile.[40] The other eleven, as described by Rufinus, "after taking counsel together, agreed to subscribe [to the Nicene Creed] with hand only, not heart."[41]

The question of Athanasius's role at the Council of Nicaea is a difficult one because of the silence of the eyewitnesses; much of what has been said about his leadership in the debate in favor of the theology enshrined in Nicene Creed is based on supposition. Gregory Nazianzen, writing soon after the death of Athanasius, is an example of this: "though not yet ranked among the Bishops, he held the first rank among the members of the Council, for preference was given to virtue just as much as to office."[42] Describing Athanasius, Theodoret wrote, "He had, at the general council, so defended the doctrines of the apostles, that while he won the approbation of all the champions of the truth, its opponents learned to look on their antagonists as a personal foe and public enemy. He had attended the council as one of the retinue of Alexander, then a very young man, although he was the

38. Ibid.
39. Sozomen, *Church History* I.20, *NPNF*, vol. II, 255.
40. Socrates, *Church History* I.8, *NPNF*, vol. II, 10.
41. Rufinus, *Church History* X.5, 13.
42. Gregory Nazianzen, *Oration* 21.14, *NPNF*, vol. VII, 273.

principal deacon."[43] Likewise, Sozomen reported, "Many of the Bishops who were assembled [at Nicaea], and of the clergy who accompanied them, being remarkable for their dialectic skill and practiced in such rhetorical methods, became conspicuous and attracted the notice of the emperor and the court. Of that number Athanasius, who was then a deacon of Alexandria, and had accompanied his bishop Alexander, seemed to have the largest share in the counsel concerning these subjects."[44] Rufinus added that "Athanasius, at that time a deacon of Alexander of Alexandria, was there too [at Nicaea], aiding the old man with his assiduous advice."[45]

The actual source of the Nicene Creed, described by J. N. D. Kelly as an explicit reply to Arianism,[46] remains somewhat of a mystery. Philostorgius, the Arian historian, described it as principally the production of Hosius and Alexander of Alexandria: "Hosius of Cordova and Alexander and their associates had in readiness the document that everyone needed to subscribe."[47] Despite the questionable accuracy of some of his assessments, Philostorgius's account rings truer than that of Eusebius of Caesarea, whose self-congratulatory letter to his own church implies that the skeleton of the Creed came from their own confession of faith.[48]

The full text of the Nicene Creed, as given by Eusebius of Caesarea, is as follows:

> We believe in one God, the Father Almighty, Maker of all things visible and invisible: —and in one Lord Jesus Christ, the Son of God, the only-begotten of the Father, that is of the substance of the Father; God of God, Light of light, true God of true God; begotten not made, consubstantial with the Father; by whom all things were made both which are in heaven and on earth; who for the sake of men, and on account of our salvation, descended, became incarnate, was made man, suffered and rose again on the third day; he ascended into the heavens, and will come to judge the living and the dead. [We believe] also in the Holy Spirit. But those who say "There was a time when he was not," or "He did not exist before he was begotten," or "He was made of nothing," or assert that "He is

43. Theodoret, *Church History* I.25, *NPNF*, vol. III, 61.

44. Sozomen, *Church History* I.17, *NPNF*, vol. II, 253.

45. Rufinus, *Church History* X.5, 13.

46. Kelly, *Early Christian Creeds*, 234–42. See Kelly for a full exposition of the anti-Arian posture of the Nicene Creed.

47 Philostorgius, *Church History* I.9a, 12.

48. Eusebius, *Council of Nicaea* 1, *NPNF*, vol. IV, 74

of other substance or essence than the Father," or that the Son of God is created, or mutable, or susceptible of change, the Catholic and apostolic Church of God anathematizes.[49]

That the Nicene Creed was developed as an anti-Arian confession is easily discerned by close attention to four phrases in the first article (paragraph), and the "anathemas" of the concluding paragraph. The phrase "only-begotten" (which stems from John 1:14) is a hedge against saying that the Son was "made or created" before all time—as the Arians had affirmed. The phrase "is of the substance of the Father" further clarifies the Divine identity of the Son, as the Second Person of the Holy Trinity, as being a part of God, and therefore as *not* being a creature. The substance of God, while (wisely) not defined, is explained metaphorically using scriptural terms: "God of God, Light of light, true God of true God." The third phrase that has an explicitly anti-Arian ring to it is "begotten not made"—since it distinguishes the mode of the Son's generation from that of all creatures. Thus, the Son is *not* a creature. And the final term that had an overtly anti-Arian thrust was "consubstantial," which affirms that the Father and the Son are of the same divine substance (literally: "one substance"), and hence are eternally equal in their Divine natures.

The key term under debate was "consubstantial" (*homoousia*, meaning "one substance"). Eusebius indicated that it was Constantine himself who insisted upon the inclusion of this term in the Creed, and this assertion was supported by both Socrates and Theodoret (who probably followed him).[50] Constantine himself is said to have explained the meaning of *homoousia* as he intended it to be used in the Creed.[51] And certainly it was his imperial support, as much as the cogency of his explanation (which probably came from Hosius), that was determinative.[52] The term *homoousia* had a compli-

49. Socrates, *Church History* I.8, *NPNF*, vol. II, 11.

50. Eusebius, *Council of Nicaea* 4, *NPNF*, vol. IV, 75. Cf. Socrates, *Church History* I.8, *NPNF*, vol. II, 11; Theodoret, *Church History* I.12, 17.

51. Ibid. Socrates wrote, "That single word '*homoousios*' (consubstantial), an expression which the emperor himself explained, as not indicating corporeal affections or properties; and consequently that the Son did not subsist from the Father either by division or abscission; for, said he, a nature which is immaterial and incorporeal cannot possibly be subject to any corporeal affection; hence our conception of such things can only be in divine and mysterious terms. Such was the philosophical view of the subject taken by our most wise and pious sovereign; and the bishops on account of the word *homoousios*, drew up this formula of faith."

52. Kelly, *Early Christian Creeds*, 250.

cated history,[53] and it was sometimes associated with a heretical, modalistic view of the relationship of the Father and Son,[54] hence it was troubling to some people at the Council.[55] While it was protested (by the Arians) that the term was not used in the Bible, Athanasius argued that it "contains the intention of the Scriptures."[56] For Athanasius and his associates "consubstantial" (*homoousia*) had come to mean that the Son of God is co-eternal, and of the same Divine nature as the Father; this precluded any notion (of the Arians) that the Son was a creature and had a beginning. This assertion that the Son is "consubstantial" with the Father was deemed absolutely necessary for the Christian doctrine of salvation and for the appropriate worship of Christ as Divine.[57] It was viewed as an essential clarification of the relationship of the Father and the Son that truly and faithfully reflected scriptural teaching. While we have no way of drawing a direct line of connection between the Nicene Creed and Athanasius's early writings, it is clear that there are strong affinities between them, particularly in insisting upon the full Deity of God the Son, and in the process of drawing the incarnation and salvation offered by Jesus Christ closely together.

Secundus and Theonas (both of Libya) refused to sign the Nicene Creed. They were deposed by the Council and exiled to Illyricum along with Arius and the presbyters who supported them.[58] As he was leaving for exile, Secundus scolded Eusebius of Nicomedia: "You subscribed in order to avoid exile! As God is my witness, you will have to suffer banishment on my account." And indeed, Eusebius of Nicomedia and Theognis of Nicaea were also sent into exile three months later;[59] while they had reputedly signed the Nicene Creed, they ultimately would not go along with the Council's rejection of Arius.[60]

After the Council of Nicaea a series of letters were written to inform the church about the decisions made at the Council and to enforce them. Among these letters, which are preserved in the early church histories, is

53. Cf. ibid., 242–54, for an extensive discussion of the term.

54. This view was represented by Marcellus, whose use of the term implied that the Father and Son were the same being.

55. Socrates, *Church History* I.23, *NPNF*, vol. II, 26.

56. Athanasius, *Four Discourses Against the Arians* III.16, *NPNF*, vol. IV, 402–3.

57. Pelikan, *Catholic Tradition*, 1:206.

58. Philostorgius, *Church History* I.10, 13.

59. Ibid.

60. Sozomen, *Church History* I.21, 255.

one to the church of Alexandria that gives an official report of the decisions made at the Council. The following Arian theological assertions were condemned: "affirming that 'the Son of God sprang from nothing,' and that 'there was a time when he was not'; saying moreover that 'the Son of God, because possessed of free will, was capable either of vice or virtue; and calling him a creature and a work. All these sentiments the holy Synod has anathematized, having scarcely patience to endure the hearing of such an impious opinion, or, rather, madness, and such blasphemous words."[61]

Constantine also addressed a letter to the Alexandrian Christians, which reported the decisions of the Council and placed the blame for the dispute squarely upon the shoulders of Arius: "Arius alone beguiled by the subtlety of the devil, was discovered to be the sole disseminator of this mischief, first among you, and afterwards with unhallowed purposes among others also."[62] The conciliar decision of Nicaea and its Creed were to be affirmed and dissension to be put behind them, for "the judgment of three hundred bishops cannot be other than the doctrine of God."[63] In a second encyclical letter, Constantine not only anathematized Arius's doctrines but also outlawed his writings: "I decree, that if any one shall be detected in concealing a book compiled by Arius, and shall not instantly bring it forward and burn it, the penalty for this offense shall be death; immediately for this offense the criminal shall suffer capital punishment."[64] In still another encyclical letter Constantine formalized the date for the Christian Passover, Easter, and took steps to normalize their celebration.[65] A subsequent letter to the church of Nicomedia bewailed the conduct of their bishop and exhorted the church to elect a new bishop to replace him.[66]

The Meletian dispute, which at this point was not directly related to the "Arian controversy," was also addressed by the Council of Nicaea. Meletius had been present at the council and he had presented a "white paper" to Alexander that indicated that the Meletians would stand with the Catholic faith against Arianism. The Council managed to reconcile the Meletians to the faith, while prohibiting them from obtaining future longevity through the elevation of additional bishops from and for their own sect.

---

61. Socrates, *Church History* I.9, *NPNF*, vol. II, 12.

62. Ibid., 14.

63. Ibid.

64. Ibid.

65. Ibid., 15.

66. Ibid., 17.

Thus, the Council of Nicaea had—apparently—established theological and ecclesiastical unity in the fourth-century Christian church. It had resolved disputes about doctrine, the celebration of Easter, and the legitimate line of episcopal succession. Most importantly, it had bequeathed the church the Nicene faith, expressed in the Nicene Creed, which many millions of Christians still use today as apt summation of their faith. But this unity was illusionary, and, as we shall see in the chapters that follow, it was maintained only by Constantine's imperial will and power. But when the will and determination of the emperor began to waver in the face of new theological and political intrigues, the disputes that revolved around the Nicene theology would return with a vengeance—and that vengeance would be meted out upon Athanasius and those who supported him.

—————— 5 ——————

Bishop in Alexandria

The Council of Nicaea addressed several important issues that directly affected the situation in the church of Alexandria. In addition to both the Meletian schism and the "Arian controversy," the great Council also passed legislation respecting the election of bishops and the extent of the episcopal see of the bishop of Alexandria. The Meletian schism was ostensibly resolved by a tenuous compromise, and the Arian question was papered over by a Creed that at least some of the signatories accepted only because of their fear of imperial retribution. Thus there was a semblance of unity, under the influence of Constantine's indomitable will. But controversy would soon erupt again, and Athanasius would be at or near the storm's center. Socrates, the early church historian, likened this period to a battle being fought at night, in that neither party understood the agenda of their opponents or the terrain upon which they stood, and yet both sides struck out blindly and violently at each other.[1]

The Council of Nicaea had stipulated, in its fourth canon, that "a bishop should most certainly be chosen by all the other [bishops] of the province. But if this poses a difficulty, because of an urgent need, or because of the length of the journey, then at least three [bishops] shall meet in one place, and with the votes of those absent having been communicated in writing, they shall proceed to the consecration. The confirmation of what has been done, however, belongs in each province to the metropolitan."[2] This policy may have varied significantly from the long-standing tradition that had been followed in Alexandria, and the conflict between the two traditions may have helped cast Athanasius's elevation to the episcopate

1. Socrates, *Church History* I.23, *NPNF*, II, 26–27.
2. Arnold, *Early Episcopal Career*, 45.

in a poor light. Eusebius reported that "all were at peace" yet "among the Egyptians alone an implacable contention still raged, so as once more to disturb the emperor's tranquility, though not to excite his anger."[3] Ever the supporter of Constantine, Eusebius reported that the emperor "treated all the contending parties with respect, as fathers, nay rather, as prophets of God."[4] Constantine responded to this contention by summoning the warring parties into his imperial presence and acting as a mediator between them. He exhorted them "not to distract and rend the Church, but to keep before them the thought of God's judgment. And these injunctions the emperor sent by a letter written with his own hand."[5]

Meanwhile, Eusebius of Nicomedia and Theognis, both of whom had been deposed and exiled for siding with Arius at the Council of Nicaea, had published retractions of their earlier views, and assented to the Nicene Creed. Constantine, pursuing his policy of unity and toleration, had them reinstated in their respective sees.[6] They soon began lobbying for the return of Arius himself. Addressing a letter to Constantine, in which he stated his faith in closely guarded terms, Arius affirmed, "We confess in writing before God that we and all those with us believe as it has been submitted." The telltale Arian phrases and doctrines were omitted as he asserted, "We believe in one God, the Father, all-sovereign: and in Lord Jesus Christ his only-begotten Son who came into existence from him before all ages, God the Word, through whom all things in the heavens and on earth came into existence, who came down and assumed flesh and suffered, rose and went up into the heavens and comes again to judge the living and the dead."[7] Avoiding any precise language about the nature of the Son and the Son's relationship to the essence of the Father, like that which was used in the Nicene Creed, Arius's statement camouflaged the true theology of its signatories, and it satisfied Emperor Constantine. Arius and his colleagues were subsequently recalled from exile. The Arians also lobbied the emperor for reentry into the church of Alexandria, but this approach was staunchly opposed by Bishop Alexander.[8]

3. Eusebius, *Life of Constantine* III.23, *NPNF*, vol. I, 526.

4. Ibid.

5. Ibid.

6. Socrates, *Church History* I.14, *NPNF*, vol. II, 19–20, and Sozomen, *Church History* II.14, *NPNF*, vol. II, 268.

7. Cf. Rusch, *Trinitarian Controversy*, 61.

8. Sozomen, *Church History* II.14, *NPNF*, vol. II, 268. Cf. Socrates, *Church History* I.26.

The Alexandrian church was deeply enmeshed in controversy as Catholics (the Nicene party), Meletians, and Arians all struggled for control and leadership in the city and in local churches. This three-way strife was exaggerated by Bishop Alexander's death on April 17, 328. Controversy soon surrounded Athanasius's election as Alexander's successor. Athanasius was not elected and inducted into the office until June 8 of the same year. The two-month delay in his elevation signals that much controversy surrounded Athanasius's election.[9] Socrates reported that the Arians held "bitter animosity against Athanasius . . . because he had so vigorously withstood them in the Synod [of Nicaea] while the articles of faith were under discussion. And in the first place they objected to the ordination of Athanasius [as bishop] partly as a person unworthy of the prelacy, and partly because he had been elected by disqualified persons."[10] In the tumult that followed both the Arian and Meletian factions sought to elect a prelate from their own party to succeed Alexander. In his third *Festal Letter*, Athanasius admitted that controversy attached itself to his elevation as bishop, but he attributed it to the fact that he was considered to be too young to be qualified for the office.[11]

Since the bishop of Alexandria was both chief cleric of the city and metropolitan (archbishop) over Egypt and Libya, the positon combined the normal duties of a pastor with those of a chief administrator and significant leader in the church. The bishop of Alexandria also had many civil responsibilities and obligations. Athanasius was well qualified for this role because of the years he had spent at the side of his father in the faith, Bishop Alexander. He proved himself to be both an able cleric and an effective administrator.

Several conflicting traditions survive to describe how Athanasius came to the prestigious and important office of bishop of Alexandria. One stems from the Catholic (pro-Nicene) church historians Socrates and Sozomen, and from Epiphanius the heresy-hunter. The second tradition was reported in the *Church History* of the Arian historian Philostorgius. A third was delivered by Gregory Nazianzen in his *Oration* 21, "On the Great Athanasius." Socrates and Sozomen remind their readers that Athanasius had been virtually raised and mentored by Alexander to be his successor. The elderly bishop's selection was subsequently ratified by a council of bishops, and

9. Hanson, *Christian Doctrine of God*, 248–49.

10. Socrates, *Church History* I.23, NPNF, vol. II, 26.

11. Athanasius, *Festal Letter* 3, NPNF, vol. IV, 503.

hence, in their minds, Athanasius had been properly elected and ordained. Sozomen explained the two-month hiatus between Alexander's death and Athanasius's elevation on June 8, 328—a sign of significant controversy in the church over his election—by saying that in deep humility, Athanasius had absented himself from the city in order to "escape the honor."[12]

Epiphanius writing in his *Panarion* (ca. 373) described the tumultuous situation with Athanasius's absence and Alexander's death. In the absence of Athanasius, and in violation of the Nicene agreement, the Meletians elected a rival bishop named Theonas, who died a few months later. Epiphanius reported, "Athanasius arrived shortly after the death of Theonas, and a council of the orthodox from every place was convened. And thus he was ordained and the See was given to him who was worthy, the one for whom it had been made ready according to God's will and the testimony and command of [the] blessed Alexander."[13] In this way, Athanasius was thrust into the midst of controversy from the very inception of his episcopate. Epiphanius described him as striving mightily for unity and harmony among the Christians in Alexandria, although without much tangible success. He wrote,

> Athanasius now began to be distressed and grieved on account of the division of the church between the Meletians and the Catholic church. He tried persuasion and exhortation, but they would have none of it. He tried force and compulsion, [but they would not obey]. Now he used often to inspect the nearby churches, especially those of the Mareotis. And once when the Meletians gathered for worship, it happened that a deacon from the crowd with Athanasius went in with some others of the people and broke a lamp, as the report has it, and a fight broke out. This was the beginning of a plot against Athanasius, with the Meletians charging and calumniating him and [crying] one thing after another, and the Arians plotting and giving themselves to their cause out of jealousy of the holy faith of God and orthodoxy. And they referred the matter to the emperor Constantine.[14]

Philostorgius told an interesting though unprovable story that allegedly took place during the election of Athanasius as bishop. He indicated that during a deadlock in the vote for bishop, Athanasius and his supporters broke into the church of Dionysius. Finding several Egyptian bishops

12. Sozomen, *Church History* II.17, *NPNF*, vol. II, 269.

13. Epaphanius, *Panarion* 68.7, 251.

14. Ibid.

there, they barred the doors to prevent interference, and secretly ordained him. In this way, Philostorgius reported, "Athanasius got what he wanted. The other assembly of bishops that was there condemned him for this reason. But when Athanasius had secured his position, he sent the emperor an announcement of his elevation to the archbishopric that was made to seem as though it had come from the city itself. The emperor, thinking that the letter had been written by the city council, endorsed his possession of the episcopal throne."[15] This report presents Athanasius's elevation to the episcopate in a very negative light, and in that way reflects the Arian plot against him, mentioned by Epiphanius.

Gregory of Nazianzus's account reported that Athanasius came to the episcopal chair "by the vote of the whole people, not in the evil fashion which has since prevailed, nor by means of bloodshed and oppression, but in an apostolic and spiritual manner, he is led up to the throne of Saint Mark, to succeed him in piety, no less than in office; in the latter indeed at a great distance from him, in the former, which is the genuine right of succession, following him closely."[16] Gregory's oration continued depicting Athanasius as being conciliatory towards the warring factions in Alexandria, mildly attempting to reconcile them to one another and to the Nicene faith. After a period of leniency and reconciliation many of the clergy who had opposed him (chiefly the Meletians) were received into fellowship. Avoiding the extremes of leniency and harshness, Gregory reported that Athanasius as bishop was

> sublime in action, lowly in mind; inaccessible in virtue, most accessible in intercourse; gentle, free from anger, sympathetic, sweet in words, sweeter in disposition; angelic in appearance, more angelic in mind; calm in rebuke, persuasive in praise, without spoiling the good effect of either by excess, but rebuking with the tenderness of a father, praising with the dignity of a ruler, his tenderness was not dissipated, nor his severity sour; for the one was reasonable, the other prudent, and both truly wise; his disposition sufficed for the training of his spiritual children, with very little need of words; his words with very little need of the rod, and his moderate use of the rod with still less for the knife.[17]

---

15. Philostorgius, *Church History* II.11, 26–27.

16. *Oration* 21.8, *NPNF*, vol. VII, 271.

17. *Oration* 21.9, *NPNF*, vol. VII, 271–72.

While his praise may seem excessive, even for a eulogy, Gregory leaves the reader with two salient points—that Athanasius was elected to the episcopate with the support of the people and in apostolic and holy manner; and secondly, that he was a moderate, reforming and reconciling leader over the clergy who served under him. Nazianzen's oration also lauds Athanasius's personal piety and prayer disciplines, which earned the respect of the holy monks and virgins. Additionally, his deep spirituality and humble demeanor won the respect of the masses. Athanasius was, as Gregory described him, a protector to the widows, father to the orphans, benefactor to the poor, and entertainer of strangers; to the brethren in faith, he was a man of brotherly love, to the sick a physician, and to the healthy a guardian of their health.

It was in the midst of the ecclesiastical disturbances in Alexandria that the so-called "Eusebians" began to mount contention against Athanasius and the legitimacy of his episcopal administration in Alexandria. Socrates, who admitted that he did not completely understand the theological implications of the tumult that was brewing, indicated that no small part of the problem stemmed from the efforts of Eusebius of Nicomedia and those who supported him. This group of clergy, which Athanasius subsequently dubbed "the Eusebians" (literally "those around Eusebius"), opposed Athanasius and his work for two main reasons. First, they showed "bitter animosity" toward him for having opposed them so "vigorously in the Synod [Council of Nicaea] while the articles of faith were under discussion."[18] The second reason was Athanasius's persistent contention for the Nicene faith and his unwillingness to readmit Arius and the Arians (who, he believed, had not really changed their theological views) into the Alexandrian church. Hence, Eusebius and those allied with him disputed Athanasius's election to the episcopate, charged him with abuses of his authority with respect to the Meletians, and tried to force him to resume communion with Arius. Socrates reported, "Eusebius therefore wrote to Athanasius, desiring him to re-admit Arius and his adherents into the church. Now the tone of his letter indeed was that of entreaty, but openly he menaced him. And as Athanasius would by no means accede to this, he endeavored to induce the emperor to give Arius an audience, and then permit him to return to Alexandria . . ."[19] Athanasius stoutly refused these efforts, and this set him

---

18. Socrates, *Church History* I.23, *NPNF*, vol. II, 26.
19. Ibid.

on a collision course with Emperor Constantine's desire for harmony and unity in the church.

It was during this same time, Socrates reported, that a major theological controversy erupted in the church over the use of the term *homoousia* ("same substance"). Those who objected to the term believed that it favored the heretical opinions of Sabellius and Montanus, and therefore called those of the Nicene party (who affirmed it) blasphemers and heretics. Those of the Nicene party who advocated for the term *homoousia* decried their opponents as polytheists and corrupters of the faith. This situation was further complicated by the fact that Eustathius, who had ably defended the "same substance" formula at the Council of Nicaea, was found to be a Sabellian, and therefore heretical on the doctrine of the Trinity. Hence, Socrates explained, "In consequence of these misunderstandings, each of them wrote as if contending against adversaries; and although it was admitted on both sides that the Son of God has a distinct person and existence, and all acknowledged that there is one God in three Persons, yet from what cause I am unable to divine, they could not agree among themselves, and therefore could in no way endure to be at peace."[20]

Recent research suggests that we should not too readily assume, as Athanasius himself certainly did, that the Eusebians were Arians in their theology.[21] Their opposition to the *homoousia* ("same substance") formula of the Nicene Creed and their sympathy for Arius may have simply signaled that Eusebius of Nicomedia and his "fellow Lucianists" sought to hold a middle ground between the Nicene faith and Arianism, and were (like Constantine himself) advocates for peace and harmony in the church. Thus, within a few years of his exile, Arius and his supporters were recalled, reinstated, and their reputations were rehabilitated largely through the efforts of Eusebius and his allies. Hanson rightly saw Eusebius of Nicomedia as the most influential church leader of the period immediately after the Council of Nicaea: "Eusebius," he wrote, "was a man of strong character and great ability; Eusebius of Caesarea calls him 'the great Eusebius.' It was he who virtually took charge of affairs of the Greek-speaking church from 328 until his death."[22]

If we ask whence came the great influence of the "great Eusebius," the question becomes more complicated. His episcopal see was at Nicomedia,

20. Ibid., 27.

21. Gwynn, *The Eusebians*, and Barnes, *Athanasius and Constantius*.

22. Hanson, *Christian Doctrine of God*, 29.

where one of Constantine's favorite imperial palaces was located, so he had frequent and rather immediate access to the seat of imperial power. The early historians also indicate that Eusebius was a favorite pastor of Constantia, the sister of Constantine, and may have exerted significant influence through her patronage and support.[23] Eusebius's significant support may also indicate that the theologians and bishops of the fourth century were not as easily lumped into two opposing camps as Athanasius seems to suggest. For Athanasius, it seemed that one supported the Nicene theology or not, and hence one was either "orthodox" or "Arian." But in truth, there may have been a significant number of clergy, like Eusebius, who sought to stand in the middle ground between those two extreme opposites, and they may have lent their support to the bishop of Nicomedia. This is certainly the situation implied by Timothy Barnes when he writes, "No fourth-century thinker who is normally regarded as 'Arian' or 'Neo-Arian' would ever have applied the term to himself. The label was a term of abuse; Athanasius and his allies habitually employed a broad definition that turned all their enemies into 'Arians.'"[24] In a similar fashion, Colm Luibheid urges, "It is essential to recognize, as many apologists refuse to do, the difference between Eusebius' theological convictions on the one hand, and, on the other hand, the fact that he showed sympathy for Arius . . . [and] had reservations about the *homoousion* formula."[25] While it is difficult to reconstruct Eusebius's theology from the few surviving remnants of his writings, his thought does seem to have some significant kinship with that which has been attributed to Arius. In his letter to Paulinus, for example, Eusebius interpreted Proverbs 8:22 as a proof text that the Son is a creature (*ktisma*) and cannot be considered to be of the same substance as the Father.[26] Socrates pointed out that Eusebius of Nicomedia—even in his recantation—did not use the phrase "same substance" (*homoousia*) and did not use it in his own written works, although he did not formally reject the Nicene Creed.[27]

While Eusebius's theological posture may have placed him in a middle ground somewhere between Athanasius and Arius, his ecclesiastical

---

23. Socrates, *Church History* I.25, *NPNF*, vol. II, 28; Sozomen, *Church History* II.27, *NPNF*, vol. II, 277. They assert, for example, that it was through Constantia's support and intervention that Arius was recalled by Constantine.

24. Barnes, *Athanasius and Constantius*, 15.

25. Luibheid, "Arianism of Eusebius of Nicomedia," 5; quoted in Gwynn, *Eusebians*, 211.

26. Ibid., 214–15. We examine this letter in chapter 3.

27. Socrates, *Church History* I.14, *NPNF*, vol. II, 20.

politics clearly turned him into a staunch opponent of Athanasius and his administration in Alexandria. Hence, Theodoret wrote subsequently, "the exiled bishops, employing their customary artifices, abused the benevolence of the emperor, renewed the previous contests, and regained their former power."[28] Eusebius not only returned to the see of Nicomedia, he was eventually elevated to the episcopacy of Constantinople. It was from that location that he "acquired great power in that city, frequently visiting and holding familiar [communication] with the emperor, he gained confidence and formed plots against those who were foremost in the support of the truth."[29] Theodoret, who embraced Athanasius's theology and accepted his polemical construal of the "Eusebians," illustrated Eusebius's subterfuge by pointing to the plot he concocted against Eustathius, bishop of Antioch. Eusebius hired a lewd woman, who had a child out of wedlock, to claim that the bishop was the father of her child. This campaign, said Theodoret, was supported by Eusebius of Caesarea, and bishops Patrophilus, Aetius, Theodotus, and others "who had imbibed the Arian sentiments."[30] A council of bishops was called in Jerusalem, and they succeeded in obtaining the banishment of "this champion of piety and chastity, as an adulterer and a tyrant."[31] In his campaign against the Nicene theology and its chief supporters, Eusebius of Nicomedia (and Constantinople) would become one of the chief ecclesiastical adversaries of Athanasius.

Athanasius's *Exposition of the Faith* was probably written in 328, either before or soon after his elevation to the office of the bishop. The brief treatise, which reads like a creed or confession of faith, may have been written as a position paper for his ordination or as a catechetical document to be used in his teaching ministry among the Alexandrians. It is clearly a document that could serve both purposes very well. The fact that the treatise does not explicitly attack the positions of Arius suggests that it may stem from the period leading up to Athanasius's elevation to the episcopate, and signals that he intended to sound a conciliatory note at the outset of his tenure. Paragraphs 1 and 2 of the *Exposition* make Arianism untenable by asserting that the Father and Son share the same essence (*homoousia*) and that the Son is eternal and not created. After affirming the full relationship and full equality of the Father and the Son, and a brief statement about

28. *Church History* I.19, *NPNF*, vol. III, 56–57.
29. *Church History* I.20, *NPNF*, vol. III, 57.
30. Ibid.
31. Ibid.

his belief in the Holy Spirit, Athanasius added, "we anathematize doctrines contrary to this."[32] This statement clearly shows an awareness that there are conflicting views circulating in the church, and that they are to be avoided.

The first paragraph of the *Exposition of Faith* contains a long statement of the full equality of the Father and the Son, without recourse to the Nicene Creed. Athanasius's confession:

> We believe in one Unbegotten God, Father Almighty, maker of all things both visible and invisible, that hath His being from Himself. And in one Only-begotten Word, Wisdom, Son, begotten of the Father without beginning and eternally; word not pronounced nor mental, nor an effluence of the Perfect, nor a dividing of the impassible Essence, nor an issue; but absolutely perfect Son, living and powerful (Heb 4:12), the true Image of the Father, equal in honor and glory. For this, he says, "is the will of the Father, that as they honor the Father, so they may honor the Son also" (John 5:23); very God of very God, as John says in his general Epistles, "And we are in Him that is true, even in His son Jesus Christ: this is the true God and everlasting life" (1 John 5:20): Almighty of Almighty. For all things which the Father rules and sways, the Son rules and sways likewise: wholly from the Whole, being like the Father as the Lord says, "he that hath seen Me hath seen the Father" (John 14:9). But He was begotten ineffably and incomprehensibly, for "who shall declare his generation?" (Isa 53:8), in other words, no one can.[33]

This long and fairly elaborate exploration of the common substance and co-eternality of the Father and the Son was probably engendered (at least in part) by the recent controversy over those same points of doctrine. It is followed by a strong affirmation of the Incarnation ("taking flesh") of the Word, and the deep theological connection between the Incarnation and the salvation of humanity. Athanasius wrote,

> He had descended from the bosom of the Father, took from the undefiled Virgin Mary our humanity, Christ Jesus, whom He delivered of His own will to suffer for us, as the Lord saith: "No man taketh My life from Me. I have power to lay it down, and have power to take it again" (John 10:18). In which humanity He was crucified and died for us, and rose from the dead, and was taken up into the heavens, having been created as the beginning of ways

32. *Exposition of Faith* 1, NPNF, vol. IV, 84.
33. Ibid.

for us (Prov 8:22), when on earth He showed us light from out of darkness, salvation from error, life from the dead, an entrance to paradise, from which Adam was cast out . . .[34]

In holding the Incarnation of Christ and Christian salvation so closely together, Athanasius seemed to be offering another echo of the dictum of *On the Incarnation*, which he wrote (perhaps) a decade before: "He became what we are to make us what He is."

Paragraph 2 of the *Exposition* explicitly attacks the modalist Christology of Sabellianism, which taught that God was in one Substance, Who went through three separate forms called "Father, Son, and Holy Spirit" in chronological succession. Ostensibly while attacking the Sabellians, Athanasius clarified the relationship between the Father and Son in ways that made Arian Christology untenable:

> But just as a river, produced from a well, is not separate, and yet there are in fact two visible objects and two names. For neither is the Father the Son, nor the Son the Father. For the Father is Father of the Son, and the Son, [is] Son of the Father. For like as the well is not a river, nor the river a well, but both are one and the same water which is conveyed in a channel from the well to the river, so the Father's deity passes into the Son without flow and without division. For the Lord says, "I came out from the Father and am come" (John 16:28). But He is ever with the Father, for He is in the bosom of the Father, nor was ever the bosom of the Father void of the deity of the Son . . . All things to wit were made through the Son; but He Himself is not a creature, as Paul says of the Lord: "In Him were all things created, and He is before all" (Col 1:16). Now He says not, "was created" before all things, but "is" before all things. To be created, namely, is applicable to all things, but "is before all" applies to the Son only.[35]

Apparently once again interacting with the Arian theology, in the third paragraph of the *Exposition*, Athanasius examined the problematic text from Proverbs 8 ("The LORD created me at the beginning of his work . . .") that the Arians took to mean that the Son was created by the Father before the beginning of creation. Athanasius argued that the Son, speaking through Wisdom in this passage, was not Himself created, since the Second Person of the Trinity is uncreated and eternal. But Jesus's physical body was

34. Ibid.

35. *Exposition of Faith* 2, NPNF, vol. IV, 84–85.

of a creaturely nature—a nature that He shared with us, in assuming our humanity, was created. Athanasius explained, "For it would be inconsistent with His deity for Him to be called a creature. For all things were created by the Father through the Son, but the Son alone was eternally begotten from the Father, whence God the Word is 'first-born of all creation' [Col 1:15], unchangeable from unchangeable. However, the body which He wore for our sakes is a creature . . ."[36] Following the Septuagint (Greek) version of Jeremiah 31:22, "The LORD created for us for a planting a new salvation, in which salvation men shall go about," Athanasius interpreted the Virgin Birth of Jesus in human flesh as that "new salvation" that was predicted and created for our benefit. Returning to the text in Proverbs 8:22, he argued, "Nothing new was created in woman, save the Lord's body, born of the Virgin Mary without intercourse, as also it says in the Proverbs in the person of Jesus: 'The Lord created me, a beginning of His ways for His works' (Prov. viii 22). Now He does not say, 'created me before His works,' lest any should take the text of [to refer to] the deity of the Word."[37] This was an inventive solution to the problem posed by an Arian reading of Proverbs 8:22 by postulating that, in the Proverbs passage, Wisdom was speaking as the *Logos* and referring to God's future plan of salvation through the creation of a human body for the Second Person of the Trinity. This approach had as its primary goal the preservation of the full deity of Christ, and an unwillingness to view the Second Person of the Trinity (the *Logos*) as a creature; it also sought to make sense of the phraseology of the passage that the Arians cited in support of their alternative view (that Christ is a creature created by the Father).

Athanasius concluded, in his fourth paragraph of the *Exposition*, "Each text then which refers to the creature [with respect to the Son] is written with reference to Jesus in a bodily sense. For the Lord's humanity was created as 'a beginning of ways,' and He manifested it to us for our salvation. For by it we have our access to the Father. For He is the way (John 14:6) which leads us back to the Father. And a way is a corporeal visible thing, such as is the Lord's humanity."[38] The Son, therefore, should not be viewed or termed as "created" but as "an offspring. For He [God] created none of the created things equal or like unto Himself. But it is the part of a Father to beget, while it is a workman's part to create. Accordingly, that a body is a

36. *Exposition of Faith* 3, NPNF, vol. IV, 85.

37. Ibid.

38. *Exposition of Faith* 4, NPNF, vol. IV, 85.

thing made and created, which the Lord bore for us, which was begotten for us, as Paul says, 'wisdom from God, and sanctification and righteousness, and redemption'; while yet the Word was before us and before all Creation, and is, the Wisdom of the Father."[39]

The *Exposition* ended with a brief affirmation of the full deity of the Holy Spirit, Who "proceeds from the Father, is ever in the hands of the Father Who sends and of the Son Who conveys Him, by Whose means He filled all things."[40] And then Athanasius registered another corrective against the Arian theology that affirms that the Son is a creature: "The Father, possessing His existence from Himself, begat the Son, as we said, and did not create Him, as a river from a well and as a branch from a root, and as brightness from a light, things which nature knows to be indivisible; through whom to the Father be glory and power and greatness before all ages, and unto all the ages of ages. Amen."[41] And with this *Exposition*, we have a consistent and comprehensive statement of the foundational theology of the new bishop of Alexandria.

39. Ibid.
40. Ibid.
41. Ibid.

6

Athanasius's First Exile

The mood of the first three years of Athanasius's episcopate in Alexandria was chronicled, to some degree, by his *Festal Letters* from that period. The *Festal Letters* were pastoral encyclicals written each year for the churches in his jurisdiction about the proper date and mode of celebration for Easter. In his first *Festal Letter*, written in 329, Athanasius made no mention of the tumult in Alexandria. His focus was entirely upon the appropriate celebration of Easter, "the Christian Passover." Using the theme of sounding a trumpet, Athanasius reminded his readers that even as Moses and the Levitical priests urged the sounding of a trumpet and the keeping of holy feasts, "blessed Paul" raised up his voice like a trumpet, saying, "Christ our Passover is sacrificed, therefore let us keep the feast, not with old leaven, neither with the leaven of malice and wickedness."[1]

In a similar way, Christ our Savior, "In the first day of the great feast, stood and cried out saying, 'if any man thirst, let him come to Me and drink' [John 7:37]. For it became the Savior not simply to call us to a feast, but to 'the great feast'; if only we will be prepared to hear, and to conform to the proclamation of every trumpet."[2] While proclaiming a holy fast, in preparation for Easter, Athanasius urged that fasting with the body avails nothing, if it is not met and joined to a fasting of the soul: "Behold, my brethren," he wrote, "how much a fast can do, and in what manner the law commands us to fast. It is required that not only with the body should we fast, but with the soul. Now the soul is humbled when it does not follow wicked opinions, but feeds on becoming virtues. For virtues and vices are the food of the soul, and it can eat either of these two meats, and incline to

1. Athanasius, *Festal Letter* 1, *NPNF*, vol. IV, 507.
2. Ibid.

either of the two, according to its own will. If it is bent toward virtue, it will be nourished by virtues, by righteousness, by temperance, by meekness, by fortitude, as Paul saith; 'Being nourished by the word of truth' [1 Tim 4:6]." Likewise, Jesus Christ enjoined us to feast on God's word in the inner person: "Such was the case with our Lord, who said, 'My meat is to do the will of My Father which is in heaven' [John 4:34]. But if it is not thus with the soul, and it inclines downwards, it is then nourished by nothing but sin."[3] Since this holy celebration of Easter involves the Christian in both fasting and feasting, Athanasius enjoined, "We begin the holy fast on the fifth day of Pharmuthi [March 31], and adding to it according to the number of those six holy and great days, which are the symbol of the creation of this world, let us rest and cease (from fasting) on the tenth day of the same [month of] Pharmuthi [April 5], on the holy Sabbath of the week . . ."[4] In the midst of Easter fasting and feasting Athanasius urged the church to express their Easter faith through care for those who stood at the margins of society. One's spiritual celebration was to be met and expressed through an advocacy for the poor and the stranger. Hence, the bishop enjoined, "Let us remember the poor, and not forget kindness to strangers; above all, let us love God with all our soul, and might, and strength, and our neighbor as ourselves. So we may receive those things . . . which God hath prepared for those that love Him, through His only Son, our Lord and Savior, Jesus Christ . . ."[5]

Athanasius's second *Festal Letter* from 330 retained much of the same pastoral and celebrative spirit of the first. It began: "Again, my brethren, is Easter come and gladness; again the Lord hath brought us to this season; so that when, according to custom, we have been nourished with His words, we may duly keep the feast. Let us celebrate it then, even heavenly joy, with those saints who formerly proclaimed a like feast, and were examples to us of conversation in Christ . . ."[6] Yet by paragraph 6 of the same encyclical the bishop began to address the dangers of heretics and heresy. He urged his readers to "hold fast" to the traditions and teaching that had been first delivered to them, and to beware of the teachings of "wicked men" who "dissemble, putting on as the Lord says sheep's clothing, and appearing like unto whited sepulchers; but they took those divine words in their mouth,

---

3. Ibid., 508.

4. Ibid., 509.

5. Ibid., 510.

6. Athanasius, *Festal Letter* 2, NPNF, vol. IV, 510.

while they inwardly cherished evil intentions."[7] In paragraph 7 Athanasius seemed to announce the policy of separation and noncooperation that he pursed with the heretical Arians and schismatic Meletians. He wrote, "For there is no fellowship whatever between the words of the saints and the fancies of human invention; for the saints are the ministers of the truth, preaching the kingdom of heaven, but those who are borne in the opposite direction have nothing better than to eat, and think their end is that they shall cease to be, and they say, 'Let us eat and drink, for tomorrow we die' [Isa 22:13]."[8]

By the time he had issued his third *Festal Letter*, in 331, Arius had returned to Alexandria; with him had come "tribulation" and "affliction." The introduction to the letter combined the mood of celebration with a call to constancy in the midst of affliction:

> Again, my beloved brethren, the day of the feast draws near to us, which, above all others, should be devoted to prayer, which the law commands to be observed, and which it would be an unholy thing for us to pass over in silence. For although we have been held under restraint by those who afflict us, that, because of them, we should not announce to you this season; yet thanks be to 'God who comforteth the afflicted' [2 Cor 7:6], that we have not been overcome by the wickedness of our accusers and silenced; but obeying the voice of truth, we together with you cry aloud in the day of the feast.[9]

The faithful were urged to keep the feast in ways that would nourish their souls and give them joy and gladness, whereas "there is no peace to the wicked, saith the Lord [Isa 48:22], [for] they labor in pain and grief."[10] Athanasius urged his readers to be faithful and true: "knowing that the Lord loves the thankful, never cease to praise Him, ever giving thanks unto the Lord. And whether the time is one of ease or of affliction, they offer up praise to God with thanksgiving, not reckoning these things of time, but worshipping the Lord, the God of [all] times."[11] In this, the faithful should follow the example of St. Paul: "In times of ease, he failed not, and in afflictions he gloried, knowing that 'tribulation worketh patience, and patience

7. Ibid., 511.
8. Ibid., 512.
9. Athanasius, *Festal Letter* 3, NPNF, vol. IV, 512–13.
10. Ibid., 513.
11. Ibid., 514.

experience, and experience hope, and that hope maketh not ashamed' [Rom 5:3]."[12] Hence, he exhorted his flock, "Let us, being followers of such men, pass no season without thanksgiving, but especially now, when the time is one of tribulation, which the heretics excite against us, will we praise the Lord, uttering the words of the saints; 'All these things have come upon us, yet we have not forgotten Thee' [Ps 44:17]."[13]

Arius had returned to Alexandria, with the emperor's consent, sometime in 330, and with him had come intense controversy.[14] Eusebius of Nicomedia and those who supported him had been successful in rehabilitating the career of Arius. Arius had been received and reinstated by the Emperor Constantine based on his recantation and a carefully worded confession of faith that skirted most of the salient themes of the Arian controversy. When Arius and his party arrived in Alexandria, Athanasius refused them admission to the church and sought to deprive them of ecclesiastical function in his jurisdiction. Arius wrote to the emperor, telling him, in the words of Socrates the historian, "that it is impossible for those who had once rejected the faith, and had been anathematized, to be again received into communion on their return."[15] Barring the Arians from communion, Athanasius wrote to Constantine to inform him of his decision. Constantine's anger is clearly visible in the letter that he wrote in return (a portion of which is preserved by Socrates): "Since you have been apprised of my will, afford unhindered access into the church to all those who are desirous of entering it. For if it shall be intimated to me that you have prohibited any of those claiming to be reunited to the church, or have hindered their admission, I will forthwith send some one who at my command shall depose you, and drive you into exile."[16]

It was in the context of Athanasius's staunch refusal to bend his will to Emperor Constantine's wishes for unity and harmony in the church that "the Eusebians" (as Athanasius styled them) found a vantage point from which to harass and afflict him. Socrates, following Athanasius's own assessment, linked this opposition from Eusebius of Nicomedia and others to their antipathy towards the bishop of Alexandria because of his defense of the Nicene theology. Hence, Socrates reported, "On this account they

12. Ibid.

13. Ibid., 514–15.

14. Socrates, *Church History* I.27, NPNF, vol. II, 29.

15. Ibid.

16. Ibid.

raised a great disturbance, endeavoring to eject him from his bishopric; for they entertained the hope that the Arian doctrine would prevail only upon the removal of Athanasius."[17] The "dirty tricks" played by the Eusebians began with their lodging charges against Athanasius with Emperor Constantine, at the very time he was already running afoul of the imperial policy of reconciling with the "former" heretics. Sozomen confided to his readers that "the various calamities which befell Athanasius were primarily occasioned by Eusebius and Theognis. As they possessed great freedom of speech and influence with the emperor, they strove for the recall of Arius, with whom they were on terms of concord and friendship, to Alexandria, and at the same time the expulsion from the Church of him who was opposed to them. They accused him before Constantine of being the author of all the seditions and troubles that agitated the Church, and of excluding those who were desirous of joining the Church; and alleged that unanimity would be restored were he alone to be removed."[18] Socrates reported that they bribed the Meletians to fabricate and file charges against Athanasius with the emperor. He wrote, "These persons suborn by bribes certain of the Melitian heresy to fabricate various charges against Athanasius; and first they accuse him through the Melitians Ision, Eudaemon and Callinicus, of having ordered the Egyptians to pay a linen garment as tribute to the church at Alexandria."[19] Given the level of internal conflict that was brewing in the church of Alexandria, it is not difficult to imagine that the Meletians, who were smarting under Athanasius's attempts to force them into compliance with the Nicene compromise, were willing to take steps to oppose and undermine his authority as bishop. Nor does it require a large leap of faith to assume that they were willing to work with the Eusebians to that end. It was a classic case of "the enemy of my enemy is my friend."[20]

It just so happened, however, that two of Athanasius's supporters (presbyters Alypius and Macarius) were at royal court at this time, and they convinced the emperor that these charges stemmed from prejudice against Athanasius and were utterly false. Socrates reported that the emperor "severely censured [Athanasius's] accusers, but urged Athanasius to

17. Ibid.

18. Sozomen, *Church History* II.22, *NPNF*, vol. II, 272. Cf. Socrates, *Church History* I.23, *NPNF*, vol. II, 26–27.

19 Socrates, *Church History* I.27, *NPNF*, vol. II, 29.

20. Sozomen opines that from this period onward, the summer of 330, the Meletians received and supported the Arian theology (*Church History* II.21, *NPNF*, vol. II, 272).

come to him."[21] Before Athanasius was able to appear before Constantine, however, the Eusebians mounted another set of charges against him, this time attempting to charge him with treason through Athanasius's alleged financial support of one of Constantine's political rivals (one Philumenus). Once again the emperor mounted an inquiry, and once again he found that the Alexandrian bishop was being falsely accused.

Theodoret recorded "a portion" of the letter that Constantine wrote to the church at Alexandria vindicating their bishop and ecclesiastical leader: "Believe me, my brethren," the emperor wrote, "the wicked men were unable to effect anything against your bishop. They surely could have had no other design than to waste our time, and to have themselves no place for repentance in this life. Do you, therefore, help yourselves and love that which wins your love; and exert all your power in the expulsion of those who wish to destroy your accord. I joyfully welcomed Athanasius your bishop; and I have conversed with him as with one whom I know to be a man of God."[22] This interview seems to have occurred in the spring of AD 332, since Athanasius's fourth *Festal Letter* mentions that he is at the court of Constantine to answer charges that have been brought against him. The letter was delivered to the Alexandrian church by the Prefect of the Praetorian Guard. Athanasius's letter concluded by stating, "For I am at the Court, having been summoned by the emperor Constantine to see him. But the Meletians, who were present there, being envious, sought our ruin before the Emperor. But they were put to shame and driven away thence as calumniators . . ."[23]

The third set of charges brought against Athanasius and his administration as bishop of Alexandria stemmed from an incident surrounding a Meletian named Ischyras, a person who, Socrates reported, "had been guilty of an act deserving of many deaths."[24] According to Socrates's chronicle, Ischyras was acting as a priest in Alexandria even though he had not been ordained into holy orders. This breach of ecclesiastical law soon came to the attention of Bishop Athanasius, who dispatched his presbyter Macarius to look into the matter. Macarius's visit to Ischyras's church devolved into conflict and violence, in which it was alleged that the altar was overturned, a sacred chalice was broken, sacred books were burnt and Ischyras

21. Socrates, *Church History* I.27, NPNF, vol. II, 29.
22. Theodoret, *Church History* I.25, NPNF, vol. III, 61.
23. Athanasius, *Festal Letter* 4, NPNF, vol. IV, 517.
24. Socrates, *Church History* I.27, NPNF, vol. II, 30.

was injured. Being forced to flee from Alexandria by Athanasius, Ischyras made his way to the episcopate of Eusebius, in Nicomedia, where he was promised an episcopate of his own, if he would testify against Athanasius as being the one behind the violence and sacrilege.[25] In his defense against these charges, Athanasius refuted the notion by showing that the building was not properly a church and that Ischyras was not properly ordained as a priest.[26] The charges that there was violence involved, however, were not addressed, and that gives the impression (as Hanson points out) that "his opponents cried 'Violence and sacrilege' and Athanasius replies 'No: only violence.'"[27] Ischyras subsequently withdrew the charges, in a letter published by Athanasius in his *Defense Against the Arians*. Hanson discredits that admission because it was probably made under duress.[28]

At this same time, the Eusebians accused Athanasius of having murdered one of the Meletian bishops, a man named Arsenius. Athanasius had chopped off his hand, the Eusebians alleged, then used it in the performance of diabolical magic. They even produced a severed hand, of unknown origin, which, they claimed, belonged to Arsenius and had been employed by Athanasius for occult practices.[29] The emperor delegated this case to his half-brother, a man named Dalmatius, who as a "censor" was ruling the East and was located in Antioch of Syria. Dalmatius was empowered to banish or acquit after due investigation of the charges. Bishops Eusebius and Theognis were also ordered to the trial, "that the case might be tried in their presence."[30] This clearly implicated them in having pressed the charges against Athanasius. Having heard about these new charges mounted against him, and knowing that Arsenius was actually alive and in hiding somewhere, Athanasius began to make a thorough search for the allegedly murdered Meletian bishop. In the meantime, however, he did not appear before the tribunal, no doubt convinced he could not get a fair hearing before them.

Emperor Constantine called a council of bishops at Jerusalem, in order to celebrate the thirtieth year of his reign as well as the establishment and consecration of a new cathedral that he caused to be erected there.

25. Ibid.

26. Athanasius, *Defense Against the Arians* 11, *NPNF*, vol. IV, 106.

27. Hanson, *Christian Doctrine of God*, 257.

28. Ibid., 256.

29. Socrates, *Church History* I.27, *NPNF*, vol. II, 30.

30. Ibid.

As a secondary matter, he ordered the bishops to reconvene at the coastal city of Tyre to hear, examine and to adjudicate the charges brought against Athanasius and his colleague Macarius. Macarius had been arrested in Alexandria and was brought to the meeting in chains, under military guard, and Athanasius was threatened with the same fate, if he did not present himself willingly before the assembly.[31]

As providence would have it, Arsenius was also in Tyre, having fled Alexandria and gone into hiding so that the charges against Athanasius would seem all the more credible. Agents of the governor, Archelaus, overheard whispers that Arsenius was alive and well in Tyre, concealed in the house of one of the citizens there. A search was made and Arsenius was quietly discovered and taken into custody. The "murdered man" initially denied his true identity, but Paul the bishop of Tyre knew him by sight and identified Arsenius as the person in question. Athanasius was soon brought before the Synod of Tyre to answer the charges against him. As soon as he was brought forth, his accusers confronted him with the charge of murder and magic and presented him with the evidence of the severed hand. Conducting the testimony with a sense of high courtroom drama, Athanasius asked whether there were among his accusers any who knew Arsenius, and several of them professed to know him. He then caused Arsenius to be introduced to the court, with his hands covered by his cloak. He then asked them, "'is this the person who lost a hand?' All were astonished at the unexpectedness of this procedure, except those who knew whence the hand had been cut off; for the rest thought that Arsenius was really deficient of a hand, and expected that the accused would make his defense in some other way."[32] Athanasius dramatically threw back the cloak to expose one of Arsenius's hands; then after a long, pregnant pause he then turned back the cloak to expose the other hand as well. Addressing himself to the assembly, Athanasius said, "Arsenius, as you see, is found to have two hands; let my accusers show the place whence the third [hand] was cut off."[33] During the tumult caused by these dramatic developments, Athanasius's chief accusers, including Achab (who is also called John Archaph), slipped away.[34]

The charges involving sacrilege and violence in the case of Macarius's attack upon Ischyras were not so easily set aside. Athanasius argued that

---

31. Scorates, *Church History* I.28, *NPNF*, vol. II, 30.

32. Socrates, *Church History* I.29, *NPNF*, vol. II, 31.

33. Ibid.

34. Socrates, *Church History* I.30, *NPNF*, vol. II, 31.

Ischyras was not properly ordained and that the place had not really been a church on that basis; in essence, as noted above, he addressed the charge of sacrilege but not the element of violence. A commission was appointed by the judges to go to the Mareotis section of Alexandria, where the incident occurred, so that the disputed points could be examined by them on location. When Athanasius saw that this commission was made up entirely of his accusers and opponents, and that they were set at liberty while Macarius was detained in bonds, he appealed to the governor about the impropriety of these developments. But when those appeals went unheeded, Athanasius secretly withdrew from the synod and made his way to the emperor.[35] Sozomen reported that

> Athanasius was filled with apprehension when he reflected upon these subjects and began to suspect that his enemies were secretly scheming to effect his ruin. After several sessions, when the Synod was filled with tumult and confusion and the accusers and a multitude of persons around the tribunal were crying aloud that Athanasius ought to be deposed as a sorcerer and a ruffian, and as being utterly unworthy [of] the priesthood, the officers who had been appointed by the emperor to be present at the Synod for the maintenance of order, compelled the accused to quit the judgment hall secretly; for they feared lest they might become his murderers, as is apt to be the case in the rush of a tumult.[36]

The Synod of Tyre, upon hearing the report of the commission sent to Mareotis, deposed Athanasius in his absence, but were wholly silent about the disgraceful defeat of the charge of murder against him. Moreover, they received into communion the Meletian Arsenius, and even allowed him to vote against Athanasius in the proceedings.[37]

London Papyrus 1914 (LP 1914) purports to be a letter written by one Callistus, a Meletian cleric in Alexandria. It bewails in some detail the violence perpetrated against the Meletians by Athanasius's adherents and Athanasius himself. It is written in very awkward Greek, by someone whose native language was probably Coptic. It details a violent attack upon the Meletian bishops by a drunken mob of Athanasius's supporters, augmented by soldiers. They were beaten "all bloody" and in fear of death, when they were cast out of the city by the mob. Five others were arrested, and two

---

35. Socrates, *Church History* I.31, *NPNF*, vol. II, 31.

36. Sozomen, *Church History* II.25, *NPNF*, vol. II, 276.

37. Socrates, *Church History* I.32, *NPNF*, vol. II, 31–32.

Meletian clergy were imprisoned in the meat market. Athanasius, who was apparently abroad at the time, was said to be "anxious and despondent" because of news that Macarius (his assistant) had been taken into custody by the emperor and that reports were circulating about his violent administration of matters in Alexandria. This manuscript, which is fragmentary and (apparently) of Meletian origin, gives some of the background of the events that led up to the Council of Tyre (335). Indeed, Hanson, who accepts the complete authority and authenticity of LP 1914, points to the strong similarity between the charges against Athanasius in it and those mounted at the Synod of Tyre.[38] It is also worth noting, as Maurice Wiles does, that the charges brought against Athanasius were not of a theological nature, but rather had to do with what was regarded as "his oppressive and sometimes violent exercise of ecclesiastical authority."[39] With Constantine, who had actively supported the "same substance" language of the Nicene Creed, still on the imperial throne, it might have seemed unwise to attack Athanasius—the chief defender of that formula—on theological grounds. Hence, the opposition against Athanasius, which may have been theologically motivated at basis, was actually voiced in terms of his ecclesiastical authority and its alleged abuses.[40]

Soon after these developments Constantine summoned the assembled bishops to Constantinople, saying that Athanasius had fled to him for protection and that it was necessary for them to come to the capital so that he could carefully examine the charges against the Alexandrian bishop. In a lengthy letter, preserved by Socrates, Constantine urged the bishops to put aside "this jealous rivalry" and to judge these matters without partiality and prejudice.[41] Athanasius, for his part, had repeatedly entreated for an audience before the emperor, and petitioned for nothing more than a fair hearing of the charges against him in the presence of his accusers. Hence, Constantine concluded, "Wherefore as this seems reasonable, and consistent with the equity of my government, I willingly gave instructions that these things should be written to you. My command therefore is, that all, as many as composed the Synod convened at Tyre, should forthwith hasten to

38. Hanson, *Christian Doctrine of God*, 254.

39. Wiles, *Archetypical Heresy*, 6.

40. Arnold, *Early Episcopal Career*, 103, agrees with this assessment, but Hanson, *Christian Doctrine of God*, 275, accepts the charges against Athanasius as being valid and not motivated by theological bias.

41. Socrates, *Church History* I.34, NPNF, vol. II, 32.

the court of our clemency, in order that from the facts themselves you may make clear the purity and integrity of your decision in my presence, whom you cannot but own to be a true servant of God."[42]

Instead of hastening to Constantinople, as the emperor ordered, most of the bishops assembled at Tyre went home to their respective cities. But several of Athanasius's chief accusers, including Eusebius of Nicomedia, Theognis, Maris, Patrophilus, Ursacius, and Valens, did go up to Constantinople, but they would not allow further inquiry to proceed on the charges of violence and sacrilege with respect to the breaking of the communion chalice, and the murder of Arsenius. Instead, they brought a new charge with them, one that was designed to trouble the emperor more than matters of ecclesiastical unity and propriety: "they had recourse to another calumny, informing the emperor that Athanasius had threatened to prohibit the sending of corn which was usually conveyed from Alexandria to Constantinople. They affirmed also that these menaces were heard from the lips of Athanasius by the bishops Adamantius, Anubion, Arbathion and Peter, for slander is most prevalent when the assertor of it appears to be a person worthy of credit."[43] Constantine was so infuriated by this new charge, which threatened the stability of the capital and therefore the entire empire, that he immediately condemned Athanasius to exile and ordered him to reside among the Gauls. And so, Socrates concluded, "He accordingly took up his abode at Treves, a city of Gaul."[44] The removal of Athanasius from his episcopal see was accompanied by widespread riots in Alexandria and letters of protest from the saintly Antony of the Desert.[45]

Athanasius's fourth *Festal Letter* (332) was composed while he was at the court of the emperor and was delivered to the Alexandrian church by a solider. He apologized for the lateness of his correspondence, bewailing the difficulty of his long journey and his subsequent illness. Despite mounting persecution, the bishop urged his readers, "Let us not fulfill these days like those that mourn, but, by enjoying spiritual food, let us seek to silence our fleshly lusts. For by these means we shall have strength to overcome our adversaries, like blessed Judith, when having first exercised herself in fastings and prayers, she overcame the enemies . . ."[46]

42. Ibid.

43. Socrates, *Church History* I.35, *NPNF*, vol. II, 33.

44. Ibid.

45. Sozomen, *Church History* II.31, *NPNF*, vol. II, 280.

46. *Festal Letter* 4, *NPNF*, vol. IV, 516.

In his own written defense against various charges, which Athanasius subsequently mounted in *Defense Against the Arians* (*Apologia contra Arianos*), he reported, "It was proved also by the anger of the Emperor; for although he had written the preceding letter, and had condemned their injustice, as soon as he heard such a charge as this, he was immediately incensed, and instead of granting me a hearing, he sent me away into Gaul."[47] Sozomen reported that "the emperor, either believing their statements to be true, or imagining that unanimity would be restored among the bishops if Athanasius were removed, exiled him to Treves, in Western Gaul; and thither, therefore, he was conducted."[48] Whether Constantine believed he heard a shred of truth in the new charges against Athanasius, or whether he was simply wearied by all the controversy surrounding the troublesome Alexandrian bishop, we cannot know from this historical distance. It is clear, however, that Athanasius started on his first exile in February 336, journeying to Treves (or Treveri in Gaul). The fact that Constantine did not appoint an episcopal successor to Athanasius during his banishment suggests that perhaps the exile of the troublesome Alexandrian bishop had less to do with the charges mounted against him by the Synod of Tyre and more to do with the unity and harmony that the emperor hoped would descend upon the church during Athanasius's absence.[49] The exile may have been intended as a temporary matter, since no successor was elected, and Athanasius continued to act as episcopal leader of Egypt, albeit from exile.

The nearly two full years that Athanasius spent in the city of Treves must have seemed like an extended vacation from the tumultuous events in Alexandria and the East. The city was rapidly becoming a northern Rome. During this period Constantine II, Caesar of the West (324–37), held court there and proved to be friendly towards the exiled bishop. Athanasius testified that Constantine II provided him with "all necessaries."[50] The exiled bishop also probably received a warm welcome from the resident bishop, Maximin (322–49), who was a fellow supporter of the Nicene theology.[51] It is in this period of relative calm and repose that some scholars locate the composition of Athanasius's first major theological works, *Against the*

47. Athanasius, *Defense Against the Arians* 87, NPNF, vol. IV, 146.

48. Sozomen, *Church History* II.28, NPNF, vol. II, 279.

49. Arnold, *Early Episcopal Career*, 173, 185–86.

50. *Defense Against the Arians* 87, NPNF, vol. IV, 146.

51. *Defense Against the Arians* 50, NPNF, vol. IV, 127.

Heathen and *On the Incarnation*, although we have suggested them to be the product of an earlier phase of his ministry.

Athanasius's fifth and sixth *Festal Letters* were written in exile. The fifth letter urged its readers to celebrate Easter because it unites the cross of Jesus Christ with their own cross-bearing life in the world: God "both brought about the slaying of His Son for salvation, and gave us this reason for the holy feast, to which every year bears witness, as often as at this season the feast is proclaimed. This also leads us on from the cross through this world to that which is before us, and God produces even now from it the joy of glorious salvation, bringing us to the same assembly, and in every place uniting all of us in spirit . . ."[52] Persecution was certainly part of this "cross" that the community bore in their solidarity with Christ and one another, and though separated by distance, they were united in spirit.

The sixth letter makes no mention of the bishop's location in exile but is full of his atonement theology, which is given, perhaps, to set the Easter celebration in its appropriate theological context. He wrote, "In our commemoration of these things, my brethren, let us not be occupied with meats, but let us glorify the Lord, let us become fools for Him who died for us, even as Paul said: 'For if we are foolish, it is to God; or if we are sober-minded it is to you; since because One died for all men, therefore all were dead to Him; and He died for all, that we who live should not henceforth live to ourselves, but to Him who died for us, and rose again' [2 Cor 5:13–15]. No longer then ought we to live to ourselves, but as servants to the Lord."[53] In a similar way, the seventh *Festal Letter* (335) urged its readers to emulate Jesus Christ both in life and in death:

> In this David participated, saying in the Psalms, "For thy sake we die all the day; we are accounted as sheep for the slaughter" [Ps 44:22]. Now this is becoming in us, especially in the days of the feast, when a commemoration of the death of our Savior is held. For he who is made like Him in His death, is also diligent in virtuous practices, having mortified his members which are upon the earth, and crucifying the flesh with the affections and lusts, he lives in the Spirit, and is conformed to the Spirit. He is always mindful of God, and forgets Him not, and never does the deeds of death.[54]

52. *Festal Letter* 5, *NPNF*, vol. IV, 518.
53. *Festal Letter* 6, *NPNF*, vol. IV, 520.
54. *Festal Letter* 7, *NPNF*, vol. IV, 523.

It was also during this period that Arius himself passed from the scene. The council of Jerusalem, which met to celebrate the thirtieth year of Constantine's reign, rehabilitated Arius's career and voted to reinstate him in the church. Arius still hoped to return to Alexandria, but that was made impossible by the strong sentiments against him there. He returned instead to Constantinople, and Alexander, who was bishop of that city, refused to receive him into communion there as well.[55] A council was called at the instigation of Eusebius of Nicomedia, and during its deliberations Arius died an ignoble death, stricken by a physical ailment while visiting a public latrine. Some attributed his death to weakness of heart, and the rush of joy that Arius might have felt as events began to fall together in his favor; others attributed his death in a latrine to God's judgment for Arius's impiety; still others saw it as the result of some secret imposition of the magical arts.[56] Athanasius, in an account preserved by Sozomen, reported that Constantine viewed Arius's ignoble death as proof of his perjury, and to Athanasius it seemed appropriate that Arius did not live long enough to be fully reinstated and received into the church.[57]

---

55. Socrates, *Church History* I.37, *NPNF*, vol. II, 34.

56. Sozomen, *Church History* II.29, *NPNF*, vol. II, 279.

57. Sozomen, *Church History* II.30, *NPNF*, vol. II, 279–80. Cf. Socrates, *Church History* I.38, *NPNF*, vol. II, 34–35.

— 7 —

Athanasius's First Return

While Athanasius was on his imperially imposed "vacation" in Treves, Constantine was taken ill. The church historian, Theodoret, described the succeeding events rather succinctly: "A year and a few months afterwards [Athanasius's exile] the emperor was taken ill at Nicomedia, a city of Bithynia, and knowing the uncertainty of human life, he received the holy rite of baptism, which he had intended to have deferred until he could be baptized in the river Jordan."[1] Shortly before his death, in 335, Constantine had assigned parts of the governance of the empire to his three sons, Constantine II, Constantius II, and Constans, as well as his nephews Dalmatius and Hannibalian. His sons ruled the main part of the empire, and his nephews the frontier outposts. Constantine's will perpetuated this division of the empire. Upon his death, however, the army would have no one over them but the sons of Constantine. Constantius II (hereafter, Constantius), being the closest to Constantinople, marched on the capital and had all other relatives—excepting his own brothers—put to death. Only Gallus and Julian (sons of Julius, Constantine I's half-brother) and Nepotian (son of Eutropia, Constantine I's half-sister) escaped the slaughter. Constantius then met with his two brothers on September 9, 337, whereupon they agreed to a new partition of the Christian Roman Empire—Constantine II would rule Gaul and Africa, Constantius would lead Thrace and the East, while Constans would govern Italy and Illyricum. Of these three rulers, Constantine II and Constans were already baptized Catholic Christians, whereas Constantius was not baptized and had sympathies for Arianism.[2] Prior to his death, Constantine had ordered that, in

1. Theodoret, *Church History* I.30, *NPNF*, vol. III, 63.

2. Kidd, *History of the Church*, 2:69. The depth of Constantius's Arianism has been debated in recent years. Cf. Barnes, *Athanasius and Constantius*.

the words of Theodoret, "the great Athanasius should return to Alexandria, and expressed this decision in the presence of Eusebius [of Nicomedia], who did all he could to dissuade him."[3]

Constantine II, the eldest son of the deceased emperor, who ruled Gaul at this time, provided Athanasius with a letter of commendation to the church of Alexandria. It is carried in full in Theodoret's *Church History*. It reports, in part: "Constantine, my lord and my father, of blessed memory, intended to have reinstated him [Athanasius] in his former bishopric, and to have restored him to your piety; but as the emperor was arrested by the hand of death before his desires were accomplished, I, being his heir, have deemed it fitting to carry into execution the purpose of this sovereign of divine memory."[4] Athanasius had been absent for two years and four months by the time he reentered his home city. Constantine II, in the same letter, explained that he had treated Athanasius well during his exile because it was clear he was a man of great virtue and true piety. "I was moved to this line of conduct," the emperor wrote, "by his own great virtue, and the thought of your affectionate longing for his return. May Divine Providence watch over you, beloved brethren!"[5]

Athanasius left Gaul immediately upon receiving news of his restoration, but he traveled home by an indirect route, stopping in Constantinople and in Antioch and elsewhere along the way to drum up support for the Nicene theology and for his own restoration. Robertson suggests that he traveled east in the company of Constantine II, and met Constantius at Viminacium and then again at Caesarea, as the emperor of the East hurried off to the Persian front.[6] Furnished with the letter from Constantine II, Athanasius returned from exile and went home to Alexandria, where he was, in the words of Theodoret, "welcomed both by the rich and by the poor, by the inhabitants of cities, and by those of the provinces. The followers of the madness of Arius were the only persons who felt any vexation at his return. Eusebius, Theognis, and those of their faction resorted to their former machinations, and endeavored to prejudice the ears of the young emperor against him."[7]

---

3. Theodoret, *Church History* I.30, *NPNF*, vol. III, 63–64. Cf. Socrates, *Church History* II.39, *NPNF*, vol. II, 35.

4. Theodoret, *Church History* II.1, *NPNF*, vol. III, 65.

5. Ibid.

6. Archibald Robertson, "Prolegomena," *NPNF*, vol. IV, xli.

7. Theodoret, *Church History* II.1, *NPNF*, vol. III, 65.

B. J. Kidd compiled a verbal portrait of Constantius based upon his research in several contemporary sources:

> He had his good points. He was pure in life; sober in habits; a good soldier, with some taste for learning; by no means wanting in statecraft, for he kept peace in his own share of the Empire for four and twenty years; and in social charm and pleasantness of private life he was no unworthy son of Constantine. But he was essentially a little man. Small in stature, with short and crooked legs, his mental capacity was small too. Vacillating as a reed, he was so ridiculously conceited that he thought it dignified to sit motionless in public, and would not even clear his throat or blow his nose. He swallowed flattery wholesale; was timorous, and therefore cruel; adept at plotting, but himself the prey of scheming and unworthy favorites.[8]

Under his rule the Christian church would be plunged into further controversy and division. Ammianus Marcellinus, a Roman historian of the period, reported, "The plain and simple religion of the Christians was bedeviled by Constantius with old wives' fancies. Instead of trying to settle matters he raised complicated issues which led to much dissension, and as this spread more widely he fed it with verbal argument. Public transport hurried throngs of bishops hither and thither to attend what they call synods, and by his attempts to impose conformity Constantius only succeeded in hamstringing the post service."[9] Among Consantius's flattering favorites was Eusebius of Nicomedia, who had emerged as one of Athanasius's chief theological and ecclesiastical opponents.

The early church historians were divided in their opinions about Emperor Constantius's theological views. Socrates simply refers to him as "an Arian," and one who "had been long since imbued with Arian doctrine."[10] Philostorgius, the Arian, reported that Constantius "went over to the Arian sect" under the influence of Eusebius.[11] Sozomen, perhaps showing more theological acumen, described Constantius as one who embraced the middle position, between the extreme Arians and the orthodox, in that the term *homoiousios* ("of similar substance") was used to describe the

---

8. Kidd, *History of the Church*, 69–70. Cf. Ammianus Marcellinus, *Later Roman Empire*, ch. 21, "The Character of Constantius," 229–32.

9. Ammianus Marcellinus, *Later Roman Empire*, 232.

10. Socrates, *Church History* II.26, *NPNF*, vol. II, 54.

11. Philistorgius, *Church History* III.2a, 39.

relationship between the essence of the Father and the essence of the Son.[12] But Sozomen also added a testimonial to his assessment of Constantius, saying that he was certain that Constantius "retained the same doctrines as those held by his father and brother,"[13] and that he was "induced to adopt the use of the term '*homoiousios*,' for it was admitted by many priests who conformed to the doctrines of the Nicaean council."[14] In the final analysis Sozomen's assessment is somewhat ambiguous, since he implies that the emperor held to the Nicene theology but used semi-Arian terms to express it. It might also have been true that, like Constantine himself, Constantius was trying mightily to unify the Christians under his rule into one theological perspective, and in this regard his antipathy towards Athanasius may have been more deeply rooted in the bishop's holy intransigence than in doctrinal differences between their views.[15]

With the imposing presence of Emperor Constantine gone from the scene, the fragile ecclesiastical peace and theological compromises that had been hammered out at Nicaea (325) began to break down. Socrates, the church historian, perhaps following the writings of Athanasius himself, wrote, "After the death of the Emperor Constantine, Eusebius, bishop of Nicomedia, and Theognis of Nicaea, imagining that a favorable opportunity had arisen, used their utmost efforts to expunge the doctrine of *homoousion* [same substance], and to introduce Arianism in its place. They, nevertheless, despaired of effecting this, if Athanasius should return to Alexandria . . ."[16] Socrates described at some length how "that presbyter by whose means Arius had been recalled from exile a little while before"—presumably Eusebius of Nicomedia himself—ingratiated himself to the royal household of Constantius and managed to convert the chief eunuch of the imperial bed-chamber (also named Eusebius) and the empress to Arian views.[17] Gradually, as Socrates described it, Arianism descended like a deadly plague upon the court till it was slowly diffused throughout the

---

12. *Church History* III.18, *NPNF*, vol. II, 297.

13. *Church History* III.19, *NPNF*, vol. II, 298.

14. Ibid.

15. Frances Young and Andrew Teal (*From Nicaea to Chalcedon*, 25–26) are also of this opinion. But Jaroslav Pelikan, in his magisterial *Christian Tradition*, clearly locates Constantius in the Arian camp. Cf. Pelikan, *Christian Tradition*, 1:209–10.

16. Socrates, *Church History* II.2, *NPNF*, vol. II, 36.

17. Ibid.

administration, the capital city, and other cities of the empire.[18] Hence, Socrates reported, "As this affair increased, going from bad to worse, Eusebius of Nicomedia and his party looked upon popular ferment as a piece of good fortune. For only thus they thought they would be enabled to constitute someone who held their own sentiments bishop of Alexandria. But the return of Athanasius at that time defeated their purpose . . ."[19]

Athanasius arrived back in Alexandria on November 23, 337, amidst much joy and celebration.[20] Subsequently, in his eulogy, Gregory of Nazianzus compared Athanasius's return to Alexandria to the "triumphant entry" of Jesus Christ into Jerusalem (Matt 21:6–11) on Palm Sunday. "All the means of testifying to a city's joy," he wrote, were bestowed upon him "in lavish and audible profusion."[21] Socrates also reported that Athanasius "was most joyfully received by the people of the city. Nevertheless as many in it had embraced Arianism, combining together, entered into conspiracies against him, by which frequent seditions were excited, affording a pretext to the Eusebians for accusing him to the emperor of having taken possession of the Alexandrian church on his own responsibility, in spite of the adverse judgment of a general council of bishops."[22]

In his lengthy *Festal Letter* 10, which he seems to have begun writing while in exile in Treves (Trier), and then completed either on the road or back in Alexandria in the year 338, Athanasius lamented his recent persecutions and separation from the brethren. But he anticipated a joyous and grateful Easter celebration despite current and past troubles: "For although I have been hindered by those afflictions of which you have doubtless heard, and severe trials have been laid upon me, and a great distance has separated us; while the enemies of the truth have followed our tracks, laying snares to discover a letter from us, so that by their accusations, they might add to the pain of our wounds; yet the Lord, strengthening and comforting us in our afflictions, we have not feared, even when held fast in the midst of such machinations and conspiracies, to indicate and make known to you our saving Easter-feast, even from the ends of the earth."[23] Reminding them of the unfathomable love of Christ, he exhorted them—in the words of St.

18. Ibid., 36–37.
19. Ibid., 37.
20. Robertson, "Prolegomena," *NPNF*, vol. IV, xli.
21. Gregory Nazianzen, *Oration* 21.29, *NPNF*, vol. VII, 277–78.
22. Socrates, *Church History* II.3, *NPNF*, vol. II, 37.
23. Athanasius, *Festal Letter* 10, *NPNF*, vol. IV, 527.

Paul—that "'nothing separates us from the love of Christ; neither affliction, nor distress, nor persecution, nor famine, nor nakedness, nor peril, nor sword' [Rom 8:35]. Thus, keeping the feast myself, I was desirous that you also, my beloved, should keep it . . ."[24]

He argued strenuously that suffering in this life does not signal God-forsakenness; quite the contrary, our suffering becomes an opportunity and area for God's triumphant love and sustaining grace. Indeed, it is in the midst of our suffering, at times, that God's loving-kindness is most emphatically recognized and decisively known. In this, Athanasius saw himself and his beloved colleagues following in the way of the sufferings of Jesus Christ, "Who when He was smitten bore it patiently, being reviled He reviled not again, when He suffered He threatened not, but He gave His back to the smiters, and His cheeks to buffetings, and turned not His face from spitting; and at last, was willingly led to death, that we might behold in Him the image of all that is virtuous and immortal, and that we, conducting ourselves after these examples, might truly tread on serpents and scorpions, and on all the power of the enemy."[25]

Thus, it is through triumphant faith in Christ that the persecuted Christian finds her sanctification enhanced. Here, St. Paul becomes the Christian's example as well:

> Thus too Paul, while he conducted himself after the example of the Lord, exhorted us, saying, "Be ye followers of me, as I also am of Christ" [1 Cor 11:1]. In this way he prevailed against all the divisions of the devil, writing, "I am persuaded that neither death, nor life, nor angels, nor principalities, nor things present, nor things to come, nor powers, nor height, nor depth, nor any other creature, shall be able to separate us from the love of God that is in Jesus Christ" [Rom 8:38–39]. For the enemy draws near to us in afflictions, and trials, and labors, using every endeavor to ruin us. But the man who is in Christ, combating those things that are contrary, and opposing wrath by long-suffering, contumely by meekness, and vice by virtue, obtains the victory, and exclaims, "I can do all things through Christ Who strengtheneth me"; and "In all these things we are conquerors through Christ Who loved us" [Phil 4:13; Rom 8:37]. This is the grace of the Lord, and these are the Lord's means of restoration for the children of men.[26]

24. Ibid., 528.

25. Ibid., 530.

26. Ibid., 530–31.

Athanasius's own sufferings and those of his fellow Christians became a lens through which he came to interpret and (in his mind) better understand the gospel of Jesus Christ.

But "the Ario-manaics," who do not truly follow Jesus Christ, writes Athanasius, are devoid of these spiritual comforts in the midst of their afflictions, because they do not properly honor Christ. They "smite Him who is their Helper with their tongue, and blaspheme Him who set [them] free, and hold all manner of different opinions against the Savior."[27] Hence Athanasius urged them, "hadst thou considered what the Father is, and what the Son, thou wouldst not have blasphemed the Son, as of a mutable nature. And hadst thou understood His work of loving-kindness towards us, thou wouldst not have alienated the Son from the Father, nor have looked upon Him as a stranger, Who reconciled us to His Father."[28]

"What then is our duty," Athanasius asked his brethren, "for the sake of these things, but to praise and give thanks to God, the King of all? And let us first exclaim in the words of the Psalms, 'Blessed be the Lord, Who hath not given us over as a prey to their teeth' [Ps 124:6]. Let us keep the [Easter] feast in that way which He hath dedicated for us unto salvation—the holy day of Easter—so that we may celebrate the feast which is in heaven with the angels."[29]

When Athanasius finally arrived in Alexandria, conflict in the city between the Nicene Christians (Catholics) and Arians soon erupted. It was further fueled by the intrigues of the Eusebians, from long distance, and the hostility of the Meletians within the city. Soon the saintly Antony the Hermit and the popular desert monks were rumored to support the Arian cause as well. This falsehood was quickly put to rest by personal visit of St. Antony in July 338. While he stayed only two days (departing on July 27, 338), he denounced the Arians emphatically, taught from the scriptures, and healed many.[30]

In his *Life of Antony*, which he wrote in 356, Athanasius presented three separate instances in which the saint of the desert addressed the Arian controversy. These passages, while written as Antony's own words, must also be seen as the words of Athanasius himself. The first of these occurs in paragraph 69, which is given here in its entirety:

27. Ibid., 531.
28. Ibid.
29. Ibid.
30. Robertson, "Prolegomena," *NPNF*, vol. IV, xli.

On another occasion when the Arians falsely claimed that he [Antony] held the same view as they, he was quite irritated and angry at them. Then, summoned both by the bishops and all the brothers, he came down from the mountain, and entering into Alexandria, he publicly renounced the Arians, saying that theirs was the last heresy and the forerunner of the Antichrist. He taught the people that the Son of God is not a creature, and that He did not come into existence from nonbeing, but rather that He is eternal Word and Wisdom from the essence of the Father. "So," he asserted, "it is sacrilegious to say 'there was when he was not' for the Word coexisted with the Father always. Therefore you are to have no fellowship with the most ungodly Arians, for there is no 'fellowship of light with darkness.' You are God-fearing Christians, but they, in saying that the Son and Word of God the Father is a creature, differ in no way from the pagans, who 'serve the creature rather than the Creator.' Be assured that the whole creation itself is angrered at them, because they number among the creatures the Creator and Lord of all, in whom all things were made."[31]

We notice this brief homily stresses three of Athanasius's own chief criticisms against the Arians: (1) they say that the Son of God, the Word, is a creature; (2) they affirm that the Son had a beginning; and (3) they argue that the *Logos*—as a creature—is not "from the essence" of the Father. There is no indication, among the sayings of the Desert Fathers, that these kinds of theological fine points were important parts of St. Antony's own teaching (though they might have been), but it is undeniably clear that they were features of Athanasius's critique of Arianism. This makes one wonder to what extent Athanasius was putting his own words in Antony's mouth when he wrote the *Life of Antony*. In this same speech Antony also advocated for and supported Athanasius'ss own policy of separation and non-communion with theological heretics (Arians) and schismatics (Meletians).[32] The visit of St. Antony might have brought a modicum of peace to the tumultuous ecclesiastical situation in Alexandria, but trouble was brewing elsewhere.[33]

Meanwhile, the saintly and orthodox Paul had been ordained to the leadership of the churches of Constantinople. This was more or less in keeping with the wishes of the populace and those of his deceased predecessor. But soon thereafter, Constantius arrived in Constantinople and "was highly

---

31. Gregg, *Life of Antony*, 82.

32. Cf. ibid., 89 and 91.

33. Robertson, "Prolegomena," ch. II, *NPNF*, vol. IV, xli.

incensed at the consecration [of Paul]; and having convened an assembly of bishops of Arian sentiments, he divested Paul of his dignity, and translating Eusebius from the see of Nicomedia, he appointed him bishop of Constantinople. Having done this the emperor proceeded to Antioch."[34] Eusebius, late of Nicomedia and now of Constantinople, went with Constantius to Antioch of Syria, and together they convened a synod, ostensibly to dedicate a new church to the memory of the emperor's father, Constantine the Great, which had been completed by his son, a full ten years after the foundation had been laid. But the real reason for the synod, opined Socrates, was to subvert the doctrine of the *homoousion* ("same substance") and to depose Athanasius from Alexandria.[35]

A council at Antioch was called in the fifth year after the death of Constantine, or 340; Socrates reported that ninety bishops attended, though several important and influential bishops were absent, including Julius of Rome, Maximus of Jerusalem, and Athanasius himself.[36] The Eusebians had previously planned among themselves to bring charges against Athanasius at this gathering, and this they did, "accusing him in the first place of having acted contrary to a canon which they then constituted, in resuming his episcopal authority without the license of a general council of bishops, inasmuch as on his return from exile he had on his own responsibility taken possession of the church; and then because a tumult had been excited on his entrance and many were killed in the riot; moreover that some had been scourged by him, and others brought before the tribunals. Besides they brought forward what had been determined against Athanasius at [the council of] Tyre."[37]

Under the leadership of Eusebius, the Council of Antioch elected and ordained Gregory to become bishop of Alexandria. They then undertook to alter the Nicene Creed. As Socrates explained, "They altered the creed; not as condemning anything in that which was set forth at Nicaea, but in fact with a determination to subvert and nullify the doctrine of consubstantiality by means of frequent councils and the publication of various expositions of the faith, so as gradually to establish the Arian views."[38] Socrates included the creed of the council in his chronicle. It began with a strong

---

34. Socrates, *Church History* II.7, *NPNF*, vol. II, 38.

35. Socrates, *Church History* II.8, *NPNF*, vol. II, 38.

36. Ibid.

37. Ibid., 38–39. Cf. Sozomen, *Church History* III.5, *NPNF*, vol. II, 285.

38. Socrates, *Church History* II.10, *NPNF*, vol. II, 39.

denunciation of the notion that the bishops had become followers of Arius. This was probably in response to a letter of condemnation that had been received from Bishop Julius of Rome. The fathers gathered at Antioch wrote, "We have neither become followers of Arius—for how should we who are bishops be guided by a presbyter?—nor have we embraced any other faith than that which was set forth from the beginning. But being constituted as examiners and judges of his [Arius's] sentiments, we admit their soundness, rather than adopt them from him . . ."[39] They then proceeded to present an affirmation that avoided the language of the *homoousia* ("same substance") when speaking of the relationship of the Father and the Son. The creed also avoided saying that the Son was a creature of the Father, and therefore had a beginning. The actual creed, apart from the preamble about not following Arius and a concluding clause about the Holy Spirit, was given as follows:

> We have learned from the beginning to believe in one God of the Universe, the Creator and Preserver of all things both those thought of and those perceived by the senses: and in one only-begotten Son of God, subsisting before all ages, and co-existing with the Father who begat him, through whom also all things visible and invisible were made; who in the last days according to the Father's good pleasure, descended, and assumed flesh from the holy virgin, and having fully accomplished his Father's will, that he should suffer, and rise again, and ascend into the heavens, and sit at the right hand of the Father; and is coming to judge the living and the dead, continuing King and God for ever.[40]

After this confession was sent out in an encyclical letter, those who remained in Antioch drafted a second, much more extensive "Exposition of the Faith." While it contained many more scriptural analogies for describing God the Father and Jesus Christ the Son, it also avoided openly contradicting the Nicene Creed. But it also avoided directly stating that Jesus Christ, the Son, is of the same substance (*homoousia*) as God the Father, nor did it state that the Son is not in any sense made, as a creature, or that He did not have a beginning. Sozomen opined that much of the phraseology of this creed was taken from an earlier creed composed by Lucianus of Antioch,[41] who had been the teacher of Arius and the Eusebians. After they all subscribed to the new creed, had confirmed Gregory as bishop of Alexandria, and established some other canons, the Council of Antioch was dissolved.

39. Ibid.

40. Ibid.

41. Sozomen, *Church History* III.5, *NPNF*, vol. II, 285.

In the spring of the same year, during Lent, Gregory along with Syrianus (the military governor) and five thousand heavily armed troops marched on Alexandra, in order to take charge of the church and the city. They arrived on the night of March 18, 339, and began to look for Athanasius secretly. They just missed capturing him that night. They failed again two days later in the church of Theonas, where he had baptized many believers. On the fourth day, March 22, 339, Gregory entered the city as bishop, and Athanasius went into hiding. From his seclusion Athanasius drafted an encyclical letter to the "Bishops of the World," which detailed the illegal and abusive actions that had been taken against him and urged his readers not to succumb to the attractions of Arianism.

In this lengthy epistle, which is preserved among his own written works, Athanasius detailed the forced intrusion of Gregory into his episcopal see, with the help of Philagrius, the new imperial governor:

> With these acts of violence has the Governor seized upon the churches, and has given them up to Gregory and the Arian madmen. Thus, those persons who were excommunicated by us for their impiety, now glory in the plunder of our churches; while the people of God, and the Clergy of the Catholic Church are compelled either to have communion with the impiety of the Arian heretics, or else to forbear entering into them. Moreover, by means of the Governor, Gregory has exercised no small violence towards the captains of ships and others who pass over sea, torturing and scourging some, putting others in bonds, and casting them into prison, in order to oblige them not to resist his iniquities, and to take letters from him. And not satisfied with all this, that he may glut himself with our blood, he has caused his savage associate, the Governor, to prefer an indictment against me, as in the name of the people, before the most religious Emperor Constantius, which contains odious charges from which one may expect not only to be banished, but even ten thousand deaths.[42]

This letter was written and disseminated either just before or just after Easter (April 15, 339).[43] The letter is silent about the violence that must have also occurred when Athanasius's followers opposed the usurpation of their beloved bishop, and in the larger scheme of things the *Encyclical Letter* depicts the removal of Athanasius as being part of a larger plot to undermine

42. Athanasius, *Encyclical Epistle to the Bishops, NPNF*, vol. IV, 95.

43. Barnes surmises that the encyclical was written soon after Athanasius arrived in Rome (*Athanasius and Constantius*, 50–51).

the orthodox (Nicene) theology of the entire church.[44] Almost immediately after issuing this encyclical letter, Athanasius and a small company of associates left Alexandria and headed for safety in Rome.

Sozomen described this exodus at some length: "Athanasius, fearful lest the people should be exposed to suffering on his account, assembled them by night in the church, and when the soldiers came to take possession of the church, prayers having been concluded, he first ordered a psalm to be sung. During the chanting of this psalm the soldiers remained without and quietly awaited its conclusion, and in the meantime Athanasius passed under the singers and secretly made his escape and fled to Rome."[45] The people of Alexandria were so angry at the forced expulsion of Bishop Athanasius that they rioted throughout the city and burned down the church that bore the name of Dionysius, one of their former bishops.[46]

Athanasius's selection of Rome as the location for his self-chosen exile speaks volumes about the growing affinity between his Nicene theology and the theology of the Latin West. It also reflects well on the relationship that he had begun building with Bishop (Pope) Julius of Rome. And finally, it also indicates something of Rome's growing dominance as the seat of Catholic Christianity, and a church that was "first among equals" and vying for leadership of the Christian movement. Theodoret indicates that Athanasius's enemies had written false accusations about him to Julius, the bishop of Rome, and that Julius had summoned both the accused and the accusers to come before him. Theodoret opined that it was for this reason that the Alexandrian bishop fled to Rome.[47] This rationale provided by Theodoret, long after the fact, may have been concocted to provide a cloak of honor to Athanasius's secret and sudden departure from Alexandria. But, as Athanasius would subsequently write, in 357, describing another forced departure from his see, if it is wrong to flee, it is even worse to persecute: "They bitterly bewail themselves, that they have not effectually put me out of the way; and so they pretend to reproach me with cowardice, not perceiving that by thus murmuring against me, they rather turn the blame upon themselves."[48]

44. Athanasius, *Encyclical Epistle to the Bishops*, NPNF, vol. IV, 95–96.
45. Sozomen, *Church History* III.6, NPNF, vol. II, 286.
46. Ibid.
47. Theodoret, *Church History* II.2, NPNF, vol. III, 96.
48. Athanasius, *Defense of His Flight* 8, NPNF, vol. IV, 257.

---------— 8 ---------—

The Second Exile (Rome 338–45)

Athanasius and his entourage arrived in Rome in June or July 339. He
left a brief recollection of this period in his *Defense before Constantius*,
which was written subsequently. "When I left Alexandria," Athanasius reported, "[I] did not go to your brother's [Constans] head-quarters, or to
any other persons, but only to Rome; and having laid my case before the
Church (for this was my only concern), I spent my time in public worship."[1]
The primary concern of this portion of Athanasius's *Defense* was to deny
that he had met with the Western emperor Constans in order to gain his
support against the Eastern emperor Constantius, but the same passage
also locates Athanasius at Rome, and mentions that he was there to clear
his reputation and engage in (probably lead) public worship.

When Athanasius reported that he "laid his case before the Church,"
he was referring primarily to Bishop (or Pope) Julius of Rome. We know
from a lengthy letter that Julius wrote to the Eusebians, who were assembled in council at Antioch in 341,[2] that the Bishop of Rome had called a
church council to examine the charges raised against both Athanasius and
Marcellus, and had found them innocent of all complaints against them.
After reviewing all the charges against Athanasius, including those raised
earlier at the Synod of Tyre, Julius pointed out that the elevation of Gregory
in his place, even supposing that it "was in the position of a criminal after
the Council," was handled in a manner that was both illegal and contrary
to the rule of the church. If Athanasius was to be replaced, his removal
and replacement should have originated in the church of Alexandria, not

1. Athanasius, *Defense before Constantius* 4, *NPNF*, vol. IV, 239.

2. This letter is presented in full in Athanasius's *Defense Against the Arians*, *NPNF*,
vol. IV, 111–19.

the Council of Antioch, and among his fellow Egyptians, not among his theological opponents. "Moreover," Julius wrote,

> the account which is given of the conduct of Gregory on his entry into the city, plainly shows the character of his appointment. In such peaceful times, as those who came from Alexandria declared them to have been, and as the Bishops also represented in their letters, the Church was set on fire; Virgins were stripped; Monks were trodden under foot; Presbyters and many of the people were scourged and suffered violence; Bishops were cast into prison; multitudes were dragged about from place to place; the holy Mysteries, about which they accused the Presbyter Macarius, were seized upon by heathens and cast upon the ground; and all to constrain certain persons to admit the appointment of Gregory. Such conduct plainly shows who they are that transgress the Canons [of church law].[3]

In short, Julius surmised, "Had the appointment been lawful, he would not have had recourse to illegal proceedings to compel the obedience of those who in a legal way resisted him."[4]

Athanasius may have "laid his case before the church" in another way as well. A few contemporary scholars date his *Defense Against the Arians* (*Apologia contra Arianos*) from this same period.[5] Sozomen reported,

> Those who were opposed to the doctrines of the Nicaean Council thought this a favorable opportunity to calumniate the bishops whom they had deposed, and to procure their ejection from the church as abettors of false doctrine, and as disturbers of the public peace; and to accuse them of having sought, during the life of Constans, to excite a misunderstanding between the emperors . . . Their efforts were principally directed against Athanasius, towards whom they entertained so great an aversion that, even when he was protected by Constans, they could not conceal their enmity. Narcissus, bishop of Cilicia, Theodore, bishop of Thrace, Eugenius, bishop of Nicaea, Patrophilus, bishop of Scythopolis, Menophantes, bishop of Ephesus, and other bishops, to the number of thirty, assembled in Antioch, and wrote a letter to all the bishops of every region, in which they stated that Athanasius had returned

3. Athanasius, *Defense Against the Arians* 30, NPNF, vol. IV, 116.

4. Ibid.

5. Barnes, *Athanasius and Constantius*, 98–99. In this they are following the suggestion of Sozomen, who connected the writing of this document with the Synod of Antioch, which was held in the autumn of 349.

to his bishopric in violation of the rules of the Church, that he had not justified himself in any council, and that he was only supported by some of his own faction; and they exhorted them not to hold communion with him, nor to write to him, but to enter into communion with George, who had been ordained to succeed him.[6]

It is not clear whether or not Athanasius had returned to Alexandria, as his detractors reported. But it is sometimes assumed, based on this passage, that *Defense Against the Arians* was written during this period and sent by Athanasius to the Council of Antioch, as a defense of his actions.

The *Defense* amounted to a collection of important documents, given in support of Athanasius's case and cause. Timothy Barnes ably summarized the contents of this work:

1. the letter of the Council of Alexandria in the early months of 338 (3–19);

2. the letter of Julius in 341 replying to the synodical letter of the "Dedication Council" at Antioch (21–35);

3. three letters of the Western bishops at Serdica: the first letter addressed specifically to the church of Alexandria (37–40), the second a letter in almost identical terms to the bishops of Egypt and Libya (41), the third the synodical letter to bishops of the Catholic Church everywhere—with no fewer than 280 names appended as signatories (42–50);

4. eight letters relating to Athanasius's return to Alexandria in 346, including six written by Constantius (52–57);

5. the letters of Ursacius and Valens to Julius and Athanasius withdrawing their charges against Athanasius (58).[7]

The bishop's tenth *Festal Letter* (338) clearly reflects the location and trials of Athanasius's exile. While he wrote to inform and comfort the church, it is clear that Athanasius was feeling the pain of exile and the pressure caused by the schemes of his opponents:

> Although I have traveled all this distance from you, my brethren, I have not forgotten the custom that obtains among you, which has

---

6. Sozomen, *Church History* IV.8, *NPNF*, vol. II, 304.

7. Barnes, *Athanasius and Constantius*, 99–100. Cf. Robertson, *Works of Athanasius, NPNF*, vol. IV, 99–148.

been delivered to us by the fathers, so as to be silent without notifying to you the time of the annual holy feast, and the day for its celebration. For although I have been hindered by those afflictions of which you have doubtless heard, and severe trials have been laid upon me, and a great distance has separated us; while the enemies of the truth have followed our tracks, laying snares to discover a letter from us, so that by their accusations, they might add to the pain of our wounds; yet the Lord, strengthening and comforting us in our afflictions, we have not feared, even when held fast in the midst of such machinations and conspiracies, to indicate and make known to you our saving Easter-feast, even from the ends of the earth.[8]

He informed his congregants that he had committed all his own affairs to God and was completely confident that "'nothing separates us from the love of Christ; neither affliction, nor distress, nor persecution, nor famine, nor nakedness, nor peril, nor sword' [Rom 8:35]. Thus keeping the feast myself, I was desirous that you also, my beloved, should keep it . . ."[9] Their current sufferings were viewed as nothing when compared to what Jesus Christ suffered for them and for their salvation.[10] But the "Ario-maniacs" ignorantly "smite Him who is their Helper with their tongue, and blaspheme Him who set [them] free, and hold all manner of different opinions against the Savior."[11] The same letter also strongly warns against the doctrine and the schismatic tendencies of the opposition. "For they have learned," he wrote, "to rend the seamless coat of God; they think it not strange to divide the indivisible Son from the Father."[12]

In his eleventh *Festal Letter* (339), Athanasius reminded his readers that persecution for the truth is not to be associated with wickedness, but rather it befalls one who is godly. For that reason, too, Paul urged his readers—as Athanasius urged his own—to "avoid profane conversations, for they increase unto more ungodliness, and their word takes hold as doth a canker . . ."[13] Therefore, the saints of Alexandria should rejoice in the Easter feast, as well as in their persecutions:

8. Athanasius, *Festal Letter* 10, NPNF, vol. IV, 527.

9. Ibid., 528.

10. Ibid., 530.

11. Ibid., 531.

12. Ibid.

13. Athanasius, *Festal Letter* 11, NPNF, vol. IV, 536.

> Let us make a joyful noise with the saints, and let no one of us fail
> of his duty in these things; counting as nothing the affliction or the
> trials which, especially at this time, have been enviously directed
> against us by the party of Eusebius. Even now they wish to injure
> us, and by their accusations to compass our death, because of that
> godliness, whose helper is the Lord. But, as faithful servants of
> God, knowing that He is our salvation in the time of trouble:—for
> the Lord promised beforehand, saying, "Blessed are ye when men
> revile you and persecute you, and say all manner of evil against
> you falsely, for My sake. Rejoice, and be exceeding glad, for your
> reward is great in heaven" [Matt 5:11–12].[14]

Athanasius's thirteenth *Festal Letter*, written in 341, sounded the same clarion call to steadfast faith amidst suffering, trials, and affliction. "Let us rejoice as we keep the feast, my brethren, knowing that our salvation is ordered in the time of affliction," he wrote. "For our Savior did not redeem us by inactivity, but by suffering for us He abolished death. And respecting this, He intimated to us before, saying, 'In the world ye shall have tribulation' [John 16:33]. But He did not say this to every man, but to those who diligently and faithfully perform good service to Him, knowing beforehand, that they should be persecuted who would live godly toward Him."[15]

While we know a lot about Athanasius's attitude concerning his exile from the *Festal Letters*, we know very little about the day-to-day events of Athanasius's stay in Rome. It is clear that he enjoyed the support and fellowship of the western bishops like Julius and Hosius of Cordova. It is also clear that during this hiatus from his frenetic pastoral activities in Alexandria, Athanasius began to construct his defense of the Nicene theology, and a defense of his own character, through a literary assault upon Arianism. One of these works, which was produced either prior to leaving Alexandria or shortly after his arrival in Rome, was a homiletical treatment of Luke 10:22 (par. Matt 11:21). This sermon was probably part of his preaching ministry in Rome.

The sermon on Luke 10:22 seems to be fragmentary, at the beginning, in so far as it starts quite abruptly, but it is evidently complete throughout the length of the text. The biblical passage was chosen because it was one that the Arians used to demonstrate the subordination of the Son to the Father. In the gospel passage, Jesus explains, "All things were delivered to Me by My Father. And no one knows the Son except the Father; and no one

---

14. Ibid., 537.

15. Ibid., *Festal Letter* 13, NPNF, vol. IV, 541.

knows the Father except the Son, and anyone to whom the Son chooses to reveal Him." Read through an Arian interpretive lens this passage seems to imply that if "all things" had to be given to the Son, then there was a time when He was without them. Among these "all things," the Arians opined, were Christ's Divine Sonship; therefore, they concluded, there was a time when the Son did not have full deity, and in fact did not exist. Athanasius described the "impious" Arian argument this way: "they say, if all things were delivered (meaning by 'all' the Lordship of Creation), there was once a time when He had them not. But if He had them not, He is not of the Father, for if He were, He would on that account have them always, and would not have [been] required to receive them."[16]

Athanasius responded to the Arian interpretation by completely denying its premise. The "all things" in this passage "does not refer to the Lordship over Creation, nor to presiding over the works of God, but is meant to reveal in part the intention of the Incarnation."[17] Furthermore, if the Arian interpretation of this passage was correct, "what becomes of the text 'in Him all things consist' (Col 1:17)?"[18] No, on this basis the Arian premise is clearly wrong. In this passage the Son is speaking about His own incarnation, when the Father and the Son participated together in the creation of "all things." The delivery of "all things" to the Son, at that time, Athanasius mused, was a bit superfluous because "all things were made by Him (John 1:3)."[19] Hence, Athanasius concluded, "For in making them ["all things"] He was Lord of the things that were being originated."[20] Even if "all things" were delivered to the Son, immediately and subsequently to their having been created, this signified a shared a partnership of dominion by the Father and the Son.[21] Thus, it is clear that the Father retains dominion over creation, since "not even a sparrow falls to the ground without the Father (Matt 10:29), nor is the grass clothed without God (Matt 6:30), but at once the Father worketh, and the Son worketh hitherto (John 5:17)."[22]

In exploring to what end "all things" were delivered to the incarnate Son, Athanasius began to tell the story of Christian redemption, just as he

16. *On Luke X.22*, § 1, *NPNF*, vol. IV, 87.
17. Ibid.
18. Ibid.
19. Ibid.
20. Ibid.
21. Ibid.
22. Ibid.

had done earlier *in On the Incarnation of the Word of God.* The reason, simply stated, was human sin: "Whereas man sinned, and is fallen, and by his fall all things are in confusion: death prevailed from Adam to Moses (Rom 5:14), the earth was cursed, Hades was opened, Paradise shut, Heaven offended, man, lastly, corrupted and brutalized (Ps 49:12), while the devil was exulting against us . . ."[23] But God, "in His loving-kindness, not willing man made in His own image to perish, said, 'Whom shall I send, and who will go?' (Isa 6:8)."[24] While all in heaven held their peace, the Son said, "'Here am I, send Me.' And then it was that, saying 'Go Thou,' He 'delivered' to Him man, that the Word Himself might be made Flesh, and by taking the Flesh, restore it wholly. For to Him, as to a Physician, man 'was delivered' to heal the bite of the serpent; as to life, to raise what was dead; as to light, to illuminate the darkness; and, because He was Word, to renew the rational nature."[25] In short, "Since then all things 'were delivered' to Him, and He is made Man, straightway all things were set right and perfected."[26] Because of the saving action of the Incarnate Word, "Earth receives blessing instead of a curse, Paradise was opened to the robber, Hades cowered, the tombs were opened and the dead raised, the gates of Heaven were lifted up to await Him that 'cometh from Edom' (Ps 24:7; Isa 63:1)."[27]

Asking the question of why all things were delivered to the Son caused Athanasius to reflect upon the character of our Lord, Jesus Christ: "The Savior Himself expressly signifies in what sense 'all things were delivered' to Him, when He continues, as Matthew tells us: 'Come unto Me all ye that labor and are heavy laden, and I will give you rest' (Matt 11:28). Yes, ye 'were delivered' to Me to give rest to those who had labored and life to the dead. And what is written in John's Gospel harmonizes with this: 'The Father loveth the Son, and hath given all things into his hand' (John 3:35). Given, in order that, just as all things were made by Him, so in Him all things might be renewed."[28] Here we see, again, the basic argument that Athanasius had mounted in *On the Incarnation.*

In exploring the question, "What was 'delivered up' to the Son?" Athanasius surmised that what He did not previously possess, and what was

---

23. *On Luke X.22,* § 2, *NPNF,* vol. IV, 87.

24. Ibid.

25. Ibid.

26. Ibid.

27. Ibid., 87–88.

28. Ibid., 88.

given to Him by the Father was not His Divinity (as the Arians suggested) but His humanity, which the Son did not possess prior to the Incarnation. As he explained, "For He was not man previously, but became man for the sake of saving man. And the Word was not in the beginning flesh, but has been made flesh subsequently (John 1:1), in which Flesh, as the Apostle says, He reconciled the enmity which was against us (Col 1:20; 2:14; Eph 2:15, 16) and destroyed the law of the commandments in ordinances, that He might make the two into one new man, making peace, and reconcile both in one body to the Father."[29]

Athanasius then turned to John 16:15, in order to explain the essential relationship of the Father and the Son within the Godhead. In that passage Jesus states, "All that the Father has is mine; therefore I said that He will take what is mine and declare it to you." Using an analogy describing the way light comes from the Sun, the bishop argued that this passage shows that the Sun (the Father) and the Light (the Son) are of the same essence and nature. He wrote, "piety would have us perceive that the Divine Essence of the Word is united by nature to His own Father. For the text before us will put our problem in the clearest possible light, seeing that the Savior said, 'All things whatsoever the Father hath are Mine'; which shows that He is ever with the Father. For 'whatsoever He hath' shows that the Father wields the Lordship, while 'are Mine' shows the inseparable union."[30] This fact of the inseparable union between Father and Son belied the Arian Christology; for if the Father "is not a creature, so neither is the Son; and as it is not possible to say of Him 'there was a time when He was not,' nor 'made of nothing,' so it is not proper to say the like of the Son either."[31] Hence, Athanasius urged, "For this is why the Only begotten, having life in Himself as the Father has, also knows alone Who the Father is, namely, because He is in the Father and the Father in Him. For He is His Image, and consequently, because He is His Image, all that belongs to the Father is in Him. He is an exact seal, showing in Himself the Father; living Word and true, Power, Wisdom, our Sanctification and Redemption (1 Cor 1:30). For 'in Him we both live and move and have our being' (Acts 17:28), and 'no man knoweth Who is the Father, save the Son, and Who is the Son, save the Father' (Luke 10:22)."[32]

29. *On Luke X.22*, § 3, *NPNF*, vol. IV, 88.
30. *On Luke X.22*, § 4, *NPNF*, vol. IV, 89.
31. Ibid.
32. *On Luke X.22*, § 5, *NPNF*, vol. IV, 89–90.

In his closing paragraphs Athanasius urged that the Arians cannot even make proper sense of the *Trisagion* ("three Holies") used in Scripture and in sacred worship to refer to the Godhead. Using the term "Monad" to stress the Unity of the Godhead and the term "Triad" to explain its "Three-ness," the exiled bishop of Alexandria wrote, "For the Triad, praised, rever-enced, and adored, is one and indivisible and without degrees. It is united without confusion, just as the Monad also is distinguished without separa-tion. For the fact of those venerable living creatures (Isa. vi ; Rev. iv. 8) offering their praises three times, saying 'Holy, Holy, Holy,' proves that the Three Subsistences are perfect, just as in saying 'Lord,' they declare the One Essence."[33] Hence, the Arians blaspheme God with their assertions: "They then that depreciate the Only-begotten Son of God blaspheme God, defaming His perfection and accusing Him of imperfection, and render themselves liable to the severest chastisement."[34]

During his stay in Rome, while teaching, preaching, and leading wor-ship there, Athanasius's case had been referred to Emperor Constans by Bishop Julius. Constans was the youngest of Constantine's sons and ruler of Gaul and the West. He was an orthodox Christian and an admirer of Athanasius for that reason. Prior to leaving Alexandria for Rome, Athana-sius had sent a letter of self-defense to Constans along with the gift of sev-eral bound volumes of the Holy Scripture. Soon after his arrival in Rome, Constans invited Athanasius to come to Milan for a personal interview. Sozomen, the early church historian, reported that Constans readily sup-ported Athanasius's cause and was won to his defense because he quickly saw through the false charges of his opponents. And when a delegation ar-rived from the East to urge the excommunication of Paul of Constantinople and Athanasius, Constans refused to heed them or their charges: "Constans perceived that they had unjustly entrapped both Paul and Athanasius, and had ejected them from communion, not for charges against their conduct, as the depositions held, but simply on account of differences in doctrine; and he accordingly dismissed the deputation without giving any credit to the representations for which they had come."[35]

Apparently, Constans had decided that a general church council should be held to review Athanasius's case, and the other controversial matters that faced the church. He had already written to his brother Constantius to this

33. *On Luke X.22,* § 6, *NPNF,* vol. IV, 90.

34. Ibid.

35. Sozomen, *Church History* III.10, *NPNF,* vol. II, 289.

effect, prior to Athanasius's arrival in Milan, and then informed him of that development at that time. After that meeting, Constans hurried off to Gaul for a military campaign against the Franks. He subsequently wrote to request Athanasius's presence with him in Treveri (Treves), in Gaul; there Athanasius met the venerable Spaniard, Hosius of Cordova, and many others in the spring of 343. He also learned that the two emperors had agreed to hold the general council at Serdica (now Sophia, Bulgaria) during the next summer. Hence, Athanasius's Easter Letter for 343 may have been written from either Milan or Treves, and he must have celebrated Easter in Gaul that year.[36]

The Council of Serdica probably met for most of the month of August 343. So scant are the surviving records that we cannot ascertain the exact dates of the beginning and conclusion of the meeting. It held the promise of being a genuine ecumenical, churchwide council, with about 170 bishops in attendance; of these more than ninety-six came from the Latin West. Hosius of Cordova was the venerable leader of this delegation, and he was selected to chair the council. The Western delegation arrived first, and more than seventy bishops from the Eastern churches arrived soon thereafter. The Eastern delegation had been making plans en route, and upon their arrival reported that they would not participate in the conciliar discussions, but only report themselves "present" if Athanasius were allowed to sit in on the deliberations. To mollify the Eastern delegation they were housed in the imperial palace, while the Western delegates met in the cathedral, and several times they were urged to join the council in its deliberations. The Eastern bishops replied that Athanasius and several others had been duly deposed by Eastern synods and had no right to be at the meeting. Hosius and his colleagues retorted that the Roman synod that cleared Athanasius had as much authority as the previous Eastern synods of Tyre and Antioch (which had deposed Athanasius), and besides the emperors had both agreed to reopen the investigation of Athanasius's case, and that was the principal object of the assembly. Messages flew back and forth from the cathedral to the palace, and from the palace to the cathedral, but to no avail. No compromise could be reached. And by night, the Eastern delegation withdrew to the city of Philippopolis, on the excuse that they had just heard that Constantius had won a great military victory over the Persians, and they must hasten off to offer their congratulations. The Eastern delegation left behind an encyclical letter that reinstated the depositions of Athanasius

36. Robertson, "Prolegomena," *NPNF*, vol. IV, xlv.

and his colleagues, and added to the list several others, including Julius of Rome, Hosius of Cordova, and Maximin of Treves (all of whom were guilty of supporting Athanasius). This document, along with a creed and a long section of anathemas, was sent on to Constans. Left to their own deliberations, the remaining majority of the Council of Serdica, the Western bishops, heard the case against Athanasius, Marcellus, and others, and acquitted them all. It too issued an encyclical letter to all the bishops and established numerous important canons for the governance of the church. While the Council of Serdica was a marked victory and a vindication for Athanasius, ultimately it was a significant failure for the entire church because it had the effect of widening the chasm that had been growing between the Eastern and Western wings of the Christian church.[37]

The opinion of those in the Eastern Church who opposed Athanasius and brought charges against him has been preserved in one of the writings of Hilary of Poitiers:

> In the case of Athanasius, formerly bishop of Alexandria, you are to understand what was enacted. He was charged with the grave offense of sacrilege and profanation of the holy Church's sacraments. With his own hands he broke a chalice consecrated to God and Christ, tore down the august altar itself, overturned the bishop's throne and razed the basilica itself, God's house, Christ's house, to the ground. The presbyter himself, an earnest and upright man called Scyras, he delivered to military custody. In addition to this, Athanasius was charged with unlawful acts, with the use of force, with murder and the killing of bishops. Raging like a tyrant even during the most holy days of Easter, he was accompanied by the military and officials of the imperial government who, on his authority, confined some to custody, beat and whipped some and forced the rest into sacrilegious communion with him by various acts of torture (innocent men would never have behaved so). Athanasius hoped that in this way his own people and his own faction would get the upper hand; and so he forced unwilling people into communion by means of military officials, judges, prisons, whippings and various acts of torture.[38]

It seems that the Roman exile might have also been the period of time in which Athanasius began writing his *Four Orations Against the Arians*.

---

37. Kidd, *History of the Church*, 2:83–85.

38. *Against Valens and Ursacius* I.2, 1–29; quoted in Gwynn, *Athanasius of Alexandria*, 36.

Robertson, the editor of the largest English-language edition of Athanasius's works, reminded his readers, "There is no absolutely conclusive evidence as to the date of these Discourses, in fact they would appear from the language of ii.1 to have been issued at intervals."[39] Robertson is correct in both of these statements, but I believe (following more modern commentators[40]) that these four Discourses or Orations were begun—though perhaps not completed—during Athanasius's exile in Rome.[41] There is, furthermore, some question whether these works, although they are frequently called "Orations" or "Discourses," were intended to be delivered as homilies. The length and complicated argumentation of their contents seem to suggest otherwise. As Robertson opined, "The title 'Orations' is consecrated by long use, and cannot be displaced, but it is unfortunate as implying, to our ears, oratorical delivery, for which the Discourses were never meant."[42]

The first *Oration* sets the stage for the other three and is a lengthy document in its own right; it is comprised of thirteen chapters and sixty-three long paragraphs. Chapter 1 explained that Athanasius was writing to raise the church from her slumber about Arianism, which he terms a "heresy" and a "madness." The bishop of Alexandria believed that many pious people in the church were indifferent in their opinions about Arianism, and so he wrote to raise their consciousness of the heretical problem and the dangers it posed to the Christian community. In the first chapter we learn that Arius's *Thalia* was patterned upon the "dissolute and effeminate tone" of Sotades's *Odes*. Thus people "frolicked in his blasphemies against the Savior; till the victims of his heresy lose their wits and go foolish, and change the Name of the Lord of glory into the likeness of the 'image of corruptible man.'"[43] Because they blaspheme the Name and Nature of Jesus Christ, the Arians do not even deserve the name of "Christian." Hence, Athanasius wrote, "How then can they be Christians, who for Christians are Ario-maniacs? Or how are they of the Catholic Church, who have shaken off the Apostolic faith, and become authors of fresh evils? Who,

---

39. Robertson, introduction to *Four Discourses Against the Arians*, NPNF, vol. IV, 303.

40. For example, R. P. C. Hanson, *Christian Doctrine of God*, 419. Like most modern commentators, Hanson also doubts that Athanasius wrote the Fourth Oration.

41. In his introduction Robertson locates them in Athanasius's third exile, instead of the second.

42. Ibid., 304.

43. *Discourse I*, I.2, NPNF, vol. IV, 307.

after abandoning the oracles of divine Scripture, call Arius's *Thalia* a new wisdom? And with reason too, for they are announcing a new heresy."[44]

In the second chapter of *Discourse I* Athanasius offered extracts from Arius's *Thalia* along with theological analysis of them. According to Athanasius, the *Thalia* began with these words:

> According to faith of God's elect, God's prudent ones,
>
> Holy children, rightly dividing, God's Holy Spirit receiving,
>
> Have I learned this from the partakers of wisdom,
>
> Accomplished, divinely taught, and wise in all things.
>
> Along their track, have I been walking, with like opinions,
>
> I the very famous, the much suffering for God's glory;
>
> And taught of God, I have acquired wisdom and knowledge.[45]

After reporting Arius's pleas for special knowledge of God and piety, Athanasius detailed the Christology of the *Thalia*, which he found deeply objectionable:

> The mockeries which he utters in it, repulsive and most irreligious, are such as these:—"God was not always a Father"; but "once God was alone, and not yet a Father, but afterwards He became a Father." "The Son was not always"; for, whereas all things were made out of nothing, and all existing creatures and works were made, so the Word of God Himself was "made out of nothing," and "once He was not," and "He was not before His origination," but He as others "had an origin of creation." "For God," he says, "was alone, and the Word as yet was not, nor the Wisdom. Then, wishing to form us, thereupon He made a certain one, and named Him Word and Wisdom and Son, that He might form us by means of Him." Accordingly, he says that there are two wisdoms, first, the attribute co-existent with God, and next, that in this wisdom the Son was originated, and was only named Wisdom and Word as partaking of it. "For Wisdom," saith he, "by the will of the wise God, had its existence in Wisdom." In like manner, he says, that there is another Word in God besides the Son, and that the Son again, as partaking of it, is named Word and Son according to grace. And this too is an idea proper to their heresy, as shown in other works of theirs, that there are many powers; one of which is God's own by nature and eternal; but that Christ, on the other hand, is not the true power of God; but, as others, one of the so-called powers, one of which,

44. *Discourse I*, I.4, *NPNF*, vol. IV, 308.

45. *Discourse I*, II.5, *NPNF*, vol. IV, 308.

namely, the locust and the caterpillar, is called in Scripture, not merely the power, but "great power." The others are many and are like the Son, and of them David speaks in the Psalms, when he says, "The Lord of hosts" or "powers" [Ps 24:10]. And by nature, as all others, so the Word Himself is alterable, and remains good by His own free will, while He chooseth; when, however, He wills, He can alter as we can, as being of an alterable nature. For "therefore," saith he, "as foreknowing that He would be good, did God by anticipation bestow on Him this glory, which afterwards, as man, He attained from virtue. Thus in consequence of His works foreknown, did God bring it to pass that He, being such, should come to be."[46]

In this long and somewhat complicated paragraph, Athanasius was reporting that the *Thalia* taught that the Second Person of the Trinity, the Son or Wisdom of God, did not always exist, but that the Son was a created Being, made out of nothing by God the Father. The Son, therefore, was not eternal, as God Himself was and is, but rather had a definite beginning and origin. The song-poem further argued that what the Christian church has esteemed as the Son's deity and divine nature was really His moral goodness and virtue. His goodness being known and anticipated by God before the Son's creation allowed God to describe the Son as being godly or divine. Therefore, Athanasius concluded his summary of the *Thalia* by reporting that in it, Arius "has dared to say, that 'the Word is not the very God'; 'though He is called God, yet He is not very God,' but 'by participation of grace, He, as others, is God only in name.'"[47]

Athanasius marveled with near incredulity which pious person could accept this doctrine and not hate Arius for propounding it. As he wrote, "Who is there that hears all this, nay, the tune of the *Thalia*, but must hate, and justly hate, this Arius jesting on such matters as on a stage? Who but must regard him, when he pretends to name God and speak of God, but as the serpent counseling the woman? Who, on reading what follows in his work, but must discern in his irreligious doctrine that error, into which by his sophistries the serpent in the sequel seduced the woman?"[48]

Chapter 3 of *Discourse I* stressed, once again, the importance of this subject. It argued that while the Arians seem to use scriptural language to mount their arguments, in the final analysis their views are unscriptural.

46. Ibid., 308–9.
47. *Discourse I*, II.6, NPNF, vol. IV, 309.
48. *Discourse I*, II.7, NPNF, vol. IV, 309.

They walk in darkness and do not know the Light. In order to distinguish what would become the orthodox point of view from that of his Arian opponents, Athanasius wrote,

> For, behold, we take divine Scripture, and thence discourse with freedom of the religious Faith, and set it up as a light upon its candlestick, saying:—Very Son of the Father, natural and genuine, proper to His essence, Wisdom Only-begotten, and Very and Only Word of God is He; not a creature or work, but an offspring proper to the Father's essence. Wherefore He is very God, existing one in essence with the very Father; while other beings, to whom He said, "I said ye are Gods," had this grace from the Father, only by participation of the Word, through the Spirit. For He is the expression of the Father's Person, and Light from Light, and Power, and very Image of the Father's essence. For this too the Lord has said, "He that hath seen Me, hath seen the Father" [John 14:9].[49]

These two theologies of Christ and His Lordship are irreconcilable. One must choose between them. And the reader of the *Oration* is urged to choose the theology "that we have spoken and maintained from the Scriptures," over that which was vomited forth by Arius in his *Thalia*.[50] Athanasius also charged the Arians with duplicity. They used language and images that intentionally camouflage their heretical views.

In chapters 4 through 6 Athanasius offered three proofs for the controverted doctrine that the Son was/is eternal, that He was not a creature, was not created, and did not have a beginning. Passages such as Romans 1:20, illuminated by John 1:1–2 and Isaiah 11:28, were used to show (firstly) that "it is plain then from the above that the Scriptures declare the Son's eternity . . ."[51] The second proof of the eternality of the Word is the fact of His Divine Sonship. Because of His unique Sonship, the Word participates in the God the Father's nature, and it is in the Father's nature to be eternal; so also the Son is eternal.[52] The third scriptural proof of the Son's eternality is that His shared essence with the Father makes Him the Creator of all things, and One who with God the Father is the Creator of all that is. Belonging to the Trinity by nature and essence, the Son is before all things that were created, and is indeed the Creator of them. If the Son were gener-

49. *Discourse I*, III.9, *NPNF*, vol. IV, 311.

50. Ibid.

51. *Discourse I*, IV.13, *NPNF*, vol. IV, 313.

52. *Discourse I*, V, *NPNF*, vol. IV, 314–16.

ated by the Father, He could not be in the Image and Form of the Godhead, nor could He say, "I am Truth."[53] Chapters 7 through 10 answered various objections that the Arians raised against the doctrine of the eternality of the Son or Word.[54]

Beginning in chapter 11, Athanasius explained a series of Scripture passages that were sometimes used by his Arian opponents to assail the orthodox (or Nicene) theology of Christ. The first of these was Philippians 2:9–10.[55] Athanasius explained this passage as containing the inner logic of the Incarnation, which controverts the Arian teaching of the Son becoming more and more divine (godly) because of His virtue. The bishop wrote, "Therefore He was not man, and then became God, but He was God, and then became man, and that to deify us."[56] Here again, we meet the famous argument from his earlier work *On the Incarnation of the Word of God*. Numerous passages (including John 17:5 and Ps 28:9, 13) were used to flesh out the theology of incarnation in a way that described it not as a growth in godliness (or divinity) but as God taking human flesh in the person of God's Son. This controverted the Arian claim that the phraseology of this passage suggested that the Son gained divinity though a life of godliness, Athanasius claimed, by showing that the passage in fact described the Son's reception of true humanity, which he bore in a humble and self-giving manner that deserved the praise of God and indeed that of the entire world.

The second passage addressed in *Discoure I* was Psalm 45:7–8.[57] In his exposition of this passage Athanasius argued against the idea that the Word was being rewarded for His virtuous choices and action. The Arian notion that the Son was "anointed" with the Holy Spirit at His baptism in the Jordan River, as a way of sanctifying His human nature and therefore enabling Him to become more godly, was also attacked. The descent of the Holy Spirit at Jesus's baptism, Athanasius opined, did not have to do with the sanctification of the Word—as though He was not holy and fully divine prior to that event; rather, that event signified the sanctification of humanity, through the coming of the Word among us in real human flesh. Hence,

53. *Discourse I*, VI.

54. *Discourse I*, VII–X, *NPNF*, vol. IV, 319–27.

55. "Therefore God has highly exalted him and bestowed on him the name which is above every name" (RSV).

56. *Discourse I*, XI.39, *NPNF*, vol. IV, 329.

57. ". . . you love righteousness and hate wickedness. / Therefore God, your God, has anointed you / with the oil of gladness above your fellows . . ." (RSV).

Athanasius wrote, "If then for our sake He sanctifies Himself, and does this when He is become man, it is very plain that the Spirit's descent on Him in Jordan was a descent upon us, because of His bearing our body. And it did not take place for promotion to the Word, but again for our sanctification, that we might share His anointing, and of us it might be said, 'Know ye not that ye are God's Temple, and the Spirit of God dwelleth in you' [1 Cor 3:16]? For when the Lord, as man, was washed in Jordan, it was we who were washed in Him and by Him."[58]

The third passage that the Arians used and that was taken up by Athanasius for refutation was Hebrews 1:4.[59] Central to this argument is whether the phrase "having become" implies the creation of the Word or not. This Arian interpretation was augmented by stressing the development implied by those words. Once again, Athanasius argued, his theological opponents do not understand the meaning or take seriously the import of the Incarnation of Christ; they are either ashamed of or they ignore the text "the Word became flesh" (John 1:14). The "having become" in this passage implies *not* the creation of the Word, before the foundations of the world, but the Incarnation of the Word into real human flesh, Hence, the bishop urged, "Scripture, in speaking thus, implies, O Arians, not that the Son is originate, but rather other than things originate, and proper to the Father, being in His bosom."[60]

The exegetical case against Arianism continued throughout *Discourse II* as well. There his opponents' interpretation of Hebrews 3:2, Acts 2:36, and Proverbs 8:22 was challenged and attacked. The Rule of Faith, which demands that one scripture shall not contradict another, does not support their reading of the Hebrews passage because there are many other Scripture passages that contradict the strained Arian interpretation.[61] Of these the Proverbs 8:22 passage is the foundational one, since the Arians used it to inform and shape their interpretation of the others.[62] Athanasius explained,

58. *Discourse I*, XII:47, *NPNF*, vol. IV, 333.

59. "having become as much superior to angels as the name he has obtained is more excellent than theirs" (RSV).

60. *Discourse I*, XIII:56, *NPNF*, vol. IV, 339.

61. "He was faithful to him who made him, just as Moses also was faithful in God's house" (Athanasius's translation).

62. "The Lord created me at the beginning of His ways, for His works" (Athanasius's translation).

They misunderstand the passage in Proverbs, "The LORD hath created me a beginning of His ways for His works," and the words of the Apostle, "Who was faithful to Him that made Him," and straightway argue, that the Son of God is a work and a creature. But although they might have learned from what is said above, had they not utterly lost their power of apprehension, that the Son is not from nothing nor in the number of things originate [created] at all.[63]

Once again the Arians, in this interpretation, misunderstand passages that refer to the Incarnation of the Word, and treat them as though they refer instead to the Word having been created at the beginning, out of nothing. Indeed, Athanasius argued, a whole chain of crucial passages provide the proper theological context for interpreting the passage in Proverbs 8:22. Among these are the following:

by John, "The Word became flesh" [John 1:14], and so by Peter, "He hath made Him Lord and Christ" [Acts 2:36]; —as by means of Solomon in the Person of the Lord Himself, "The Lord created me a beginning of His ways for His works" [Prov 8:22]; so by Paul, "Become so much better than the Angels" [Heb 1:4]; and again, "He emptied Himself, and took upon Him the form of a servant" [Phil 2:7]; and again "Wherefore, holy brethren, partakers of the heavenly calling, consider the Apostle and High Priest of our profession, Jesus, who was faithful to Him that made Him" [Heb 3:1, 2]. For all these texts have the same force and meaning, a religious one, declarative of the divinity of the Word, even those of them which speak humanly concerning Him, as having become the Son of man.[64]

In taking these passages together, Athanasius argued, we see that the Son is of the essence of the Father and that this shared nature comes before the other terms (i.e., "made" or "become") that describe some subsequent work of the Son. Hence, as a Son, Christ the Word shared in the Divine essence prior to "becoming" flesh, or being "made" man, or a creature.[65] "This being so," he wrote, "when persons ask whether the Lord is a creature or work, it is proper to ask them this first, whether He is Son and Word and Wisdom.

63. *Discourse II*, XIV.1, *NPNF*, vol. IV, 348.
64. Ibid.
65. Ibid., 350.

For if this is shown, the surmise about work and creation falls to the ground at once and is ended."[66]

Beginning in chapter 16 of *Discourse II*, Athanasius mounted an extended explanation and interpretation of Proverbs 8:22, which continued through chapter 24 and was comprised of more than thirty-six large pages of text. Since Proverbs 8:22 was the exegetical foundation of the Arian assertion that the Word was created and had a beginning, he explored that assertion and interpretation with great care and acumen. His method of argumentation was to show parallel passages from Scripture (applying the Rule of Faith) that contradicted and made impossible, in his view, the Arian reading of Proverbs 8:22. As he moved towards the conclusion of his exposition, Athanasius urged, "Let the Word then be excepted from the works, and as Creator be restored to the Father, and be confessed to be Son by nature; or if simply He be a creature, then let Him be assigned the same condition as the rest one with another, and let them as well as He be said every one of them to be 'a creature, but not as one of the creatures, offspring or work, but not as one of the works or offsprings.'"[67] So if the Son is not of the essence of the Father, and partaker of the Father's Divine nature, but is a creature, then He is no different from the other created works of the Father—so saying, Athanasius argued that Scripture denied the existence of a middle place between Divine and created nature, which could, in the Arian syllogism, be occupied by the Word. Hence "God's Word is not merely pronounced, as one may say, nor a sound of accents, nor by His Son is meant His command; but as radiance of light, so is He perfect offspring from perfect. Hence He is God also, as being God's Image; for 'the Word was God' [John 1:1], says Scripture."[68]

Hence, when the text in Proverbs 8:22—a figurative text, Athanasius reminded his reader—declared that the Father "created" Him (the Word), it was not speaking of His nature, but of his work as a servant; thus this passage, in a figurative manner, also speaks of the Incarnation of the Word, just as did John 1:14, "the Word became flesh," and Philippians 2:7, "taking the form of a servant."[69] Athanasius explained, "For the very passage proves that it is only an invention of your own to call the Lord creature. For the Lord, knowing His own Essence to be the Only-begotten Wisdom and Off-

---

66. *Discourse II*, XIV.5, *NPNF*, vol. IV, 350.

67. *Discourse II*, XVI.20, *NPNF*, vol. IV, 359.

68. *Discourse II*, XVIII.35, *NPNF*, vol. IV, 367.

69. *Discourse II*, XIX, *NPNF*, vol. IV, 372ff.

spring of the Father, and other than things originate and natural creatures, says in love to man, 'The Lord created me a beginning of His ways,' as if to say, 'My Father hath prepared for Me a body, and has created Me for men in behalf of their salvation.'"[70] And this did not imply a loss of the Word's Divine nature, but it meant as the Word and Wisdom and Son, He was clothed in our flesh for our salvation. In an extensive and elegant passage Athanasius explained,

> as when John says, "The Word was made flesh," we do not conceive the whole Word Himself to be flesh, but to have put on flesh and become man, and on hearing, "Christ hath become a curse for us," and "He hath made Him sin for us who knew no sin," we do not simply conceive this, that [the] whole Christ has become curse and sin, but that He has taken on Him the curse which lay against us (as the Apostle has said, "Has redeemed us from the curse," and "has carried," as Isaiah has said, "our sins," and as Peter has written, "has borne them in the body on the wood"); so, if it is said in the Proverbs "He created," we must not conceive that the whole Word is in nature a creature, but that He put on the created body and that God created Him for our sakes, preparing for Him the created body, as it is written, for us, that in Him we might be capable of being renewed and defied.[71]

If the Word is "begotten" of the Father, then the Word is God's Son, and is a partaker of the Divine nature, and not a creature of any sort; hence the Word is without beginning, as God is without beginning. As Athanasius explained, "The being of things originate [created] is measured by their becoming, and from some beginning does God begin to make them through the Word, that it may be known that they were not before their origination; but the Word has His beginning, in no other beginning than the Father, whom they [the Arians] allow to be without beginning, so that He too exists without beginning in the Father, being His Offspring, not His creature."[72]

After extensively addressing the phrase from Proverbs 8:22, "He founded me before the world," Athanasius explained that this refers not to the Godhead of the Word but to his Incarnate Presence, which was planned and established prior to the Incarnation of the Son for our sakes.[73] He then ended the second *Discourse* or *Oration* with a note of triumph over the

70. *Discourse II*, XIX.47, *NPNF*, vol. IV, 374.

71. Ibid.

72. *Discourse II*, XXI.57, *NPNF*, vol. IV, 379.

73. *Discourse II*, XXII, *NPNF*, vol. IV, 388.

exegesis of the Arians, whom he addressed directly: "Vain then is your vaunt as is on all sides shown, O Christ's enemies, and vainly did ye parade and circulate everywhere your text, 'The Lord created me a beginning of His ways,' perverting its sense, and publishing, not Solomon's meaning, but your own comment. For behold your sense is proved to be but a fantasy; but the passage in the Proverbs, as well as all that is above said, proves that the Son is not a creature in nature and essence, but the proper Offspring of the Father, true Wisdom and Word, by whom 'all things were made,' and 'without Him was made not one thing' [John 1:3]."[74]

In *Discourse III* Athanasius continued his exegetical attack upon Arianism. It began with a vitriolic summary of what had been argued in previous books:

> The Ario-maniacs, as it appears, having once made up their minds to transgress and revolt from the Truth, are strenuous in appropriating the words of Scripture, "When the impious cometh into a depth of evils, he despiseth" [Prov 18:3, Septuagint]; for refutation does not stop them, nor perplexity abash them; but, as having "a whore's forehead," they "refuse to be ashamed" [Jer 3:3] before all men in their irreligion. For whereas the passages that they alleged, "The Lord created me" [Prov 8:22], and "Made better than the Angels" [Heb 1:4], and "First-born" [John 1:1], and "Faithful to Him that made Him" [Heb 2:17], have a right sense, and inculcate religiousness towards Christ, so it is that these men still, as if bedewed with the serpent's poison, not seeing what they ought to see, nor understanding what they read, as if in vomit from the depth of their irreligious heart, have next proceeded to disparage our Lord's words, "I in the Father and the Father in Me" [John 14:10] . . .[75]

In urging what he believed to be the true interpretation of Jesus's words, Athanasius wrote, "For the Son said, 'I am in the Father and the Father in Me,' because His discourses were not His own words but the Father's, and so of His works . . ."[76] But this relationship between the Father and the Son goes even further, Athanasius suggested, to the point of shared attributes and shared Divine essence. Hence "the Son is in the Father, as it is allowed us to know, because the whole Being of the Son is proper to the Father's essence, as radiance from light, and stream from fountain; so that whoso sees the Son, sees what is proper to the Father, and knows that

74. *Discourse II*, XXII.82, *NPNF*, vol. IV, 393.
75. *Discourse III*, XXIII.1, *NPNF*, vol. IV, 393.
76. *Discourse III*, XXIII.2, *NPNF*, vol. IV, 394.

the Son's Being, because from the Father, is therefore in the Father."[77] And respecting their shared attributes, the bishop wrote,

> And so, since they are one, and the Godhead itself one, the same things are said of the Son, which are said of the Father, except His being said to be Father:—for instance, that He is God, "And the Word was God" [John 1:1]; Almighty, "Thus saith He which was and is and is to come, the Almighty" [Rev 1:8]; Lord, "One Lord Jesus Christ" [1 Cor 8:6]; that He is Light, "I am the Light" [John 8:12]; that He wipes out sins, "that ye may know," He says, "that the Son of man hath power upon earth to forgive sins" [Luke 5:24]; and so with other attributes. For "all things," says the Son Himself, "whatsoever the Father hath, are Mine" [John 16:15]; and again, "And Mine are Thine" [John 17:10].[78]

Continuing along these lines, Athanasius explained the proper meaning of John 17:3—"And this is life eternal, that they might know thee the only true God, and Jesus Christ, whom thou hast sent"—against the Arian claim that in distinguishing between the Father ("the only true God") and the Son ("Jesus Christ"), this passage and others like it hint that the Son is not the "only true God" like the Father. Athanasius replied to this assertion by strongly affirming the Oneness of God, from passages like Deuteronomy 6:4 and Deuteronomy 32:39, and arguing—based on the preceding exegesis—that what was said of God the Father is also said of God the Son, and vice versa. Hence, "If then the Father be called the only true God, this is said not to be the denial of Him who said, 'I am the Truth' [John 14:6], but of those on the other hand who by nature are not true, as the Father and His Word are."[79] Passages like John 10:30 and John 17:11 were considered in a similar vein, as distinguishing between the nature of the Father and the Son, and this Arian interpretation was readily dismissed and textually disproved as leading to polytheism.[80]

In a new section and new line of approach, beginning in chapter 26, Athanasius set out to attack the Arian doctrines from the standpoint of the Incarnation of the Word, as Jesus Christ. He pointedly argued that the Word did not simply come into man (as the Arians suggested) but actually became human, and therefore had the actions, the feelings and the emotions

---

77. *Discourse III*, XXIII.3, *NPNF*, vol. IV, 395.
78. *Discourse III*, XXIII.4, *NPNF*, vol. IV, 395.
79. *Discourse III*, XXIV.9, *NPNF*, vol. IV, 398.
80. *Discourse III*, XXV, *NPNF*, vol. IV, 399–407.

of bearing real human flesh. This was done for us, and for our salvation, so that human flesh might be purified and humans might become more and more like God, who made them (1 Pet 4:1). Thus, for Athanasius, the Incarnation of the Word is the most important thing that can be said about the nature of our Lord Jesus Christ, that He was/is, in the words of the creed, "Very God and Very Man." The bishop marshaled a myriad of biblical passages and wove them into a tapestry of evidence for this assertion. He began this long section in this manner: "Now the scope and character of Holy Scripture, as we have often said, is this—it contains a double account of the Savior; that He was ever God, and is the Son, being the Father's Word and Radiance and Wisdom; and that afterwards for us He took flesh of a Virgin, Mary Bearer of God, and was made man."[81] Making the same point, based on a sampling of biblical passages, Athanasius affirmed,

> "In the beginning was the Word, and the Word was with God, and the Word was God. The same was in the beginning with God. All things were made by Him, and without Him was made not one thing" [John 1:1–3]; next, "And the Word was made flesh and dwelt among us, and we beheld His glory, the glory as of one Only-begotten from the Father" [John 1:14]; and next Paul writing, "Who being in the form of God, thought it not a prize to be equal with God, but emptied Himself, taking the form of a servant, being made in the likeness of men, and being found in fashion like a man, He humbled Himself, becoming obedient unto death, even the death of the Cross" [Phil 2:6–8].[82]

Thus, if the whole of scripture is read from the vantage point of this perspective, including the Gospels, it is clear that the Scriptures uniformly teach "that the Lord became man; for 'the Word,' he says, 'became flesh, and dwelt among us' [John 1:14]. And He became man, and did not come into man; for this it is necessary to know, lest perchance these irreligious men fall into this notion also, and beguile any into thinking, that, as in former times the Word was used to come into each of the Saints, so now He sojourned in a man, hallowing him also, and manifesting Himself as in the others."[83] Thus, the implicit adoptionism that Athanasius believed was part and parcel to the Arian Christology was to be undercut by a close reading

81. *Discourse III*, XXVI.29, *NPNF*, vol. IV, 409.
82. Ibid.
83. *Discourse III*, XXVI.30, *NPNF*, vol. IV, 410.

of the Holy Scriptures and by subjecting that interpretation to what the Rule of Faith teaches about the Incarnation of the Word of God.

In chapter 27, passages like Matthew 11:27 and John 3:35 were expounded and explained as not leading to Sabellianism—that is, the notion that the whole of the Godhead was subsumed into the Son during the Incarnation, and that the Trinity possessed its threefold nature only over time, with God first being the Father, then becoming the Son, and finally becoming the Holy Spirit, each in succession. This and adoptionism were wholly disproved by noticing that in the Scriptures, Jesus Christ was simultaneously both true God and true Man, or as Athanasius wrote, "He was Very God in the flesh, and He was true flesh in the Word. Therefore from His works He revealed both Himself as Son of God, and His own Father, and from the affections of the flesh He showed that He bore a true body, and that it was His own."[84]

It was in this theological context, then, that Athanasius explored the Arian assertion that passages like Mark 13:32, Matthew 24:42, and Luke 2:52, which show ignorance of some fact or information on the part of the Son, indicate a limitation to the Deity of Jesus Christ. He asserted, "For this as [said] before is not the Word's deficiency, but of that human nature whose property it is to be ignorant. And this again will be well seen by honestly examining into the occasion, when and to whom the Savior spoke thus. Not then when the heaven was made by Him, nor when He was with the Father Himself, the Word 'disposing all things' [Prov 8:27, Septuagint], nor before He became man did He say it, but when 'the Word became flesh' [John 1:14]. On this account it is reasonable to ascribe to His manhood everything which, after He became man, He speaks humanly."[85]

In a similar way, the truth of the Incarnation countered the Arian assertion that the Word could not weep or be afraid (Matt 26:39; John 12:27). The Rule of Faith, which is the overall witness of Scripture, teaches that the Word was God, and that the Word became Flesh (John 1:14); hence it was in His true human flesh that Jesus Christ experienced sadness and fear. Once again these objections became a foundation upon which Athanasius attacked the "Ario-maniacs." "Idle then is the excuse for stumbling," he wrote, "and petty the notions concerning the Word, of these Ario-maniacs, because it is written, 'He was troubled,' and 'He wept.' For they seem not even to have human feeling, if they are thus ignorant of man's nature and

84. *Discourse III*, XXVII.41, *NPNF*, vol. IV, 416.
85. *Discourse III*, XXVIII.43, *NPNF*, vol. IV, 418.

properties; which do but make it the greater wonder, that the Word should be in such a suffering flesh, and neither prevented those who were conspiring against Him, nor took vengeance of those who were putting Him to death, though He was able, He who hindered some from dying, and raised others from the dead."[86] Thus, these objections only cause us to gaze with awe at the depths of the Son's love for us in taking true humanity, with all its limitations and capacity for suffering, for our sakes and the sake of our salvation.

In chapter 30, a few concluding Arian objections were answered, such as that which says, if the Son is begotten of the Father by the Father's will, does that not make the Son a lesser God than the Father? Athanasius countered this argument by showing that this view is contrary to the Rule of Faith (that is, the whole witness of Scripture), since the Scriptures show that the Son is begotten of the Father's nature, and is in His own nature Divine. It is, of course, *with* the Father's will and good pleasure that the Word became flesh, but that does not signify that the Word which became flesh was *simply* the Father's will. Hence, the bishop concluded, "Therefore call not the Son a work of good pleasure; nor bring in the doctrine of Valentinus[87] into the Church; but be He the Living Counsel, and Offspring in truth and nature, as Radiance from the Light. For thus has the Father spoken, 'My heart uttered a good Word'; and the Son conformably, 'I in the Father and the Father in Me.'"[88]

The authenticity of the fourth *Discourse* has long been questioned by scholars on the basis of internal and external evidence.[89] It was, apparently, either not known or not quoted in Christian antiquity. The fundamental argument of *Discourse IV* is consistent with that of the other three, in that the full divinity and full humanity of the Word, Jesus Christ, are stressed, along with the Son's consubstantial nature with the Father, but the method of argumentation has changed and there seems to be no literary connection between the first three *Discourses* and the fourth.

In this treatise, unlike the others, the writer specifically used the term "consubstantial" or *homoousia* to describe the relationship of the nature of

86. *Discourse III*, XXIX.58, *NPNF*, vol. IV, 425.

87. Valentinus was an Alexandrian gnostic who taught that the Son of God was an emanation of the Father's will.

88. *Discourse III*, XXX.67, *NPNF*, vol. IV, 430.

89. For a fuller discussion of this, see Robertson, "Excursus C: Introductory to the Fourth Discourse agains the Arians," *NPNF*, vol. IV, 431–32.

the Father and the Son (§§ 9, 10, 22), and this may signal a later writer, or at least a later time of writing for this work. It states, for example, "if the two [Father and Son] are one, then of necessity they are two, but one according to the Godhead, and according to the Son's coessentiality with the Father, and the Word's being from the Father Himself; so that there are two, because there is Father, and Son, namely the Word; and one because [there is] one God."[90] After a long discussion in which the threeness of the Trinity was defended against the charge of there being three different personalities and attributes, as in the modalism of Paul of Samosata, the writer of the fourth *Discourse* concluded, "God the Word Himself is Christ from Mary, God and Man; not some other Christ but One and the Same; He before ages from the Father, He too in the last times from the Virgin; invisible before even to the holy powers of heaven, visible now because of His being one with the Man who is visible; seen, I say, not in His invisible Godhead but in the operation of the Godhead through the human body and whole Man, which He has renewed by its appropriation to Himself."[91] Athanasius, though perhaps not the author of this portion of the treatise, would have certainly agreed with its premise about the consubstantial nature of the Father and Son and its argumentation against critics of the Nicene theology.

90. *Discourse IV*, 9, *NPNF*, vol. IV, 436.
91. *Discourse IV*, 36, *NPNF*, vol. IV, 447.

9

The Golden Decade

Athanasius's Roman exile came to an end in 345, when his replacement in Alexandria, Gregory, died in June of that year. The emperor of the West, Constans, used his influence with his brother Constantius to encourage the Eastern emperor to allow Athanasius to return to his see. The bishop arrived back home in the spring of 346. He had departed Rome the previous October but took a route that was not direct. His return trip to Alexandria was punctuated by a series of other visits as well as ecclesiastical and political meetings. It seems that Athanasius spent Easter 345 in Aquileia, as a guest of Bishop Fortunatian, where he had several productive interviews with Emperor Constans. Subsequently, Constans urged—and perhaps threatened—his brother Constantius to reinstate Athanasius in Alexandria. When the interloper bishop of Alexandria (Gregory) died, the way was open for Athanasius's reinstatement, without undue turmoil—it seemed—and Constantius wrote three letters to Athanasius in which he invited him to return to Alexandria.[1]

Initially, Athanasius seemed to hesitate, and perhaps this explains the reason for the succession of letters from Constantius inviting him to return. But he subsequently began his homeward homeward journey. First, however, he went back to Rome, where Julius received him gladly and sent a warmly supportive letter to the church of Alexandria.[2] Julius of Rome had received a letter from Ursacius and Valens, the under-emperors of the East. They wrote, "Since we previously . . . made many various charges against Athanasius, the bishop, by our letters, and although we have been urged persistently by the epistles of your excellency in this matter which we

1. These letters are preserved in Athanasius's *Defense Against the Arians* 51–58, *NPNF*, vol. IV, 127–31.

2. *Defense Against the Arians* 52–53, 128.

publicly alleged and have not been able to give a reason for our accusation, therefore, we now confess to your excellency in the presence of all the presbyters, our brethren, that all that you have heard concerning the aforesaid Athanasius is utterly false and fictitious, and in every way foreign to his nature. For this reason, we joyfully enter into communion with him . . ."[3]

Athanasius soon took his leave of Rome and headed east, meeting Constantius for the third time, in April 346, in Antioch of Syria. Athanasius was graciously received, and took opportunity to ask for a public hearing of his case in order to clear his name in the imperial presence. Constantius demurred, saying that was not necessary. He promised that he would never again listen to any such accusations and that his purpose in this regard was fixed and unalterable. Athanasius recalled, "This he did not simply say, but sealed his words with oaths, calling upon God to be witness of them."[4] With this strong assurance Athanasius turned homeward, passing first through Antioch, where he visited for a time, and then Jerusalem, where a council met under Bishop Maximus to congratulate him and his church. The church of Jerusalem also sent the Alexandrian church a congratulatory letter.[5] It was on the basis of these events that Athanasius felt free to return to his see. He arrived home on October 21, 346, and was warmly received: "He was thought to be worthy of a grand reception, for . . . the people and all those in authority met him a hundred miles distant and he continued in honor."[6] Socrates, the early church historian, left a more sobering recollection: "Athanasius came to Alexandria, and was most joyfully received by the people of the city. Nevertheless as many in it as had embraced Arianism, combining together, entered into conspiracies against him, by which frequent seditions were excited, affording a pretext to the Eusebians for accusing him to the emperor of having taken possession of the Alexandrian church on his own responsibility, in spite of the adverse judgment of a general council of bishops."[7]

Thus began the so-called Golden Decade (346–56) of Athanasius's ministry in Alexandria. It was "golden" in that it was a decade of almost uninterrupted service. His position during these early years was, as Kidd

3. Sozomen, *Church History* III.23, *NPNF*, vol. II, 300.

4. Athanasius, *History of the Arians* 22, *NPNF*, vol. IV, 277.

5. Athanasius, *Defense Against the Arians* 57, *NPNF*, vol. IV, 130.

6. See "Introduction: Festal Letters, and Index," *NPNF*, vol. IV, 504. Cf. Kidd, *History of the Church*, 2:98–101, for this information and more.

7. Socrates, *Church History* II.3, *NPNF*, vol. II, 37.

described it, "impregnable."[8] Initially, Emperor Constantius was too occupied with other imperial matters to trouble himself with Athanasius and Alexandria, and the bishop had the support of many of the populace, as well as the revered monks of the Egyptian desert. The Golden Decade was a time of sustained ministry and significant literary production for Athanasius.

Despite or because of the questionable legacy left by his predecessor, Bishop Gregory, Athanasius almost certainly had hard work to do in order to consolidate his rule and try to unify the church of Alexandria behind his leadership. The priests appointed by Gregory, for example, owed him no loyalty and might have been hostile to Athanasius's rule. The new bishop's *Festal Letter* for the year 347 suggests that there were difficulties stemming from clerics offering improper and unlawful "sacrifices." Hence, in paragraph 2, for example, Athanasius reminded his church, "For actions not done lawfully and piously, are not of advantage, though they may be reputed to be so, but they rather argue hypocrisy in those who venture upon them. Therefore, although such persons feign to offer sacrifices, yet they hear from the Father, 'Your whole burnt-offerings are not acceptable, and your sacrifices do not please Me . . .'"[9]

This was also a time in which Athanasius became more deeply involved in the work of Egyptian monasticism. Two of the shining lights of Egyptian monasticism, Pachomius and Antony of the Desert, were alive and practicing their respective ministries during the Golden Decade. Pachomius lived and worked at the beginning of it, and Antony in the later part of it. Antony (ca. 250–356) had become a monk around the year 270, initially near civilization, but fifteen years later—by 285—he had withdrawn to live a solitary life in the desert at Pispir by the Nile. After living there for nearly twenty years, in 305, during the time of the last great governmental persecution of the Christians in Egypt, Antony left his cave and organized a monastic community at the Inner Mount, near the Red Sea. Pachomius (ca. 292–346) was the champion of communal monasticism (as opposed to the solitary or semi-solitary life of the hermits) and more moderate monastic rules. He established his first monastery at Tabennesi, near Denderah, on the Nile, in the south of Egypt. With the lives and work of these two luminous examples of the monastic life, one can readily summarize and epitomize the

---

8. Kidd, *History of the Church*, 2:101.

9. Athanasius, *Festal Letter* 19, NPNF, vol. IV, 545.

early development of Christian monasticism, which came to full flower in Egypt during the life and ministry of Athanasius.[10]

Hence, Egyptian monasticism was in its prime when Athanasius was bishop of Alexandria. He had occasional visits to monastic centers and was deeply influenced by monastic spirituality at a personal level. He saw himself as both a disciple of and a spiritual heir to the great St. Antony of the Desert. Athanasius was considered "one of the ascetics" even by his opponents. In 333 he had visited the Thebaid region and the monastery at Tabennesi. In 338, during the bishop's first return, Antony had visited Athanasius to offer his support and congratulations. In 340, during his exile to Rome, Athanasius took several Egyptian monks with him, and these helped him popularize monasticism in the West. When he returned from Rome, in 346, Athanasius was welcomed by a delegation from Tabennesi, who brought personal greetings from St. Antony. And Athanasius's extant correspondence during the Golden Decade was entirely directed to Egyptian monastics. These were letters of instruction, encouragement, and guidance.

The Golden Decade also saw Athanasius bring liturgical and theological unity to Alexandria. While there were a few Arians and Meletians left in the city, the orthodox Christian message once again spread rapidly and widely among the populace. In fact, the crowds at Easter 355 were so huge that services had to be held in the partially completed new cathedral that had been begun by Gregory and was being built at imperial expense. This was also a time of ecclesiastical growth and expansion of the power of the Alexandrian see, because Athanasius ordained associate bishops and presbyters for surrounding regions.[11]

The Golden Decade was a period of almost uninterrupted productivity for Athanasius. This was particularly true with regard to his literary work. While it is always difficult to precisely date his compositions, several significant works seem to have been written during this period. The important *Apologia contra Arianos* (*Defense Against the Arians*), which we reviewed in the previous chapter, is sometimes assigned to this period.[12] Two other important and interrelated works clearly stem from the early 350s, these being *De decretis Nicaenae synodi* (*Defense of the Nicene Definition*) and *De sententia Dionysii* (*Defense of Dionysius*), both of which are often dated to

---

10. Kidd, *History of the Church*, 2:101–4.

11. Ibid., 106–7.

12. Ibid., 107.

352.[13] The *Apologia ad Constantium* (*Defense before Constantius*), *Ad Amun* (*Letter to Amun*), and *Ad Dracontium* (*Letter to Dracontius*) all stem from later in this same period.

First we shall consider Athanasius's *Defense of the Nicene Definition.* The "definition" here in the title refers to the Nicene Creed, which Athanasius esteemed and explained as a sound and official definition of the orthodox Christian faith. This treatise has three main contributions to make to our understanding of Athanasius and his thought; first, it reports on the proceedings of the Council of Nicaea, and becomes one of our few primary sources for our knowledge of what transpired at that critically important council. Second, it gives further information about other figures of the period (Dionysius, Theognostus, etc.), about whom little is otherwise known. And finally, it gives an extensive study of the terms *homoousia* ("same substance"), which was used in the Nicene Creed, and "uncreated" or "unoriginated" (Gk. *agennetos*), which the Arians used in their description of the relationship of the Father and the Son.[14]

De Decretis (*Defense of the Nicene Definition*) is comprised of seven long chapters, each one of which deals with one or two major assertions. The first chapter served as an introduction and registered the Arian complaints against the Nicene Creed. "Why did the Fathers at Nicaea use terms not in Scripture, 'Of the essence' [*homoousia*] and 'One in essence'?" And then when that question was answered by learned men, they resorted to subterfuge and registered other complaints. This showed, Athanasius urged, that they were "variable and fickle in their sentiments," and he compared the Arians unfavorably to the scribes and Pharisees of the Christian gospels who heard the words of Jesus and saw His mighty works, and still were able to "imagine a vain thing" (Ps 2:1) and resort to irreligion.[15]

Chapter 2 buttressed the argument of the preceding chapter by describing the conduct of "the Eusebians" at the Council of Nicaea. It is noteworthy that by this time in the development of the controversy, "Eusebians" and "Arians" had become synonymous terms in Athanasius's mind. He wrote,

> Now it happened to Eusebius and his fellows in the Nicene Council as follows:—while they stood out in their irreligion, and attempted their fight against God, the terms they used were replete with

13. Ibid.

14. Robertson, introduction to *De Decretis*, NPNF, vol. IV, 149.

15. *De Decretis* I.1, NPNF, vol. IV, 150–51.

irreligion; but the assembled Bishops who were three hundred more or less, mildly and charitably required of them to explain and defend themselves on religious grounds. Scarcely, however, did they begin to speak, when they were condemned, and one differed from another; then perceiving the straits in which their heresy lay, they remained dumb, and by their silence confessed the disgrace which came upon their heterodoxy. On this the Bishops, having negatived the terms they had invented, published against them the sound and ecclesiastical faith; and, as all subscribed [to] it, Eusebius and his fellows subscribed [to] it also in those very words, of which they are now complaining, I mean, "of the essence" and "one in essence," and that "the Son of God is neither creature or work, nor in the member of things originated, but that the Word is an offspring from the substance of the Father."[16]

Athanasius then described the duplicity of Eusebius of Caesarea, who had initially sided with the Arians, but then made a public profession of their error and wrote a letter to his church to excuse his own conduct.[17] The Alexandrian bishop completed this chapter by asking, "Are they not then committing a crime, in their very thought to gainsay so great and ecumenical a Council?" He not surprisingly concluded that they were committing an ecclesiastical crime and urged that they should indeed keep silent instead of diabolically advocating for irreligion.[18]

In chapter 3 of the *Defense*, Athanasius began to explore the Arians' affirmation that the Word is the true Son of God. He noted that "Son" can be used in two ways, in terms of having a shared essence, or in the sense of being adopted by the Father; the former of these represents the Nicene faith, and the latter option is heresy. The Arians sought to develop a third alternative to describe the Father-God relationship in the Godhead. In their view, the Son is "only begotten" in the sense that He is the only one created first and in a unique manner by the Father. Hence they have maintained the following:

Not always Father, not always Son; for the Son was not before His generation, but, as others, came to be from nothing; and in consequence God was not always Father of the Son; but when the Son came to be and was created, then was God called His Father. For the Word is a creature and a work, and foreign and unlike the

16. *De Decretis* II.3, *NPNF*, vol. IV, 152.

17. Ibid.

18. *De Decretis* II.5, *NPNF*, vol. IV, 153.

Father in essence; and the Son is neither by nature the Father's true Word, nor His only and true Wisdom; but being a creature and one of the works, He is improperly called Word and Wisdom; for by the Word that is in God was He made, as were all things. Wherefore the Son is not true God.[19]

Several of the Bible passages that the Arians used to support this theory were explored, most notably Psalm 2:7, "Thou art my Son, this day have I begotten Thee." Where the Arians interpreted this passage as pointing to a beginning and a generation of the Word, or Son of God, Athanasius interpreted it as referring to the Incarnation of the Word of God; describing how the Word took on the flesh that God the Father had created for Him.[20] As he had earlier written in *On the Incarnation*, Athanasius urged, "And if we wish to know the object attained by this, we shall find it to be as follows: that the Word was made flesh in order to offer up this body for all, and that we partaking of His Spirit, might be deified, a gift which we could not otherwise have gained than by His clothing Himself in our created body, for hence we derive our name of 'men of God' and 'men in Christ.'"[21]

The fourth chapter developed a scriptural proof for "the Catholic sense of the word Son." This defense was mounted by marshaling passages from both testaments that evidenced the Word or Wisdom as the Son of God, Who is "unoriginate," uncreated, and eternal. The Johannine Prologue played a foundational role in Arthanasius's argumentation:

> "In the beginning was the Word, and the Word was with God, and the Word was God; the same was in the beginning with God: all things were made by Him, and without Him was not anything made" [John 1:1–3]. And the Apostle, seeing that the Hand and the Wisdom and the Word was nothing else than the Son, says, "God, who at sundry times and in divers manners spake in time past unto the Fathers by the Prophets, hath in these last days spoken unto us by His Son, whom He hath appointed Heir of all things, by whom also He made the ages" [Heb 1:1, 2].[22]

In chapter 5 of the *Defense*, Athanasius answered the Arian assertion that "from the essence" and "one in essence" (phrases that are used in the Nicene Creed) were not scriptural words, and then went on to explain the

---

19. *De Decretis* III.6, *NPNF*, vol. IV, 153–54.
20. *De Decretis* III.13, *NPNF*, vol. IV, 158.
21. *De Decretis* III.14, *NPNF*, vol. IV, 159.
22. *De Decretis* IV.17, *NPNF*, vol. IV, 161.

orthodox meaning and application of those terms. "Why then," he asked, "when they have invented on their part unscriptural phrases, for the purposes of irreligion, do they accuse those who are religious in their use of them?"[23] His argument amounted to saying that these terms capture the essence and nature of Scripture's affirmation of the shared divinity of the Father and Son, and their coeternal nature; therefore, these phrases are "equivalent language" for the words of the Bible.[24] No one, therefore, should go against the phraseology of the Council or scruple against using their definition.

In chapter 6, Athanasius drew Christian tradition into his argument by showing that Theognostus, Dionysius of Alexandria, Dionysius of Rome, and Origen all supported the use of the term "one essence" (*homoousia*) and had used it in the sense that it was applied by the Fathers of Nicaea. He quoted extensively from each of these writers to show that they stood shoulder to shoulder with the Nicene Fathers' application of the idea and phraseology of "one essence" (*homoousia*). Showing that this was the faith that was handed down from of old, the bishop of Alexandria concluded, "The faith which the Council has confessed in writing, that is the faith of the Catholic Church; to assert this, the blessed Fathers so expressed themselves while condemning the Arian heresy; and this is a chief reason why these apply themselves to calumniate the Council. For it is not the terms which trouble them, but that those terms prove them to be heretics, and presumptuous beyond other heresies."[25]

Chapter 7 explored the various meanings of the word "unoriginate," which was used by the Arians to describe their own understanding of the nature of the Son and the relationship of the Son to the Father. This was a relationship in which the Son was the firstborn creation of the Father, distinct from all other creatures, but a non-eternal creature nonetheless. The most obvious use of the term, opined Athanasius, was to describe the Father and the Son as being of "one essence," since both Persons are without origin and are uncreated. But the Arians do not wish to embrace that meaning. Their sense of the term comes from the philosophers, to describe "what exists indeed, but was neither originated nor had origin of being, but is everlasting and indestructible."[26] The bishop argued that this is not

23. *De Decretis* V.18, *NPNF*, vol. IV, 162.

24. *De Decretis* V.22, *NPNF*, vol. IV, 165.

25. *De Decretis* VI.27, *NPNF*, vol. IV, 169.

26. *De Decretis* VII.28, *NPNF*, vol. IV, 170.

a proper name for the Christian God: "It will be much more accurate to denote God from the Son and to call Him Father, than to name Him and call Him Unoriginated from His works only; for the latter term refers to the works that have come to be at the will of God through the Word, but the name of Father points out the proper offspring from His essence."[27] The Scriptures themselves teach us to call God "Father." "But," the bishop concluded, "if He wills that we should call His own Father our Father, we must not on that account measure ourselves with the Son according to nature, for it is because of the Son that the Father is so called by us; for since the Word bore our body and came to be in us, therefore by reason of the Word in us, is God called our Father."[28]

The treatise entitled *De sententia Dionysii* (*On the Opinion of Dionysius*) was written just after the *Defense*. We know this because it quotes from the latter. The letter was written as a spirited defense of the saintly bishop of Alexandria, who had preceded Athanasius's patron (Alexander) in that see. Dionysius was bishop of the city circa 247–65 and had been a student of the great Alexandrian theologian Origen. The Arians claimed that Dionysius taught their own theology of the subordination of the Son to the Father, and Athanasius wrote to counter that charge. Athanasius was not surprised: "For what marvel is it if men who have presumed to 'take counsel against the Lord and against His Christ,' are also vilifying the blessed Dionysius, Bishop of Alexandria, as a partisan and accomplice of their own?"[29] In his extensive rebuttal, Athanasius argued that the Arians made their case by appealing to but a fragment of Dionysius's writings, and they neglected to acknowledge that the writings they appealed to were written to combat Sabellianism—not to support Arianism.[30] He argued that, like the holy apostles, Dionysius wrote of Christ as both God and Man,[31] and hence did not separate the Persons of the Holy Trinity one from another.[32] The counter-case seems to reach its climax in section 19, where Athanasius demonstrated and asserted that Dionysius believed and taught that the Father and Son were of one essence.[33] He explained,

27. *De Decretis* VII.31, *NPNF*, vol. IV, 171.

28. Ibid., 172.

29. Athanasius, *On the Opinion of Dionysius*, *NPNF*, vol. IV, 176.

30. Ibid., 177.

31. Ibid., 178–79.

32. Ibid., 182–83.

33. Ibid., 183.

> While their statement that the Son has no part in the Father's
> essence, he unequivocally tramples down by saying that the Son
> is of one essence with the Father. Wherein one must wonder at
> the impudence of the irreligious persons. How can they, when
> Dionysius whom they claim as their partisan says that the Son is
> of one essence, themselves go about buzzing like gnats with the
> complaint that the Synod was wrong in writing "of one essence"?
> For if Dionysius is a friend of theirs, let them not deny what their
> partisan holds.[34]

Hence, Athanasius argued in section 24, "If the Arians agree with Dionysius let them use his language."[35] After answering a few more direct charges,
Athanasius gave an extensive (and orthodox) discussion of the theology of
the Word (*Logos*) of God, in which Dionysius overthrew the teaching of
both Sabellius and Arius, and showed "both heresies to be equal in impiety.
For neither is the Father of the Word Himself Word, nor is the offspring
of the Father a creature, but the Own-begotten of His essence."[36] In his
conclusion, Athanasius marveled once again at the impiety of "the Arian
madmen": "Convicted on this evidence, whom will they again venture to
malign?"[37]

A pair of interesting personal letters from the pen of Athanasius have
survived from this period (ca. 354)—one addressed to Amun and another
to Dracontius. The *Letter to Amun* seems to be advice to a cleric, one who
was perhaps also a monk, on issues pertaining to things "clean and unclean." Athanasius writes that "all things made by God are beautiful and
pure, for the Word of God has made nothing useless and impure."[38] Hence,
"to the pure all things are pure" (Titus 1:15), yet to those whose conscience
is defiled, all things are defiled. And this led Athanasius to a discussion of
marriage:

> There are two ways in life, as touching marriage. The one the more
> moderate and ordinary, I mean marriage; the other angelic and
> unsurpassed, namely virginity. Now if a man choose the way of the
> world, namely marriage, he is not indeed to blame; yet he will not
> receive such great gifts as the other. For he will receive, since he too
> brings forth fruit, namely thirtyfold. But if a man embrace the holy

34. Ibid.
35. Ibid., 185, section head.
36. Ibid., 186.
37. Ibid., 187.
38. Athanasius, *Letter* 48, *NPNF*, vol. IV, 556.

and unearthly way, even though, as compared with the former, it be rugged and hard to accomplish, yet it has the more wonderful gifts: for it grows the perfect fruit, namely an hundredfold.[39]

The *Letter to Dracontius* (written just prior to Easter in 354–55) was intended to urge the recipient not to flee persecution or to refuse the episcopacy but to embrace the episcopate and to remain faithful to the cause even in the face of persecution. Apparently Dracontius had fled his see and was not functioning as a bishop in the church. Athanasius wrote, "I am at a loss how to write. Am I to blame you for your refusal? Or for having regard to the trials, and hiding for fear of the Jews? In any case, however it may be, what you have done is worthy of blame, beloved Dracontius. For it was not fitting that after receiving the grace you should hide, nor that, being a wise man, you should furnish others with a pretext for flight."[40] Thus the bishop urged his absent colleague, "Do not then suffer those who give you contrary advice. But rather hasten and delay not; the more so as the holy festival is approaching; so that the laity may not keep the feast without you, and you bring great danger upon yourself. For who will in your absence preach them the Easter sermon? Who will announce to them the great day of the Resurrection, if you are in hiding? Who will counsel them, if you are in flight, to keep the feast fittingly?"[41]

The relationship between Athanasius and Emperor Constantius had been a rocky one from the very outset. But imperial intrigues and foreign wars caused Constantius to allow ecclesiastical matters to slip from the foreground of his attention during the initial years of Athanasius's return to Alexandria. In 351 the usurper Magnentius murdered the Western emperor Constans, who had been a supporter of Athanasius and the Nicene theology, and assumed his throne. After a raging civil war over the imperial throne in the West, Constantius defeated Magnentius (ca. 353) and became sole ruler of the entire Roman Empire. With his orthodox brother's influence and support for the Nicene theology gone, Constantius seemed to feel free to undertake a wholesale remaking of the theological landscape.

As early as 351 a council of (predominantly) Eastern bishops was held at Sirmium, under the direction of Basil of Ancyra. This group produced the "First Sirmium Confession," which was essentially a reworked version of the Arian Confession that had been drafted in Antioch (341). In 353,

39. Ibid., 557.
40. Athanasius, *Letter* 49, *NPNF*, vol. IV, 557–58.
41. Ibid., 560.

a council held at Arles, during the autumn of that year, revived the old charges against Athanasius and added a few new ones. It seems that it was in response to these events that Athanasius composed his *Apologia ad Constantium* (*Defense before Constanius*).

Beginning as it does with a mild and conciliatory tone, the *Defense* may have been composed in installments between 353–57, but that is by no means entirely clear. The bishop of Alexandria began thus: "Knowing that you have been a Christian for many years, most religious Augustus, and that you are godly by descent, I cheerfully undertake to answer for myself at this time . . ."[42] In the very next paragraph, however, Athanasius went on to describe the "conspiracy against me" that is clearly underway. He produced favorable quotations and recommendations from Valens and Ursacius (the under-emperors), as well as testimonials collected by them in which his Arian opponents confessed, "We lied, we invented these things; all the accusations against Athanasius are full of falsehood."[43]

The balance of the treatise sought to answer the charges made against Athanasius, and this is an important window into our understanding of the case against him. The first of these was that Athanasius had poisoned the mind of Constans (Constantius's imperial brother) against him. The second was that Athanasius had written to, encouraged, and supported Magnentius. Third, the bishop had used the new and unconsecrated cathedral (Caesareum) without imperial approval or permission during Easter 355. Fourth, and finally, Athanasius had directly disobeyed an imperial summons to the Council of Milan (July 31, 353). In his *Defense*, Athanasius sought to show himself innocent of these charges, either by outright denial or by an extensive explanation of his own actions.

The first charge, that he had tried to turn Constans against Constantius, was answered, in part, by pointing out that he never conversed with the Western emperor alone, but always in the presence of witnesses; and these could and should be amply interviewed. He also put himself under oath: "'The Lord is witness, and His Anointed is Witness' [1 Sam 12:5], I have never spoken evil of your Piety before your brother Constans, the most religious Augustus of blessed memory. I did not exasperate him against you, as these have falsely accused me."[44] In order to substantiate this point, Athanasius gave a literary itinerary of his movements with respect to

42. *Defense before Constantius* 1, NPNF, vol. IV, 238.
43. Ibid.
44. *Defense before Constantius* 3, NPNF, vol. IV, 239.

meeting with Constans. The upshot of this was that there was "no possible time or place for the alleged offense."[45]

The second charge, of corresponding with and thereby supporting "the tyrant" Magnentius, was flatly denied by Athanasius. He wrote, "Believe me, most religious Prince, many times did I weigh the matter in my mind, but was unable to believe that any one could be so mad as to utter such a falsehood. But when this charge was published abroad by the Arians, as well as the former, and they boasted that they had delivered to you a copy of the letter, I was the more amazed, and I used to pass sleepless nights contending against the charge, as if in the presence of my accusers."[46] This letter, if there really was one, he urged, must have been a complete and utter forgery. Once again, Athanasius put himself under oath, and denied any acquaintance with Magnentius, let alone having written to him. In contrast to his supposed friendship with Magnentius, Athanasius pointed to and swore his complete loyalty to Constantius and his brother.[47]

As to the third charge, of using an undedicated church, at Easter, Athanasius pled that the pragmatic need for more room—due to the huge crowds desiring to worship—was his justification. No disrespect toward the emperor (who was building the church) or toward ecclesiastical propriety was intended. This pragmatic reply was buttressed by several sub-points: "[it is] better to pray together than separately," "[it is] better to pray in a building than in the desert," and "prayers first do not interfere with dedication afterwards."[48] Hence, he wrote to Constantius, "The place is ready, having been already sanctified by the prayers that have been offered in it, and requires only the presence of your Piety. This only is wanting to its perfect beauty."[49]

Taking up the fourth charge of having disobeyed an imperial order, Athanasius gave a history of his actions preceding his refusal to come to the Council of Milan. The people who ordered him to leave Alexandria and travel west presented no letter of introduction from Constantius. Hence, he wrote, "I acted rightly then, most religious Augustus, that as I had returned to my country under the authority of your letters, so I should only leave it by your command; and might not render myself liable hereafter to a charge

---

45. *Defense before Constantius* 5, *NPNF*, vol. IV, 240.

46. *Defense before Constantius* 6, *NPNF*, vol. IV, 240.

47. *Defense before Constantius* 10, *NPNF*, vol. IV, 241.

48. *Defense before Constantius* 16–18, *NPNF*, vol. IV, 244–45.

49. *Defense before Constantius* 18, *NPNF*, vol. IV, 245.

of having deserted the Church, but as receiving your order might have a reason for my retiring."[50] When the proper documents and letter arrived, Athanasius set out for the West, but as he traveled he met rumors that his supporters in the West (including Pope Liberius of Rome and the venerable Hosius of Spain) had been banished for failing to support the trumped-up charges against Athanasius and for refusing to deny the Nicene theology.[51] Soon after this Athanasius learned of his own proscription from office, and that George was elected bishop and sent to replace him.[52] In the closing sections of the *Defense*, Athanasius defended his flight into hiding, upon hearing the news of his banishment. Seeing that people were seeking to arrest and kill him, Athanasius decided, "It was better for me to hide myself, and to wait for this opportunity [to make a defense]."[53] And he detailed the dishonors, abuses, and scandals against the holy Virgins of his church that were perpetrated when the Arians assumed power.[54] The *Defense* closed with Athanasius imploring Constantius to do his imperial, Christian duty in the face of all these abuses.[55]

The *Defense* seemed not to have much effect upon the imperial attitude toward Athanasius. And events, as they are described by Sozomen, quickly spun out of control. The emperor called a council at Milan (referenced above) in 355, which condemned and deposed Athanasius. When the Nicene supporters protested against these measures they were threatened with immediate banishment, and among those banished was Hilary of Poitiers. Athanasius, who had been summoned to the council, did not go, but instead sent five Egyptian bishops (including Serapion, bishop of Thumis) and three presbyters who could answer adequately in his behalf. Sozomen reported, "Athanasius, being apprised that plots had been formed against him at court, deemed it prudent not to repair to the emperor himself, as he knew that his life would be thereby endangered, nor did he think that it would be of any avail."[56] Shortly after this party had departed for their voyage, Athanasius received a series of letters from Emperor Constantius summoning him to the royal palace. Athanasius and the people of the Al-

50. *Defense before Constantius* 24, *NPNF*, vol. IV, 247.

51. *Defense before Constantius* 27, *NPNF*, vol. IV, 248–49.

52. *Defense before Constantius* 28–29, *NPNF*, vol. IV, 249.

53. *Defense before Constantius* 35, *NPNF*, vol. IV, 253.

54. *Defense before Constantius* 33, *NPNF*, vol. IV, 252.

55. *Defense before Constantius* 35, *NPNF*, vol. IV, 253.

56. Sozomen, *Church History* IV.9, *NPNF*, vol. II, 305.

exandrian church were "greatly troubled at this command" since they saw no safety in obeying the emperor's command, because of his "heterodox sentiments."[57] On this basis, the bishop once again considered it more prudent to disobey the emperor and remain in Alexandria.

The following summer another letter arrived for Athanasius from the emperor, summoning him to court. This letter arrived with the governor of the provinces, and "he was charged to urge the departure of Athanasius from the city, and to act with hostility against the clergy." This summons too came to naught, when the governor "perceived, however, that the people of the Church were full of courage and ready to take up arms, he also departed from the city without accomplishing his mission." A third time, the emperor sought to extricate Athanasius from Alexandria, this time sending Roman legions, which were quartered in Egypt and Libya, to remove him by force under the leadership of General Syrianus. It was rumored that the bishop could be found in the church known as "Theonas." When the troops burst open the doors and sought to arrest him, Athanasius could not be found. Sozomen remarked, "It is said that he escaped this and many other perils by the Divine interposition; and that God had disclosed this previously; directly as he went out, the soldiers took the doors of the church, and were within a little [time] of seizing him."[58] Athanasius narrated these events in his *Apologia de fuga* (*Defense of His Flight*), which was written during his subsequent exile:

> It was now night, and some of the people were keeping a vigil preparatory to a communion on the morrow, when the General Syrianus suddenly came upon us with more than five thousand soldiers, having arms and drawn swords, bows, spears, and clubs . . . With these he surrounded the Church, stationing his soldiers near at hand, in order that no one might be able to leave the Church and pass by them. Now I considered that it would be unreasonable in me to desert the people during such a disturbance, and not to endanger myself in their behalf; therefore I sat down upon my throne, and desired the Deacon to read a Psalm, and the people to answer, "For His mercy endureth forever," and then all to withdraw and depart home. But the General having now made a forcible entry, and the soldiers having surrounded the sanctuary for the purpose of apprehending us, the Clergy and those of the laity, who were still there, cried out, and demanded that we too

57. Ibid.
58. Ibid.

should withdraw. But I refused, declaring that I would not do so, until they had retired one and all. Accordingly, I stood up, and having bidden prayer, I then made my request of them, that all should depart before me, saying that it was better that my safety be endangered, than that any of them should receive hurt. So when the greater part had gone forth, and the rest were following, the monks who were there with us and certain of the Clergy came up and dragged us away. And thus (Truth is my witness), while some of the soldiers stood about the sanctuary, and others were going round the Church, we passed through, under the Lord's guidance, and with His protection without observation, greatly glorifying God that we had not betrayed the people, but had first sent them away, and then had been able to save ourselves, and to escape the hands of them that sought after us.[59]

For a time Athanasius hid in the city of Alexandria while the troops sought to arrest him. Initially he hid in an underground cistern, which had at one time been used as a reservoir for water. When that place of hiding became known through bribing the servants who were helping him, he eventually escaped from the city by sailing up the Nile to the distant parts of the region. But when his pursuers learned of this he sailed back south, as his assailants rowed past him in the darkness. Exactly when the bishop fled the city is not clear, but most commentators locate Athanasius in exile among the desert monks of Egypt in the summer of 356. An Arian bishop named George was installed as head of the church, with the support of imperial forces. Sozomen reported that he was regarded with "great aversion" because of the means of his elevation and his "many evil deeds." He quickly forfeited the support of the populace and the respect of the Egyptian monks, who "openly declared him to be perfidious and inflated with arrogance." "The opinions of these monks," Sozomen reported, "were always adopted by the people, and their testimony was universally received."[60]

59. *Defense of His Flight* 24, *NPNF*, vol. IV, 263–64.

60. Sozomen, *Church History* IV.9, *NPNF*, vol. II, 306

10

The Third Exile (356–62)

After hurriedly and secretly leaving Alexandria in the spring of 356, Athanasius took up residence among the monks of the Egyptian desert. If we are to judge this period of his life by his literary production, which is one of the few barometers available to us, then one must say that this was one of the most significant and productive periods of his life and ministry. While he was sequestered in the desert, however, events in the wider world went on without him. Emperor Constantius's campaign against the Eastern bishops who supported the Nicene Creed continued, and even the Roman Pope Liberius and Hosius of Cordova were driven into exile. The Council of Sirmium (357) emphasized the subordination of the Son to the Father, but maintained the Son's eternal existence. It developed a view that was called "Anomianism," and stressed the Son was "unlike" (*anomoios*) the Father. Bishop Basil of Ancyra emerged as an opponent of this approach, and he called the Council of Ancyra, in 358, to affirm the "likeness" of the Father and the Son and to deny that the Son was a creature. This new, third option between Arianism and the Nicene party was termed *homoiousian* ("similar substance") because it argued that the Son was of "similar substance" as the Father. There was an attempt to find common ground between the "similar substance" party and the Nicene supporters, but this too fell apart when the Western bishops refused to affirm anything other than the Nicene Creed.

Meanwhile, back in Alexandria, George the Cappadocian, who replaced Athanasius as bishop, strenuously persecuted Athanasius's followers in the city and threw the church into conflict and turmoil:

> For on a sudden the Church was surrounded by soldiers, and sounds of war took the place of prayers. Then George of Cappadocia who was sent by them, having arrived during the season of Lent, brought an increase of evils which they had taught him.

For after Easter week, Virgins were thrown into prison; Bishops were led away in chains by soldiers; houses of orphans and widows were plundered, and their loaves taken away; attacks were made upon houses, and Christians thrust forth in the night, and their dwellings sealed up; brothers of clergymen were in danger of their lives on account of their brethren. These outrages were sufficiently dreadful, but more dreadful than these followed.[1]

It was probably during his "desert period" that Athanasius completed his *Defense before Constantius*, which he had begun as early as 353 and intended to deliver to the emperor in person, but events quickly eclipsed that hope. Now he also found himself writing a *Defense of His Flight* (*Apologia de fuga* [357]) to answer critics who charged him with cowardice for leaving the fray, and a *Circular to Bishops of Egypt and Libya* (*Ad episcopos Aegypti*) giving them instructions for how to conduct themselves in his absence.

His Flight (*De Fuga*) began by stating the problem, as Athanasius saw it: "I hear that Leontius, now at Antioch, and Narcissus of the city of Nero, and George, now at Laodicea, and the Arians who are with them, are spreading abroad many slanderous reports concerning me, charging me with cowardice, because forsooth, when I myself was sought by them, I did not surrender myself to their hands."[2] After arguing that the charge against him is based in "insincerity," Athanasius presented his own persecution as being part of a larger conspiracy by the Arian party to rid themselves of bishops who supported the Nicene Creed. After detailing the persecutions, beatings, murders, and other atrocities perpetuated by George the Cappadocian against the orthodox believers of Alexandria, Athanasius implied that similar things—including death—were also meant for him. "They accuse me," he wrote, "because I have been able to escape their murderous hands."[3]

The exiled bishop's first defense was a simple one: if it is wrong to flee, it is much worse to persecute. He wrote, "For if it be a bad thing to flee, it is much worse to persecute: for the one party hides himself to escape death, the other persecutes with a desire to kill; and it is written in the Scriptures that we ought to flee; but he that seeks to destroy transgresses the law, nay, and is himself the occasion of the other's flight."[4] And so he

1. Athanasius, *Defense of His Flight* 6, NPNF, vol. IV, 257.
2. *Defense of His Flight* 1, NPNF, vol. IV, 255.
3. *Defense of His Flight* 8, NPNF, vol. IV, 257.
4. Ibid.

concluded the real grievance that his accusers had against him was not that he was a coward but that he was alive and free; in this the bishop did not do more than what Jacob did when he fled the anger of Esau, or Moses when he withdrew to Midian in fear of Pharaoh's revenge. In fact, the holy Scripture is replete with examples of saints who fled extreme danger in order to preserve their lives and ministries.[5]

Our Lord Jesus Christ, opined Athanasius, was himself an example of one who withdrew to avoid arrest and death, when "his hour had not yet come" (John 7:30). "He neither suffered Himself to be taken before the time came, nor did He hide Himself when it was come; but gave Himself up to them that had conspired against Him, that He might show to all men that the life and death of man depend upon the divine sentence; and that without our Father which is in heaven, neither a hair of man's head can become white or black, nor a sparrow ever fall into the snare"[6] (Matt 5:36; 10:29). And while there comes a "time and an hour" for all men to die, that time is in God's hands, not the hands of his theological and ecclesiastical opponents. Thus, there is an appropriate time to flee and a time to stay; God alone helps one know when it is time to face death or martyrdom. For this reason, then, the saints (both then and now) who have fled persecution are not to be looked upon as cowards—for they too endured hardship, and they too have received the blessing and favor of God as a sort of verification of their righteousness in fleeing.[7] In fact, those who fled did so for the sake of others, and for their ministry, and not because of cowardice and fear of death. In stark contrast to the selfless and holy spirit of the persecuted who flee is the diabolical attitude of those who persecute them. Hence, Athanasius wrote, "seeing. . . . that such is the conduct of the Saints, let these persons, to whom one cannot give a name suitable to their character—let them, I say, tell us, from whom they learnt to persecute? They cannot say, from the Saints. No, but from the Devil (that is the only answer which is left to them) . . ."[8] And this realization should be of some comfort to those who are being persecuted.

After recounting his providential and miraculous escape from the clutches of the military governor Syrianus (see the preceding chapter), Athanasius urged, "Now when Providence had delivered us in such an

5. *Defense of His Flight* 10, NPNF, vol. IV, 258.
6. *Defense of His Flight* 15, NPNF, vol. IV, 260.
7. *Defense of His Flight* 18–19, NPNF, vol. IV, 261–62.
8. *Defense of His Flight* 23, NPNF, vol. IV, 263.

extraordinary manner, who can justly lay any blame upon me, because we did not give ourselves up into the hands of them, that sought after us, nor return and present ourselves before them? This would have been plainly to show ingratitude to the Lord, and to act against His commandment, and in contradiction to the practice of the Saints."[9] Therefore, in conclusion, those who oppose and persecute Athanasius and the other Alexandrian Christians are doing so because "they are enemies of Christ, and are no longer Christians, but Arians. They ought indeed to accuse each other of the sins they are guilty of, for they are contrary to the faith of Christ, but they rather conceal them [their sins] for their own sakes."[10] The treatise ended with a prayer: "May they continue to be injured in such sort, that they may lose the power of inflicting injuries, and that those whom they persecute may give thanks unto the Lord, and say in the words of the twenty-sixth Psalm, 'The Lord is my light and my salvation; whom then shall I fear? The Lord is the strength of my life; of whom then shall I be afraid?'"[11]

Athanasius's letter *To the Bishops of Egypt* (*Ad episcopos Aegypti*) was written in 356, thirty-one years after the Council of Nicaea.[12] It seems to have been composed soon after the bishop's expulsion by the Roman governor Syrianus (February 8, 356) and before the arrival of George the Cappadocian as bishop. The encyclical letter had several purposes; the first and most obvious was to deliver the news of his own expulsion and exile, and beyond that, to give a strong warning against a new creed being circulated (perhaps the Sirmian Creed of 351) for the bishops' acceptance on pain of imperial banishment. The creed was not, strictly speaking, Arian, but it was substandard from the standpoint of Nicene orthodoxy, and through its careful wording left room for Arianism. The long second part of the *Letter* amounts to another restatement and rebuttal of Arian theology. The letter concluded with a strong call to steadfastness in the face of persecution. Athanasius closed with the opinion that Emperor Constantius would ultimately put an end to these ecclesiastical disputes and outrages, once he became aware of the true facts of the matter: "when our gracious Emperor shall hear of it, he will put a stop to their wickedness, and they will not continue long . . ."[13] In this latter hope, the *Letter* seems to breathe the same

9. *Defense of His Flight* 25, NPNF, vol. IV, 264.
10. *Defense of His Flight* 27, NPNF, vol. IV, 264-65.
11. Ibid., 265.
12. *To the Bishops of Egypt* 22, NPNF, vol. IV, 234.
13. *To the Bishops of Egypt* 23, NPNF, vol. IV, 235.

optimism as the opening of Athanasius's *Defense before Constantius*—an optimism that was soon eroded by the passage of time and ongoing imperial persecution.

Athanasius's argument against this "new" creed was very direct. He viewed it as wrong to take only part of the Holy Scriptures, and reject the other part, and that is what the Arians and the framers of this creed were doing. He viewed the party of Acacius as Arians in disguise who were trying to make room for "the Arian madness" within the pale of orthodoxy. In this they had become accomplices with "Eusebius and his fellows" in "advocating this Antichristian heresy . . ."[14] Their words, though scriptural, were evil because they came from heretical intentions, and therefore became a cloak for false teaching. Hence, Athanasius wrote, "They disguise their real sentiments, and then make use of the language of Scripture for their own writings, which they hold forth as a bait for the ignorant, that they may inveigle them into their own wickedness."[15]

Chapter 2 of the same epistle begins with a full paragraph (12) of Arian theological statements and phrases. Among these were the following:

> God was not always a Father: The Son was not always: But whereas all things were made out of nothing, the Son of God also was made out of nothing: And since all things are creatures, He also is a creature and a thing made: And since all things once were not, but were afterwards made, there was a time when the Word of God Himself was not; and He was not before He was begotten, but He had a beginning of existence: For He has then originated when God has chosen to produce Him: For He also is one among the rest of His works.[16]

These assertions were all answered from Scripture in the next three long paragraphs (13–15). The writings of the Fourth Gospel and St. Paul figured largely in Athanasius's rebuttal. The Arians imply and argue that the Son is not true God, and in the bishop's opinion, "he who holds these opinions can no longer be even called a Christian."[17] They call Him a creature, Whom Scripture calls the Creator, "while they perceive not the absurdity of this."[18] Upon comparing the Christology of Arianism disfavorably with

---

14. *To the Bishops of Egypt* 7, *NPNF*, vol. IV, 226.

15. *To the Bishops of Egypt* 9, *NPNF*, vol. IV, 228.

16. *To the Bishops of Egypt* 12, *NPNF*, vol. IV, 229.

17. *To the Bishops of Egypt* 13, *NPNF*, vol. IV, 230.

18. Ibid.

the adoptionism of the Manichees (16), Athanasius turned to rebuke both groups from the Scriptures (17). In the latter instance they err greatly in misunderstanding the Incarnation of the Word of God. He wrote, "These last are in error either concerning the body or the Incarnation of the Lord, falsifying the truth, some in one way and some in another, or else they deny that the Lord has sojourned here at all . . . But this one alone more madly than the rest has dared to assail the very Godhead, and to assert that the Word is not at all, and that the Father was not always a father; so that one might reasonably say that that Psalm was written against them; 'The fool hath said in his heart, there is no God [Ps 53:1]. Corrupt are they, and become abominable in their doings.'"[19]

In paragraph 19, Arius's ignoble death in a public latrine also was turned to apologetic value, since it evidenced divine retribution for his theological "perjury" and it was even seen as such by Emperor Constantine. Thus, Athanasius wrote, "It was shown too that the Arian madness was rejected from communion by our Savior both here and in the Church of the first-born in heaven."[20] In vain will the friends of Arius convince the orthodox with their more moderate words so long as they fail to renounce his sentiments, and in so doing they participate in his impiety and will receive his punishment (20). In perpetuating Arius's heresy, they have become the "seducing spirits" against which the Scriptures warn us: "For we know that, as it is written, 'in the latter times some shall depart from the sound faith, giving heed to seducing spirits, and doctrines of devils, that turn from the truth' [1 Tim 4:11; Titus 1:14]; and 'as many as will live godly in Christ shall suffer persecution. But evil men and seducers shall wax worse and worse, deceiving and being deceived.' But none of these things shall prevail over us, nor 'separate us from the love of Christ' [Rom 8:35], though the heretics threaten us with death. For we are Christians, not Arians . . ."[21]

In his concluding sections Athanasius compared taking a stand for the true faith with a kind of martyrdom and urged the bishops of Egypt to remain faithful to the Nicene Creed. "I exhort you," he wrote, "keeping in your hands the confession which was framed by the Fathers at Nicaea, and defending it with great zeal and confidence in the Lord, be examples to the brethren everywhere, and show them that a struggle is now before us in support of the Truth against heresy, and that the wiles of the enemy are

19. *To the Bishops of Egypt* 17, *NPNF*, vol. IV, 232.
20. *To the Bishops of Egypt* 19, *NPNF*, vol. IV, 233.
21. *To the Bishops of Egypt* 20, *NPNF*, vol. IV, 233.

various. For the proof of a martyr lies not only in refusing to burn incense to idols; but to refuse to deny the Faith is also an illustrious testimony of a good conscience."[22] Where their opponents follow the example of Judas and Jezebel, Athanasius urged his readers to follow the example of St. Paul, and the other orthodox Fathers, so that they shall be able to say, "We have 'kept the Faith'; and ye shall receive the 'crown of life,' which God 'hath promised to them that love Him' [2 Tim 4:7; Jas 1:12]."[23]

Athanasius wrote the *Life of Antony* (*Vita Antonii*) soon after the saintly monk's death in 356. He viewed Antony as an example, mentor and friend, so it was quite natural that Athanasius would receive inquiries about Antony's life and death. The *Life of Antony* was composed, as a letter, in reply to one of these inquiries: "Since you have asked me about the career of the blessed Antony, hoping to learn how he began the discipline, who he was before this, and what sort of death he experienced, and if the things said concerning him are true—so that you might also lead yourselves in imitation of him—I received your directive with ready good will. For simply to remember Antony is a great profit and assistance for me also."[24] Seen through the eyes of Athanasius, the life of Antony becomes the ideal example of the redeemed Christian, and hence the *Life of Antony* provides the reader with Athanasius's own understanding of what the life of grace looks like when it is lived out robustly and meaningfully.[25]

The *Life of Antony* quickly became Athanasius's most popular work. It was composed in Greek and quickly translated into Latin (in at least two separate editions) and was widely circulated throughout the Eastern and Western churches. It was widely read by Christians everywhere, but the *Life of Antony* was particularly formative for those Christians interested in or drawn to the rigors of monasticism. At a time when monasticism was replacing martyrdom as the epitome of the Christian life of selflessness and sacrifice, the *Life of Antony* showed Christians like Basil the Great, Gregory Nazianzen, and Augustine of Hippo how to follow the monastic path. In fact, Antony's sudden and dramatic conversion to robust Christian faith was a model as well as a spur to Augustine's own spiritual transformation.[26]

22. *To the Bishops of Egypt* 21, *NPNF*, vol. IV, 234.

23. *To the Bishops of Egypt* 23, *NPNF*, vol. IV, 235.

24. Gregg, *Life of Antony*, 9.

25. Anatolios, *Athanasius: The Coherence of His Thought*, 166.

26. Cf. Augustine's *Confessions* VIII.28, *NPNF*, first series, vol. I, 127.

A middle-class Egyptian born to prosperous Christian parents, Antony lived a carefree early life, with few concerns about spiritual matters. But when he was in his late teens, his parents died suddenly, leaving him alone with his younger sister. Six months later he found himself, as was his custom, attending worship in the Lord's house. On this occasion he found himself contemplating how the apostles of Christ had given up everything to follow the Savior, and how—in the book of Acts—the early believers sold what they possessed and took the proceeds and laid them at the feet of the apostles for distribution among those who were in need. As he went to church pondering these things, Antony heard the words of the gospel lesson with new ears: "He heard the Lord saying to the rich man, *If you would be perfect, go, sell what you possess and give to the poor, and you will have treasure in heaven* [Matt 19:21]. It was as if by God's design he held the saints in his recollection, and as if the passage were read on his account. Immediately Antony went out from the Lord's house and gave to the townspeople the possessions he had from his forebears . . . And selling all the rest that was portable, when he had collected sufficient money, he donated it to the poor, keeping a few things for his sister."[27] Upon returning to church, when Antony "heard in the Gospel the Lord saying, *Do not be anxious about tomorrow*, he could not remain any longer, but going out he gave those remaining possessions also to the needy. Placing his sister in the charge of respected and trusted virgins, and giving her over to the convent for rearing, he devoted himself from then on to the discipline rather than the household, giving heed to himself and patiently training himself."[28]

Antony received ascetical training ("the discipline") from a monastic hermit in a neighboring village, and then continued to learn from others throughout the region. Athanasius wrote, "All the desire and all the energy he possessed concerned the exertion of the discipline. He worked with his hands, though, having heard that he who is idle, *let him not eat* [2 Thess 3:10]. And he spent what he made partly for bread, and partly on those in need. He prayed constantly, since he learned that it is necessary to pray unceasingly in private [1 Thess 5:17; Matt 6:7]. For he paid such close attention to what was read that nothing from Scripture did he fail to take in—rather he grasped everything, and in him the memory took the place of books."[29] Living in this manner bore significant spiritual fruit in Antony's

27. Gregg, *Life of Antony*, 31.

28. Ibid., 31–32.

29. Ibid., 32.

life; he "was loved by all. He was sincerely obedient to those men of zeal he visited, and he considered carefully the advantage in zeal and in ascetic living that each held in relation to him. He observed the graciousness of one, the eagerness for prayers in another; he took careful note of one's freedom from anger, and the human concern of another . . . And having been filled in this manner, he returned to his only place of discipline, from that time gathering the attributes of each in himself, and striving to manifest in himself what was best from all."[30] Thus, in the life of Antony, the reader found exemplified many, if not all, of the virtues of desert monastics, distilled down into one exceptionally spiritually attuned life.

The *Life of Antony* was primarily a holy biography for Christian instruction, but be assured that the reader is being instructed in Athanasius's own orthodox brand of Christianity. Without saying so, Athanasius's depiction of the saintly monk shows him to be a supporter of the Nicene theology; for Antony, Jesus Christ is, in words of the Nicene Creed, "very God and very Man." The moral life that Antony hungered and thirsted for, and that he exemplified, was for Athanasius part and parcel of the process of Christian sanctification. It was Christ at work in Christians by the Word and Spirit of God. Sanctification involved the process of deification, in which "He became what we are, in order to make us what He is." This vision of moral transformation by the Incarnation of Christ within Christians, which was first lauded in his *On the Incarnation*, stood in stark contrast to the Arian approach to salvation through moral effort, in which the disciple strives to become increasingly moral and godly, and thereby participates in the life of God. Indeed, the saintly monk was enlisted as an ally in Athanasius's own ecclesiastical and theological struggles. Antony was reported as saying, for example, "'Be zealous in protecting the soul from foul thoughts, as I said before, and compete with the saints, but do not approach the Meletian schismatics, for you know their evil and profane reputation. Nor are you to have any fellowship with the Arians, for their impiety is evident to everyone."[31] Antony died as he lived: poor, penniless, and utterly dedicated to life in Jesus Christ. After distributing his clothing to the poor, two sheepskins upon which he slept were his sole remaining possessions, save the clothes in which he was buried, and the sheepskins he bequeathed to Athanasius and his Egyptian friend, Bishop Serapion.[32]

30. Ibid., 33.
31. Ibid., 95.
32. Ibid., 97.

During this same period, Athanasius addressed a letter to Serapion concerning the death of Arius.[33] Arius had died in 336, so the role of this particular letter was not so much to deliver "new news" as it was to put a new orthodox apologetic spin on old news. Athanasius reported that he was replying to an earlier letter from Serapion, in which the bishop had requested information about the "most impious heresy of the Arians, in consequence of which I have endured these sufferings, and also the manner of the death of Arius."[34] While Athanasius was not a firsthand observer of the events he narrated, he reported hearing this account from one Macarius, who had been at Constantinople.[35]

In his epistle Athanasius recounted the excommunication of Arius by Bishop Alexander and the appeal that Arius made to the emperor. Arius professed, in his *Account of the Faith*, that he held none of the views for which he was excommunicated. When Emperor Constantine ordered Alexander to reinstate Arius and to receive him into communion, the Alexandrian bishop refused, because he did not believe that Arius's recantation was genuine. When he was about to receive communion in distant Constantinople, Alexander fervently prayed that Arius would be taken from the world prior to contaminating the church with his heresy and blasphemy. The Alexandrian bishop's prayer was answered, as Arius was "urged by the necessities of nature" to withdraw to a public latrine where, as he tried to relieve himself, he "'burst asunder in the midst' [Acts 1:18], and immediately expired as he lay, and he was deprived both of communion and of his life together."[36] Intentionally paralleling Arius's ignoble death with that of Judas in the Scriptures (Acts 1:18), Athanasius opined, "So the antichristian gang of the Arian madmen has been shown to be unpleasing to God and impious; and many of those who before were deceived by it changed their opinions."[37] Athanasius urged Serapion to share this letter with the monks who were with him, so that they might all strongly condemn the Arian heresy and not be led astray by the wickedness of the "Arian madmen."

In his letter to Athanasius, Serapion requested three specific items: a history of recent events, an exposition of the Arian heresy, and an exact

33. Letter 54, *To Serapion, Concerning the Death of Arius*, NPNF, vol. IV, 564–66.
34. Ibid., 564–65.
35. Ibid., 565.
36. Ibid.
37. Ibid.

account of the death of Arius.[38] The letter itself fulfilled the third request. Johannes Quasten suggested that the Alexandrian bishop sent copies of his *Arian History* and *Orations Against the Arians* to answer the other aspects of this request.[39] There is considerable cogency to this assessment, and some scholars date the composition of all three works (the *Letter,* the *Arian History,* and the *Orations*) to this same exile.[40] It is my feeling, however, that the *Orations* were composed earlier (hence they were treated in an earlier chapter), though they might have been employed at this time, as Quasten suggests. This leaves us with the consideration of Athanasius's magnum opus, *History of the Arians.*

History of the Arians is an extensive (more than thirty double-column pages in translation) and comprehensive work. It presents the emergence and growth of Arianism in the Christian Roman Empire in an orderly and chronological format. It presents Athanasius's own particular "slant" on this history, in that it views Arianism as a heinous and heretical belief system that became an international conspiracy against the Nicene faith in the hands of the Eusebians and Emperor Constantius. The work gives a cross-section of the years 335 (and the aftermath of the Council of Nicaea) up through recent actions by Constantius against Pope Liberius (358) and Hosius of Cordova. It ends by returning to Alexandria and chronicling the further persecution of the church in Egypt (357–58). A close examination of the contents of the work, therefore, suggests that it was composed around 358, during Athanasius's third exile.

While written as an historical account, *History of the Arians* should be viewed as an apology for the orthodox Nicene faith. Gone, now, was Athanasius's early optimism, registered in his *Defense before Constantius,* that the Christian emperor meant well and was only trying to bring peace and unity to the Christian church. Now, Constantius is depicted as being "worse than Saul, Ahab, and Pilate"—all arch-villains of the Bible who vehemently opposed God and God's people.[41] In his *History* Athanasius even went so far as to describe the recent episcopal appointments made by Constantius as being "a mark of the Antichrist."[42] And a later section of the same document described the emperor as "the precursor of Antichrist." If Constantius

---

38. Ibid., 564.

39. Quasten, *Patrology,* 3:27.

40. Robertson, introduction to *Against the Arians,* NPNF, vol. IV, 303.

41. *History of the Arians* 68, NPNF, vol. IV, 295.

42. *History of the Arians* 74, NPNF, vol. IV, 297.

is not the forerunner of the Antichrist, "Else wherefore is he so mad against the godly? Wherefore does he contend for it as his own heresy, and call everyone his enemy who will not comply with the madness of Arius, and admit gladly the allegations of the enemies of Christ, and dishonor so many venerable Councils? Why did he command that the Churches should be given up to the Arians? Was it not that, when that other comes, he may thus find a way to enter into them, and may take to himself him who has prepared those places for him?"[43] As the *History* came to a close, Athanasius urged the orthodox Christians to remain separate from the Arian heretics, and he mounted a call for a spirited protest against the ecclesiastical and political authorities who were perpetuating the Arian heresy.[44]

Timothy Barnes considers *History of the Arians* to be "a systematically deceptive work" that exaggerates the degree to which Constantius supported Arianism.[45] Like David Gwynn,[46] Barnes seems to suspect that Athanasius has linked his own ecclesiastical problems (which, in his mind, stemmed from abuse of his office) with opposition to the Arian theology, through efforts of self-justification and self-preservation. While it is helpful to read Athanasius's work with a critical eye, the preponderance of the evidence (as it is given by the Christian church historians) seems to underscore the Alexandrian bishop's presentation of the situation. Although one cannot conclusively know the emperor's own beliefs from the distance of so many years, it is clear that he took strenuous steps to oppose Athanasius and his theology; seen from the standpoint of his deeds, Athanasius seemed justified in doubting Constantius's theological orthodoxy as well as his good intentions toward the church. Where unity and religious harmony meant more to Constantius than theological precision, with respect to Arianism and the full deity and equality of the Father, Son, and the Holy Spirit, Athanasius valued theological accuracy more than false harmony and theological unity with those whom he considered heretics. The struggle between Athanasius and the emperor clearly also involved questions of the extent of political authority with respect to the governance of the church and theological questions. Athanasius saw himself as being charged with the task of being a guardian of theological truth and ecclesiastical purity, and was

43. *History of the Arians 77*, NPNF, vol. IV, 299.

44. *History of the Arians 80–81*, NPNF, vol. IV, 300–302.

45. Barnes, *Athanasius and Constantius*, 128–29.

46. Cf. Gwynn, *The Eusebians*.

for that reason willing to disobey and oppose the harmonizing efforts of Constantius.

In circa 358–60 Athanasius also addressed an open letter *To the Monks* (*Ad Monachos I*). It began in this fashion: "To those in every place who are living a monastic life, who are established in the faith of God, and sanctified in Christ, and who say, 'Behold, we have forsaken all, and followed Thee' [Matt 19:27], brethren dearly beloved and longed for, heartiest greeting in the Lord."[47] His allegiance and admiration for this faith community could hardly be more complete! Once again, the exiled bishop wrote in reply to a request for information—this time his recipients long to know about the sufferings of the church and those that are being endured by Athanasius himself for refuting, "according to my ability, the accursed heresy of the Arian madmen, and proving how entirely it is alien from the Truth."[48] Attempting to crystalize the debate between himself and the Arians, Athanasius wrote,

> For although it be impossible to comprehend what God is, yet it is possible to say what He is not. And we know that He is not as man; and that it is not lawful to conceive of any originated nature as existing in Him. So also respecting the Son of God, although we are by nature very far from being able to comprehend Him; yet it is possible and easy to condemn the assertions of the heretics concerning Him, and to say, that the Son of God is not such; nor is it lawful even to conceive in our minds such things as they speak, concerning His Godhead; much less to utter them with the lips.[49]

With respect to the condemnation of Arius, Athanasius pointed once again to his ignoble death in a public latrine: "For what the Holy God hath purposed, who shall scatter [Isa 14:27]?' and whom the Lord condemned who shall justify [Rom 8:33, 34]?"[50] So dangerous were the sentiments he voiced in this letter that Athanasius asked his readers to make no copy of it, and to return it to him upon reading it as many times as they wished.

In late 359 or early 360 the bishop in exile continued his literary production through the composition of the *Letters to Serapion on the Holy Spirit*. These treatises clearly belong to the third exile, since in paragraph

47. Athanasius, *Letter 52*, *NPNF*, vol. IV, 563.
48. Ibid.
49. Ibid.
50. Ibid.

33 their author mentioned "dwelling as I do in a desert place . . ."[51] Athanasius wrote these epistles because a new heresy had arisen in the Egyptian church, and it was his duty as bishop and defender of the Nicene theology to expose and attack it. This new heresy was, as Shapland described it, "a crisis within a crisis."[52] The heretical group Athanasius called "the Tropici" because they invented new "tropes" or teachings.[53] They had extended the Arian supposition that the Son of God was a creature and applied it instead to the Holy Spirit. Even though the Nicene Creed, at this time, affirmed only one meager statement about the Holy Spirit ("We believe . . . also in the Holy Spirit"), Athanasius realized that the Trinitarian theology that constituted orthodox faith required the full deity and equality of the Father, Son and the Holy Spirit. So in this sense, Athanasius's insight about the Holy Spirit went much further than the formal words of the Nicene Creed of his day, and anticipated the addition to the Nicene Creed that was made at the Council of Constantinople in 381: "We believe . . . also in the Holy Spirit, the Lord and Giver of life, who proceedeth from the Father, who with the Father and the Son together is worshiped and glorified, who spake by the prophets." While the writings of Basil the Great, the Cappadocian bishop, are generally considered to be the primary influence behind this expansion in the Nicene Creed, it is also clear that through his correspondence with Basil (which is not extant) and his *Letters to Serapion on the Holy Spirit* Athanasius anticipated and contributed to this important theological development.

Letters to Serapion on the Holy Spirit is comprised of four rather lengthy letters, but only the first three of these are considered to be authentic. The fourth letter, which may be the compilation of an original writing by Athanasius combined with another's work, evidences a different concern and a variant theology, and hence is generally discounted.[54] Shapland, for example, considered the first half of it as stemming from the pen of Athanasius, but looked upon it as "an independent work."[55] The occasion of these letters is the request from Bishop Serapion for instruction and direction about the teaching of the heretical Tropici. This group, which might have

51. Shapland, *Letters of Saint Athanasius*, 141.

52. Ibid., 36.

53. Ibid., 85.

54. For this reason we will treat only the first three letters here.

55. Shapland, *Letters of Saint Athanasius*, 13.

been limited to the locale of Egypt,[56] accepted the full deity and full equality of the Father and Son, but refused to extend that equality to the person of the Holy Spirit.

The contents of the first three letters are rather direct. Letter I begins with a presentation of the view of the Holy Spirit (pneumatology) advanced by the Tropici. Athanasius asserted that their teaching would utterly destroy the orthodox understanding of the Holy Trinity, and if one postulated that the Holy Spirit is merely a creature, then the obvious connection between the Son and the Holy Spirit would certainly lead to making a similar assertion about the Son—and that road leads directly back to Arianism. Hence, Athanasius described his opponents as "having forsaken the Arians on account of their blasphemy against the Son of God, yet [they] oppose the Holy Spirit, saying that He is not only a creature, but actually one of the ministering spirits, and differs from the angels only in degree."[57] Thus, employing a "slippery slope" argument, the exiled bishop urged, "For if they thought correctly of the Word, they would think soundly of the Spirit also, who proceeds from the Father, and, belonging to the Son, is from Him given to the disciples and all who believe in Him. Nor, erring thus, do they so much as keep sound their faith in the Father. For those who 'resist the Spirit,' as the great martyr Stephen said, deny also the Son. But those who deny the Son have not the Father."[58]

Athanasius next examined the biblical exegesis that the Tropici used to support their position. This amounted to two main passages: Amos 4:13 (in the Septuagint reading) and 1 Timothy 5:21. The Amos 4:13 text reads, "For behold, I am he that strengthens the thunder, and creates spirit [or wind], and proclaims to man his Christ."[59] It was employed by the Tropici to assert that like the thunder and the other elements of nature, the Holy Spirit was "created" by God and therefore was not co-eternal and consubstantial with the Father. Marrying this insight to that of 1 Timothy 5:21 ("In the presence of God, and of Christ Jesus, and the elect angels, I charge you to keep these rules without favor . . .") was said to provide new insight into the nature of the Trinity—as being constituted by God the Father, Christ Jesus, and the elect angels. The Tropici viewed 1 Timothy 5:21 as a new, al-

56. Ibid., 27, and Ayres, *Nicaea and Its Legacy*, 212.

57. Shapland, *Letters of Saint Athanasius*, 59–60.

58. Ibid., 64–65.

59. In the RSV, this passage reads, "For lo, he who forms the mountains, and creates the wind, and declares to man what is his thought . . ."

ternative Trinitarian formula, to counterbalance the one in Matthew 28:19, which had long been used as the basis of orthodox Trinitarian theology.[60]

Bishop Athanasius attacked the heretical use of the Amos 4:13 passage because it presents "the spirit" without article or descriptive phrase, and every other time the Holy Spirit is referred to in the Scriptures, He/She is called "the Spirit," "the Holy Spirit," "the Spirit of God," etc., and never simply "spirit." As he wrote, "To sum up, unless the article is present, or the above-mentioned addition, it cannot refer to the Holy Spirit."[61] He attacked the heretical exegesis on 1 Timothy 5:21 in a similar manner: "The Tropici, true to their name, having made a compact with the Arians and portioned out with them the blasphemy against the Godhead, so that these may call the Son a creature, and those the Spirit—the Tropici, in their own words, have dared to devise for themselves tropes and to pervert also the saying of the Apostle that he blamelessly wrote to Timothy . . . They say that because he mentions God and Christ and then the angels, the Spirit must be counted with the angels, and belong himself to their category, and be an angel greater than the others."[62] Once again, their assertion is without scriptural basis: "Where in the Scriptures have they found the Spirit referred to as an angel?"[63] After thoroughly surveying what the Scriptures *do* say about the nature of the Holy Spirit, Athanasius concluded, "For this reason too, it is madness to call Him a creature. If He were a creature, He could not be ranked with the Triad. For the whole Triad is one God. It is enough to know that the Spirit is not a creature, nor is He numbered with the things that are made. For nothing foreign is mixed with the Triad; it is indivisible and consistent. These things are sufficient for the faithful. Thus far human knowledge goes."[64] After a lengthy and full discussion, again from Scripture passages, that the Holy Spirit is not created but in fact shares in the full Divine nature of the Father and Son, Athanasius asserted, "The Spirit, therefore, is distinct from the creatures, and is shown rather to be proper to the Son and not alien from God."[65] His final significant argument was to assert that because of the Holy Spirit's equality and shared nature, the three

60. Matt 28:19: "Go therefore and make disciples of all nations, baptizing them in the name of the Father and of the Son and of the Holy Spirit . . ."

61. Shapland, *Letters of Saint Athanasius*, 69–70.

62. Ibid., 86.

63. Ibid., 87.

64. Ibid., 103–4.

65. Ibid., 128.

Persons of the Holy Trinity act completely in concert with one another. Hence "the activity of the Triad [Trinity] is one. The Apostle does not mean that the things which are given are given differently and separately by each Person, but that what is given is given in the Triad, and that all are from the one God."[66]

Letters II and III are often taken together, as Shapland does in his edition, because they represent two halves of the same argument against the Tropici.[67] Letter II is actually more about Jesus Christ than it is about the Holy Spirit; the burden of Athanasius's argument there is to reiterate his attack upon the Arian notion that Jesus Christ, Son of God, is a creature (§§ 1–9). At the outset of Letter III, the bishop explained that he took his theological detour through Christology, in defense of the Holy Spirit, because "our Lord himself said that the Paraclete 'shall not speak from himself but what things soever he shall hear, these shall he speak . . . for he shall take of mine and shall declare it unto you'; and, 'having breathed on them,' he gave the Spirit to the disciples out of himself, and in this way the Father poured him out 'upon all flesh,' as it is written. It is natural, therefore, that I should have spoken and written first concerning the Son, that from our knowledge of the Son we may be able to have true knowledge of the Spirit. For we shall find that the Spirit has to the Son the same proper relationship as we have known the Son to have with the Father."[68] After mounting another spirited defense of the Holy Spirit, as being fully God and not a creature, Athanasius concluded Letter III by writing, "Therefore the Spirit is not a creature. As it always was, so it now is; as it now is, so it always was. It is the Triad, and therein Father, Son, and Holy Spirit. And God is one, the Father, who is 'overall and through all and in all,' who is blessed forever. Amen."[69] The exiled bishop closed by apologizing for anything that might be lacking in his epistle, and urging his reader to read it "to them that are of the household of faith [Gal 6:10], and refute those who love contention and evil speech."[70]

World politics and ecclesiastical intrigue did not come to a standstill while Athanasius was in exile among the monks of the Egyptian desert. Emperor Constantius continued in his pursuit of a unified Christian church, and to that end continued to call church councils that were designed to

66. Ibid., 142.

67. Ibid., 52–53.

68. Ibid., 169–70.

69. Ibid., 177.

70. Ibid., 178.

develop a consensus theology around the Arian doctrines that he seemed to favor. In May 359 the Fourth Council of Sirmium was convened, and it produced a compromise creed (called the Dated Creed) that was written in nontechnical terms and was designed to please all parties enmeshed in the christological debate. The result, however, was that the Dated Creed was so theologically innocuous that none of the warring parties could embrace it fervently. Later in the same year the emperor summoned two additional councils, each with the goal of completing what Nicaea had started in 325—that is, developing a unifying creed for all Christians. The Synod of Ariminum (Rimini) was held in the West during the same May, and was attended by more than four hundred bishops. The Synod of Seleucia was held in the East in October, and was attended by more than 160 bishops. Both councils developed what have been termed, over time, "semi-Arian" creeds, which affirmed that the Son, Jesus Christ, is "like the Father" (*homoi*) in substance (*ousia*); thus, *homoiousia* ("similar substance") was set forth as an alternative to the more divisive "same substance" (*homoousia*) language of the Nicene Creed. It was these developments and the decisions of the councils of Ariminum and Seleucia, which rejected the Nicene Creed and its terminology, that caused St. Jerome to pen these memorable lines: "The Nicene Faith stood condemned by acclamation. The whole world groaned, and was astonished to find itself Arian."[71]

These events drew forth from Athanasius's pen still another important document in his attack upon Arianism and apologetic campaign for the Nicene Creed: the *Councils of Ariminum and Seleucia* (*De Synodis*). It was written in 359, after the October 1 adjournment of the Council of Seleucia. Two sections of the lengthy treatise, sections 30–31, were subsequently added after the death of Constantius, in 361, and inserted into the document. The treatise is comprised of three main parts and fifty-five sections. The first part reported the background and events that led up to the two councils in question, including letters, creeds, and supporting documents. The second lengthy part surveyed the history of the Arian creeds—beginning with the *Thalia* running through the Dated Creed and the creed published by the Council of Antioch (361). In the final part, "An Appeal to the Semi-Arians," Athanasius examined the terms used in the debate, especially those that described the Son as "like the Father," and therefore "coessential" (§ 34). The Arian objection regarding the use of non-scriptural language in the creed was addressed (§ 36) and laid aside, as was the objection that

71. Jerome, *Dialogue Against the Luciferians*, NPNF, vol. VI, 329.

the Nicene Creed was obscure and liable to misunderstanding (§ 40). The balance of the third part of *De Synodis* took an apologetic posture toward those who affirmed that the Son is "of similar substance" or "like" the Father in that Athanasius sought to win over those who affirmed that both the Father and Son were "unoriginated" (§§ 46–47) and shared "like" attributes (§ 48). In short, then, "the Son is all that the Father is, except being Father" (§ 49), and if the Son is not affirmed as being "coessential" *(homoousia)* with the Father, then the fundamental unity of the Godhead is lost (§ 50).[72]

Once again, the argument about Christology and shared Divine essence was linked by Athanasius to the process of salvation (soteriology), as he argued that the Son cannot communicate to us what He does not possess within Himself—for example, the Divine essence by which we believers become "partakers of the Divine nature" through justification and sanctification. He explained, "It follows that He, being the deifying and enlightening power of the Father, in that all things are deified and quickened, is not alien in essence to the Father, but coessential. For by partaking of Him, we partake of the Father; because that the Word is the Father's own."[73] Based on this argumentation, Athanasius concluded that "coessential" was a term much more suited for correct affirmation of the relationship of the Father and the Son (§ 53), and therefore that "this is why the Nicene Council was correct in writing, what it was becoming to say, that the Son, begotten from the Father's essence, is coessential with Him."[74] If those who affirm the "likeness" *(homoiousia)* of the Father and Son are really affirming the same doctrine as those who assert that they are "coessential" *(homoousia)*, then they should not scruple in using the more appropriate terms of the Nicene Creed to affirm their "coessential" unity.[75]

About this same period of time, Athanasius penned a second letter to the monks, "to those who practice a solitary life, and are settled in faith in God, most beloved brethren . . ."[76] In this brief epistle he continued his attack against Arianism by warning the monks against the doctrine of Arian evangelists who go about among the monasteries to try to win them over to their own point of view. Furthermore, they should be careful not to worship with the Arians, so that others are not led astray by their example: "For

72. See *NPNF*, vol. IV, 449–77.
73. *Councils of Ariminum and Seleucia* 51, *NPNF*, vol. IV, 477.
74. *Councils of Ariminum and Seleucia* 54, *NPNF*, vol. IV, 479.
75. Ibid.
76. *Letter* 53, *NPNF*, vol. IV, 564.

when any sees you, the faithful in Christ, associate and communicate with such people . . . certainly they will think it is a matter of indifference and will fall into the mire of irreligion."[77] Therefore, the monks must have no fellowship or communion with the heretics, and they should admonish those among themselves who do; if such a person persists in their wrong-doing, then they should separate themselves from him as well.[78]

Athanasius's "third exile," in the Egyptian desert, was one of his most productive periods from a literary and theological standpoint. He kept well abreast of events in the Egyptian church and directed the orthodox community from afar through his various friends and associates there. Given his own monastic proclivities, his four years away from his post in the city might have actually been more like a lengthy sabbatical that rekindled his own spiritual strength and was a tonic to his resolve. In his monastic seclusion Athanasius not only produced some of his most important and popular theological works, but he also contributed significantly to the theological reflection upon the full divinity and equality of the Holy Spirit—a conversation that was absolutely necessary for the subsequent affirmation of the Nicene doctrine of the Holy Trinity, at the Council of Constantinople, in 381.

77. Ibid.
78. Ibid.

11

The Final Years

World events marched on as the great Athanasius worked in seclusion in the Egyptian desert. Sozomen, the gossipy Christian historian, reported that the bishop lived in seclusion in the home of a holy virgin in the city of Alexandria, though the duration of seven years Sozomen mentioned is unprovable. However, there is an indication that the bishop may have visited the city and hidden himself there from time to time during his exile.[1] But once again world politics intervened in Athanasius's life and ecclesiastical fortunes.

"Julian the Philosopher" was a cousin of Constantius and Caeasar in the West. He was extremely successful in his military campaigns in Europe and was immensely popular with his Gallic troops. After a significant military victory he was proclaimed "Emperor" by his troops, in Thrace, and began to march on Constantinople to claim the capital and throne as his prize. Constantius, who was living in Antioch at this time, had taken ill. He was so ill that he had himself baptized by the Arian bishop of Antioch, Euzoius, and then immediately prepared to undertake a military expedition against Julius. But he died en route, on November 3, 361, having reigned for thirty-eight years, twenty-five of which he was sole emperor of the entire Roman world.[2] He begrudgingly left the throne to his uncle Julian.

Julian had been raised as a Christian but was seduced into paganism through his extensive studies in classical Greco-Roman literature and philosophy. And though he had also studied the sacred texts of the Christians, he considered himself a philosopher more than a Christian. Julian had passed himself off as a practicing Christian when that was advantageous to

1. Sozomen, *Church History* IV.6, *NPNF*, vol. II, 330.
2. Socrates, *Church History* II.47, *NPNF*, vol. II, 75.

him. He eventually showed his true colors, however, and he began persecuting Christians and favoring the traditional religions of Rome. This practice earned Julian the distasteful epithet of "the Apostate" from the Christian historians, since apostasy describes the process of willfully renouncing one's Christian faith.

Upon becoming sole emperor, Julian initially pursued a policy of toleration toward both Christians and non-Christians in the empire. This encouraged both Christians and pagans, in Alexandria, to struggle for control of the city. George the Cappadocian, who had been appointed bishop of the city following the exile of Athanasius, attempted to lead the Christians in transforming a site that had been dedicated to Mithra—a location of human sacrifice—into a sacred site for Christian worship and for the construction of a new church. When the Christians discovered human remains in their excavation of the site, they marched through the streets of the city, displaying human skulls to shame and embarrass the pagans with the atrocities and abominations of the Mithraeum. The non-Christians of the city responded with much violence and attacked the Christians with whatever weapon came to hand: "Some they killed with the sword, others with clubs and stones; some they strangled with ropes, others they crucified, purposely inflicting this last kind of death in contempt of the cross of Christ."[3] Neither friends nor relatives, nor women and children, were spared by the wrath of the mob and the shedding of blood. Hence, the Christians stopped trying to cleanse the site of Mithrite worship, and "the pagans meanwhile having dragged George out of the church, fastened him to a camel, and when they had torn him to pieces, they burnt him together with the camel."[4] Julian remonstrated the people of Alexandria through an imperial letter telling them to behave better than this, as their heritage as Greeks would befit them, but he did not otherwise intervene in those events.

With the rise of Emperor Julian and the violent passing of Bishop George, Athanasius returned to the city of Alexandria and took possession of the episcopal see. As Socrates reported, "Athanasius returning from his exile, was received with great joy by the people of Alexandria. They expelled at that time the Arians from the churches, and restored Athanasius to possession of them. The Arians meanwhile assembling themselves in low

---

3. Socrates, *Church History* III.2, *NPNF*, vol. II, 79.
4. Ibid.

and obscure buildings, ordained Lucius to supply the place of George. Such was the state of things at that time at Alexandria."[5]

Soon after his return to Alexandria, Athanasius called a synod, with the cooperation of the Western bishop known as Eusebius (a third person named Eusebius!). Bishops assembled from various cities to consider matters that were of "the utmost importance." Socrates summarized their work in this way: "They asserted the divinity of the Holy Spirit and comprehended him in the consubstantial Trinity; they also declared that the Word in being made man, assumed not only flesh, but also a soul, in accordance with the views of the early ecclesiastics. For they did not introduce any new doctrine of their own devising into the church, but contented themselves with recording their sanction of those points which ecclesiastical tradition has insisted on from the beginning, and wise Christians have demonstratively taught."[6] This synod also directed an epistle to the church at Antioch that urged them to remain faithful to the Nicene faith and to overcome the divisions by which that church was riven. Bishops Eusebius and Asterius were sent bearing the synodical letter to Antioch "for many reasons, but chiefly that we might embrace your affection and together enjoy the said peace and concord."[7]

The letter detailed orthodox teaching in the face of the current heresies, particularly with respect to the blasphemy against the Holy Spirit that had been perpetuated by the Meletians (3), and "to anathematize those who say that the Holy Spirit is a Creature and separate from the Essence of Christ. For this is in truth a complete renunciation of the abominable heresy of Arius, to refuse to divide the Holy Trinity, or to say that any part of it is a creature."[8] This same letter expressed joy (4) at the prospect of theological reunion among those who embraced the theology of "the Old church" and who did not teach anything else than "the Nicene definition."[9] The creed of the Council of Serdica was attacked (5) as being unauthorized and deficient, since it left room for the beliefs of "the Arian madmen." And once again, the Nicene Creed was upheld as the only suitable and authorized definition of the relationship of the three persons of the holy Trinity.[10]

5. *Church History* III.4, *NPNF*, vol. II, 80.

6. *Church History* III.7, *NPNF*, vol. II, 81.

7. Athanasius, *Letter to the Church of Antioch* 2, *NPNF*, vol. IV, 483.

8. *Letter to the Church of Antioch* 3, *NPNF*, vol. IV, 484.

9. *Letter to the Church of Antioch* 4, *NPNF*, vol. IV, 484.

10. *Letter to the Church of Antioch* 5, *NPNF*, vol. IV, 484.

The question of whether there is one "substance" (*hypostasis*) or three was viewed as a divine mystery that need not be pressed so long as one affirms that there is one God, Who has one nature, and Who takes expression in three consubstantial persons, as Father, Son and Holy Spirit (6). The full and true humanity of Jesus Christ was affirmed (7) in terms that paraphrased the Scriptures: "And being Son of God in truth, He became also Son of Man, and being God's Only-begotten Son, He became also at the same time 'firstborn among many brethren' [Rom 8:29]."[11]

Once these fundamental Christian truths are affirmed, questions of particular terminology must not be allowed to divide those Christians who think alike in orthodox doctrine (8). So saying, the letter, sent under the leadership of Athanasius, urged that the disputes among them should not amount to a discussion about mere words or pet phrases but should in fact be focused upon the unity that is to be found in apostolic, orthodox doctrine. The epistle mused, "Perhaps God will have pity on us, and unite what is divided, and, there being once more one flock, we shall all have one leader, even our Lord Jesus Christ."[12] These things were universally agreed upon by the synod, and the letter closed by once again holding up the Nicene Creed as a rallying point and a foundation upon which to build Christian unity. The epistle declared, "These things, albeit there was no need to require anything beyond the synod of Nicaea, nor to tolerate the language of contention, yet for the sake of peace, and to prevent the rejection of men who wish to believe aright, we enquired into."[13] These questions, therefore, have been adequately answered in the Creed, and insofar as Christians can embrace the doctrine of the Nicene Creed, they should also be able to embrace each other, regardless of the terms and phrases they might use to explain it. The letter was received and signed by Paulinus, the bishop, and by other representatives of the church of Antioch, and returned to Alexandria along with a highly orthodox statement of faith attached. Not only did that statement affirm the full deity and consubstantial nature of all three persons of the Trinity, it also anathematized those who affirmed otherwise.[14]

Meanwhile, Julian had begun earning his nickname, "the Apostate," by bringing persecution upon the Christians. He had come to the conclusion that his previous policy of toleration had not had its desired effects,

---

11. *Letter to the Church of Antioch 7, NPNF*, vol. IV, 485.

12. *Letter to the Church of Antioch 8, NPNF*, vol. IV, 485.

13. *Letter to the Church of Antioch 9, NPNF*, vol. IV, 485.

14. *Letter to the Church of Antioch 10–11, NPNF*, vol. IV, 486.

namely, the weakening of Christianity (through division) and the return to the traditional Greco-Roman religions. Not only did he single out individual Christians for persecution, he passed laws that dealt unfairly with Christians. This was done through taxation of church property and through various prohibitions—such as forbidding Christians to embark upon literary pursuits.[15] Socrates described how Julian carried out this process, partly by interdicts, partly by flattery, and partly by outright oppression:

> He moreover interdicted such as would not abjure Christianity, and offer sacrifice to idols, from holding office at court: nor would he allow Christians to be governors of provinces; "for," said he, "their law forbids them to use the sword against offenders worthy of capital punishment." He also induced many to sacrifice, partly by flatteries, and partly by gifts. Immediately, as if tried in a furnace, it at once became evident to all, who were the real Christians, and who were merely nominal ones. Such as were Christians in integrity of heart, very readily resigned their commission, choosing to endure anything rather than deny Christ. Of this number were Jovian, Valentinian, and Valens, each of whom afterwards became emperor.[16]

The non-Christians, being now free to practice their impious rites, including even human sacrifice, returned to them in vast numbers. Socrates reported that "these infamous rites were practiced in other cities, but more particularly at Athens and Alexandria; in which latter place, a calumnious accusation was made against Athanasius the bishop, the emperor being assured that he was intent on desolating not that city only, but all Egypt, and that nothing but his expulsion out of the country could save it. The governor of Alexandria was therefore instructed by imperial edict to apprehend him."[17] Sozomen reported the same event, in greater detail:

> The emperor, on being informed that Athanasius held meetings in the church of Alexandria, and taught the people boldly, and converted many pagans to Christianity, commanded him, under the severest penalties, to depart from Alexandria. The pretext made use of for enforcing this edict, was that Athanasius, after having been banished by Constantius, had resumed his episcopal see without the sanction of the reigning emperor [Julian]; for Julian

---

15. Socrates, *Church History* III.11–12, *NPNF*, vol. II, 84–85; Sozomen, *Church History* V.15–20, *NPNF*, vol. II, 336–42.

16. Socrates, *Church History* III.13, *NPNF* vol. II, 85.

17. Ibid., 86.

declared that he had never contemplated restoring the bishops who had been exiled by Constantius to their ecclesiastical functions, but only to their native land.[18]

Hence, eight months after returning from his exile in the desert, Athanasius began his fourth exile; once again he retired to the Egyptian desert. During this period of exile, the tenor of the Eastern Church began to change, and Athanasius's efforts on behalf of Christian orthodoxy began to change with it. As Barnes pointed out, "Between 356 and 362 the exiled bishop was transformed from a proud prelate with a dubious reputation into an elder statesman renowned for his heroic defense of Nicene orthodoxy."[19]

Emperor Julian's reign was nearly as brief as was Athanasius's return to Alexandria. In summer of the year following the bishop's exile, on June 26, 363, Julian died of wounds he received in battle during his unsuccessful military campaign against Persia. Timothy Barnes pointed out, "Julian's death in Persia soon provided [Athanasius] with yet another proof that God intervened actively in human affairs to protect both the true faith and Athanasius himself."[20] In a quandary, the army declared Jovian to be the next Roman emperor, and he immediately sued for peace with the Persians, which was achieved on the basis of humiliating terms. An orthodox Christian, Jovian established Christianity as the state religion of the empire and recalled the influential Christian bishops who had been exiled by his predecessor. Athanasius was among those bishops who received a letter of recall from Emperor Jovian, and the text of that letter is carried in Athanasius's collected works:

> Admiring exceedingly the achievements of your most honorable life, and of your likeness to the God of all, and your affection toward our Savior Christ, we accept you, most honored bishop. And inasmuch as you have not flinched from all labor, nor from the fear of your persecutors, and, regarding dangers and threats of the sword as dung, holding the rudder of the orthodox faith which is dear to you, are contending even until now for the truth, and continue to exhibit yourself as a pattern to all the people of the faithful, and an example of virtue:—our imperial Majesty recalls you, and desires that you should return to the office of the teaching of salvation. Return then to the holy Churches, and tend the people of God, and send up to God with zeal your prayers for our

18. Sozomen, *Church History* V.15, *NPNF*, vol. II, 136.
19. Barnes, *Athanasius and Constantius*, 152.
20. Ibid., 159.

clemency. For we know that by your supplication we, and all who hold with us [the Christian faith], shall have great assistance from the Supreme God.[21]

Athanasius responded to Jovian's epistle with gratitude and with celebration. He was particularly glad that, unlike his predecessor, the new emperor desired "to learn from us the faith of the Catholic Church, giving thanks for these things to the Lord, we counselled above all things to remind your Piety of the faith confessed by the Fathers at Nicaea. For this certain [people] set at nought, while plotting against us in many ways, because we would not comply with the Arian heresy, and they have become authors of heresy and schisms in the Catholic Church."[22]

Athanasius's epistle to Jovian gave a brief recounting of the roots and teaching of Arianism and urged Jovian to stand against it as well as the new heresy that taught that the Holy Spirit was also merely a creature: "since now certain [people] who wish to renew the Arian heresy have presumed to set at nought the faith confessed at Nicaea by the Fathers, and while pretending to confess it, do in fact deny it, explaining away the 'Coessential' [*homoousia*], and blaspheming of their own accord against the Holy Spirit, in affirming that It is a creature, and came into being as a thing made by the Son, we hasten as of bounden duty, in view of the injury resulting to the people from such blasphemy, to hand to your Piety the faith confessed at Nicaea . . ."[23] Thus, the Nicene Creed, which was enclosed in this epistle, was to be esteemed as a foundation for orthodox Christian unity, as well as a bulwark against heresy (both old and new).

The letter closed by reiterating the absolute necessity, demonstrated by the Fathers of Nicaea, that the church affirm the "coessential" nature of the Father, Son, and Holy Spirit. "For they have not merely said that the Son is like the Father, lest He should be believed merely [to be] like God, instead of Very God from God; but they wrote 'Coessential,' which was peculiar to a genuine and true Son, truly and naturally from the Father. Nor yet did they make the Holy Spirit alien from the Father and the Son, but rather glorified Him together with the Father and the Son, in the one faith of the Holy Triad, because there is in the Holy Triad also one Godhead."[24]

---

21. *Letter 56, NPNF*, vol. IV, 567.

22. Ibid.

23. Ibid., 568.

24. Ibid.

Jovian recalled all of the Christian bishops who had been exiled by Julian for religious reasons. He decreed that the pagan temples be shut up, and the philosophers who had been granted special privileges under Julian had them taken away. Some of the Christian bishops tried to extract a new creed from Jovian, but he refused to promulgate a new creed; being a proponent of the "consubstantial" theology of the Nicene Creed, he pointed these bishops to it as the basis of orthodoxy and Christian unity. It was also at this time that the churches of Macedonia and Acacia met together in synods and declared their assent to the *homoousian* theology of the Nicene Creed.[25]

In the immediate context of Athanasius's letter and its sentiments, several Alexandrian Arians (principally Lucius and Bernicianus) made petitions to the new emperor, against Athanasius. The first of these was: "May it please your Might and your Majesty, give us a Bishop." The emperor replied by saying, "I ordered the former one, whom you had before, Athanasius, to occupy the See." The Arians retorted, "May it please your Might: he has been many years both in banishment, and under accusation." A solider who was standing nearby interjected, "May it please your Majesty, enquire of them who they are and where from, for these are the leavings and refuse of Cappadocia, the remains of that unholy George who desolated the city and the world." Upon hearing this, Jovian spurred on his horse and began to ride away from the petitioners.[26]

But a second petition came quickly after the first: "We have accusations and clear proofs against Athanasius, in that ten and twenty years ago he was deprived by the ever memorable Constantine and Constantius, and incurred banishment under the most religious and philosophical and blessed Julian." Emperor Jovian replied, "Accusations ten, twenty, and thirty years old are now obsolete. Don't speak to me about Athanasius, for I know why he was accused, and how he was banished."[27]

The Arians urged, a third time, "May it please you, any one you will except Athanasius." The emperor replied, "I told you that the case of Athanasius was already settled . . . I took pains, and ascertained that he holds right opinions and is orthodox, and teaches aright." The Arians replied, "With his mouth he utters what is right but in his soul he harbors guile." The Emperor retorted, "That will do, you have testified of him, that he utters

25. Socrates, *Church History* III.24, *NPNF*, vol. II, 94.

26. Appendix to *Letter* 56, *NPNF*, vol. IV, 568.

27. Ibid.

what is right and teaches aright, but if he teaches and speaks aright with his tongue, but harbors evil thoughts in his soul, it concerns him before God. For we are men, and hear what is said; but what is in the heart God knows." Upon being charged with the same duplicity they would cast upon Athanasius, the Arians requested, "Authorize our holding communion together." To that the emperor replied, "Why, who prevents you?" The Arians replied, "May it please you, he proclaims us as sectarians and dogmatizers." To this Jovian retorted, "It is his duty and that of those who teach aright." Exasperated, the Arians pleaded, "May it please your Might; we cannot bear this man, and he has taken away the lands of the Churches." The emperor then concluded, "Oh, then it is on account of property you are come here, and not on account of the faith . . . Go away to the Church. Tomorrow you have a Communion, and after the dismissal, there are Bishops here . . . [and] Athanasius is here too; whoever does not know the word of faith, let him learn from Athanasius."[28]

Two lawyers among the Arians made charges against Athanasius as well; one claimed that the bishop had authorized the Receiver-General to seize his place of residence. To the one, Jovian responded curtly, "What has that to do with Athanasius?" To the other man, "What have you to do with Christians, being a heathen?" When the emperor learned that Lucius himself wanted to become bishop of Alexandria, he concluded the interview with a benediction of sorts: "May the God of the world, and the radiant sun, and moon, be angry with those men that made the voyage with you, for not casting you into the sea; and may that ship never again have fair winds, nor find a haven with her passengers when in a storm." After that, it is said, Jovian had those eunuchs punished who had granted the Arians access to him, and said, "If anyone wants to make a petition against Christians let this be his fate."[29]

Rufinus, the Christian historian, summarized the reign of Jovian succinctly: "He did not act heedlessly like Constantius; warned by his predecessor's fall, he summoned Athanasius with a respectful and most dutiful letter. He received from him a creed and a plan for ordering the churches. But an early death ruined these so religious and happy beginnings; eight months after his accession, he died in Cilicia."[30] The means of Jovian's sudden death is debated; it is sometimes said to have come from eating poison

28. Ibid., 568–69.
29. Ibid., 569.
30. Rufinus, *Church History* XI.1, 63.

mushrooms, while others suggest that he died in his sleep from the carbon monoxide fumes of his charcoal fire.[31] Be that as it may, Jovian's sudden death brought Athanasius's stay in Alexandria to an equally sudden end.

Upon the death of Jovian, the army declared Valentinian emperor in 364, and the new emperor named his brother Valens to be his colleague in ruling the world. Valentinian ruled the West, whereas Valens oversaw the East, from his dominion in Constantinople. As Socrates reported, "They both professed Christianity, but did not hold the same Christian creed; for Valentinian respected the Nicene Creed; but Valens was prepossessed in favor of the Arian opinions."[32] While both men were zealous for their own theological position and religious party, they conducted themselves and their public religious policy differently. "Valentinian, while he favored those who agreed with him in sentiment, offered no violence to the Arians; but Valens in his anxiety to promote the Arian cause, grievously disturbed those who differed from them . . ."[33] After consolidating his rule in the East by defeating the "usurper" Procopius of Constantinople, Valens began to suppress orthodox Christianity in the East and instituted Arianism wherever he could. His vengeance against the recent synods of Antioch and Macedonia (which had affirmed the Nicene Creed) and its framers was particularly acute. The Christian historian Rufinus reported that "during this time the church shone with a purer light than gold in the fire of persecution. For the faith of each was tried not in words but in exiles and imprisonments, since being Catholic was not a matter of honor but of punishment, especially in Alexandria, where the faithful were not even free to bury the bodies of the dead."[34] As orthodox bishops were being arrested, exiled, and banished throughout the East, Athanasius spent four months hiding in an ancestral tomb. Once again Athanasius escaped the clutches of his political and ecclesiastical enemies by what seemed to be an imposition of divine providence. Sozomen explained,

> The governor of Egypt and the military chief took possession of the church in which Athanasius generally dwelt, and sought him in every part of the edifice, and even on the roof, but in vain; for they had calculated upon seizing the moment when the popular commotion had partially subsided, and when the whole city was

31. Sozomen, *Church History* VI.6, *NPNF*, vol. II, 349.

32. Socrates, *Church History* IV.1, *NPNF*, vol. II, 96.

33. Ibid.

34. Rufinus, *Church History* XI.6, 67–68.

wrapped in sleep, to execute the mandate of the emperor, and to transport Athanasius from the city.

Not to have found Athanasius naturally excited universal astonishment. Some attributed his escape to a special revelation from above; others to the advice of some of his followers; both had the same result; but more than human prudence seems to have been requisite to foresee and to avoid such a plot.[35]

The people of the city had so much affection for their bishop and were so perplexed by his absence that they petitioned the emperor in support of Athanasius's work in Alexandria. Valens soon wrote to grant permission for Athanasius to return to his see. Sozomen opined that the influence of Valentinian that might have caused this change in policy: "I rather imagine that, on reflecting on the esteem in which Athanasius was universally held, he feared to excite the displeasure of the Emperor Valentinian, who was well known to be attached to the Nicene doctrines; or perhaps he was apprehensive of a commotion on the part of many admirers of the bishop, lest some innovation injure the public affairs."[36] Socrates embraced the latter opinion, reporting that since "the people, on account of their affection for him, became seditious in impatience of his absence, the emperor, on ascertaining that on this account agitation prevailed at Alexandria, ordered by his letters that Athanasius should be suffered to preside over the churches without molestation; and this was the reason why the Alexandrian church enjoyed tranquility until the death of Athanasius."[37] Despite his sympathy and actions in support of the Arian position, Valens preferred tranquility to riots and insurrection, so he allowed Athanasius to finish his days in Alexandria and at peace.

During these later years Athanasius's literary work and ecclesiastical leadership continued nearly unabated. In circa 369 he called a synod of the African bishops that was attended by more than ninety clerics from Egypt and Libya. The purpose of this synod was to affirm the finality of the Nicene Creed as the preeminent definition of Christian orthodoxy and unity, over against the deficient creed that had been recently produced by the Council of Ariminum. The report of the bishops of Africa was summarized as an encyclical letter (titled *Ad Afros Epistola Synodica*) and sent west to Pope Damasus of Rome, to confirm the orthodox faith and to confess their own

35. Sozomen, *Church History* VI.12, *NPNF*, vol. II, 354.
36. Ibid.
37. Socrates, *Church History* IV.13, *NPNF*, vol. II, 103.

faith, as enshrined in the Nicene Creed. Athanasius is generally credited with writing *To the Africans* (*Ad Afros*), and he stated his purpose quite clearly: "Since we have heard that certain [people] wishing to oppose it [the Nicene Creed] are attempting to cite a synod supposed to have been held at Ariminum, and are eagerly striving that it should prevail rather than the other, we think it right to write and put you in mind, not to endure anything of the sort; for this is nothing else but a second growth of the Arian heresy. For what else do they wish for who reject the synod held against it, namely the Nicene, if not that the cause of Arius should prevail?"[38] The lengthy letter that followed falls into ten additional subsections:

1. The Ecumenical Synod of Nicaea was contrasted with the local synods that had been held ever since.

2. The true nature of the proceedings of the Synod of Ariminum was disclosed.

3. The Nicene Creed and its Trinitarian theology were demonstrated as being completely in accordance with holy Scripture.

4. It was explained how the term "consubstantial" (*homoousia*) came to be used and adopted by the Council of Nicaea.

5. This "consubstantial" test was proven not to be unscriptural, and was not a theological novelty.

6. It was demonstrated that the position that the Son is a Creature is inconsistent with Christian teaching and is untenable.

7. It was demonstrated that the Son's relationship to the Father is one of shared essential nature, and not only of ethical loyalty.

8. It was urged that the full repudiation of Arianism involves the acceptance of the Nicene test (*homoousia*) and Creed.

9. It was admitted that one purpose of this letter was to warn against the false teaching of Auxentius of Milan.

10. The full Deity of the Holy Spirit was also affirmed in the Nicene Creed.

This was an important synodical letter, sent under the direction (and probably pen) of Athanasius of Alexandria. It was a summary and repudiation of the Arian heresy that both looked back to Nicaea and the Creed that the first ecumenical council produced, but also looked ahead to the second

38. Athanasius, *To the Bishops of Africa* 1, *NPNF*, vol. IV, 489.

ecumenical council, which would be called at Constantinople in 381. There the Nicene Creed would be embraced and affirmed and language about the full Deity and equality of the Holy Spirit would be added.

Among his other literary production were several extant letters to various bishops and church leaders. A notable example of these was his letter to "Adelphius, Bishop and Confessor: Against the Arians."[39] In this epistle Athanasius wrote to confirm the faith of Adelphius, bishop of Onuphis, and to urge him to remain resolute against the Arian heresy. In this lengthy letter the bishop repeatedly attacked the "error [that] belongs to heathens and Arians" that Christians worship a creature. He wrote, "But we worship the Lord of Creation, Incarnate, the Word of God. For if the flesh also is in itself a part of the created world, yet it has become God's body. And we neither divide the body, being such from the Word, and worship it, by itself, nor when we wish to worship the Word do we set Him apart from the Flesh, but knowing, as we said above, that 'the Word was made flesh,' we recognize Him as God also, after having come in the flesh."[40] In fact, the flesh of Jesus Christ, the Word, is indispensable, not only as part of His Incarnation, but as a part of God's plan of salvation: "For the flesh did not diminish the glory of the Word; far be the thought: on the contrary, it was glorified by Him. Nor, because the Son that was in the form of God took upon Him the form of a servant was He deprived of His Godhead. On the contrary, He is thus become the Deliverer of all flesh and of all creation."[41] And so with a characteristic emphasis, which he had maintained since writing *On the Incarnation* at the beginning of his journey, Athanasius wrote, "For He has become Man, that He might deify us in Himself, and He has been born of a woman, and begotten of a Virgin, in order to transfer to Himself our erring generation, and that we may become henceforth a holy race, and 'partakers of the Divine Nature.'"[42]

In a second letter, this one to Maximus, the Cynic philosopher, perhaps written in 371, Athanasius urged a similar theological connection between Incarnation and Salvation: "For neither does Nature know of a virgin bearing apart from a man. Whence by the good pleasure of the Father, being true God, and Word and Wisdom of the Father by nature, He became man in the body for our salvation, in order that having somewhat to offer

---

39. Athanasius, *Letter 60*, *NPNF*, vol. IV, 575–78.

40. Ibid., 575.

41. Ibid., 576.

42. Ibid.

for us He might save us all, 'as many as through fear of death were all their lifetime subject to bondage' [Heb 2:15]."[43] Hence, the bishop pointed his reader to the Nicene Creed as an apt summary of the Christian faith: "For let what was confessed by the Fathers at Nicaea prevail. For it is correct, and enough to overthrow every heresy however impious, and especially that of the Arians which speaks against the Word of God, and as a logical consequence profanes His Holy Spirit."[44]

During these same closing years Athanasius seemed increasingly drawn to study of and commentary on the Holy Scriptures. In his thirty-ninth *Festal Letter* (367), he criticized the Meletians for using non-inspired books and delineated—in an authoritative manner—the scope of the New Testament canon. In one of the first delineations of what would become the canonical New Testament, the bishop wrote,

> Again, it is not tedious to speak of the [books] of the New Testament. These are, the four Gospels, according to Matthew, Mark, Luke and John. Afterwards, the Acts of the Apostles and Epistles (called Catholic), seven, viz. of James, one; of Peter, two; of John, three; after these, one of Jude. In addition, there are fourteen Epistles of Paul, written in this order. The first, to the Romans; then two to the Corinthians; after these, to the Galatians; next, to the Ephesians; then to the Philippians; then to the Colossians; after these, two to the Thessalonians, and that to the Hebrews; and again, two to Timothy; one to Titus; and lastly, that to Philemon. And besides, the Revelation of John.[45]

As to the authority of these canonical books, Athanasius added, "These are the fountains of salvation, that they who thirst may be satisfied with the living words they contain. In these alone is proclaimed the doctrine of godliness. Let no man add to these, neither let him take ought from these."[46] He also penned an important and lengthy (more than thirty pages in translation) pastoral letter to an ill friend, Marcellinus, on how to interpret the Psalms. Marcellinus, reported the writer, had set himself to learning what was truly taught in each psalm, and Athanasius—his archbishop—wrote to help him along in that commendable task. Marcellinus had embraced the

---

43. Athanasius, *Letter* 51, *NPNF*, vol. IV, 579.

44. Ibid.

45. Athanasius, *Festal Letter* 39, *NPNF*, vol. IV, 552.

46. Ibid.

study of the Psalms as a part of his "discipline," which implies it was a part of his daily monastic regimen.

The *Letter to Marcellinus on the Interpretation of the Psalms* begins with a strong affirmation of the inspiration and usefulness of the Psalms. Athanasius wrote, paraphrasing 2 Timothy 3:16, "All Scripture of ours, my son—both ancient and new—is inspired by God and profitable for teaching, as it is written. But the book of Psalms possesses a certain winning exactitude for those who are prayerful. Each sacred book supplies and announces its own promise . . . Yet the book of Psalms is like a garden containing things of all these kinds, and it sets them to music, but also exhibits things of its own that it gives in song along with them."[47] The bishop saw the Psalms as a repository of biblical truth and promises that encompassed the rest of the Hebrew Scriptures and set their salient themes to song, as well as making their own unique spiritual contribution. Thus, Athanasius spent considerable time and care delineating how it was that the individual psalms reflected the main themes of the various books of the Old Testament (in §§ 1–14), encompassing and including the Law, Prophets, and historical books.

The second major concern and interpretive lens he urged upon Marcellinus was to look at the Psalms from the standpoint of the "soul's course of life." He wrote, "For as one who comes into the presence of a king assumes a certain attitude, both of posture and expression, lest speaking differently he be thrown out as boorish, so also to know the one who is running the race of virtue and wishing to know the life of the Savior in the body the sacred book first calls to mind the emotions of the soul through the reading and in this way represents the other things in succession, and teaches the readers by those words."[48] Thus the Psalms are to be sung and prayed as expressions of one's own soul's quest for Christian virtue and truth. There are some that teach us how to pray with confession and petition (Pss 18, 43, 48, 49, 72, 76, 88, 89, 106, 113, 126, and 136).[49] Other psalms urge and prescribe along with prophecy (Pss 28, 32, 80, 94–97, 102, 103, and 113), while some combine the expression of exhortation with praise of God (Ps 149). Many simply express praise (Pss 90, 112, 116, 134, 144, 145, 146, 148, 150), while

47. Gregg, *Life of Antony and the Letter to Marcellinus*, 101–2.

48. Ibid., 112–13.

49. Athanasius's numbers are taken from the Septuagint (LXX) or Greek translation of the Psalms; to find these psalm numbers in a modern English version, add one to the LXX number.

others involve the singer and prayer in the expression of joyful thanksgiving (Pss 8, 9, 17, 33, 45, 63, 76, 84, 114, 115, 120, 121, 123, 128, and 143). And a few psalms promise blessedness to the singer (Pss 1, 31, 40, 118, and 127). Some psalms exhort the singer to courage (Ps 80), while others lay charges against those who are impious and lawless (Pss 2, 13, 35, 51, and 52). There are psalms that teach a person to announce supplications to God (Pss 19 and 63), as well as those that teach one to boast in the Lord (Pss 22, 26, 38, 39, 41, 61, 75, 83, 96, 98, and 151).[50] A few psalms are designed to arouse a sense of shame in their singers (Pss 47, 64), and one (Ps 65) speaks of resurrection in words of exultation.[51] Thus, the Psalter is to be employed as a handbook and a model, as well as a tool for instilling Christian spiritual life within a person.

For the circumspect reader, singer and prayer, the Psalms are a medicine for what ails the human soul. They give voice to our yearnings to thank and praise God, as well as our supplications in times of need and extremity. Hence, Athanasius urged, "When you behold the Savior's grace, which has been extended everywhere, and the human race, which has been rescued, if you wish to address the Lord, sing the eighth [Psalm]."[52] Or, "Let us say you stand in need of a prayer because of those who have oppressed you and encompass your soul: sing Psalms 16, 85, 87, and 140."[53] And again, "But you sinned, and being ashamed, you repent and you ask to be shown mercy. You have in Psalm 50 the words of confession and repentance."[54] And, "Whenever you want to celebrate God in song, recite the things in Psalm 64. And if you wish to instruct some people about the resurrection, sing the words in Psalm 65."[55]

For Athanasius and those who followed him in this practice of reading and singing the Psalms with an eye to their spiritual expression and theological payload, the Psalter became a living handbook for growing Christian spirituality and for gaining full salvation. He concluded of this process for studying the Psalms,

> "I will meditate on Your ordinances; I will not forget your words" [Ps 118:6]. And again, "Your ordinances were my songs in the place

50. Gregg, *Life of Antony and the Letter to Marcellinus*, 113–14.

51. Ibid.

52. Ibid., 115.

53. Ibid.

54. Ibid., 118.

55. Ibid., 119.

of my sojourning" [Ps 118:54]. For in those they were gaining salvation, saying, "Were it not that your law is my meditation, then I should have perished in my affection" [Ps 118:92]. It was for this reason also that Paul fortified his own disciple [Timothy] by these things, saying "Practice these duties, devote yourself to them, so that your progress may become manifest" [1 Tim 4:15]. You too, practicing these things and reciting the Psalms intelligently in this way, are able to comprehend the meaning of each, being guided by the Spirit. And the kind of life the holy, God-bearing men possessed who spoke these things—this life you also shall imitate.[56]

The great Athanasius died peacefully on May 3, 373. The Christian historian Rufinus of Aquileia recorded his passing with these words: "During this time, then, in the forty-sixth year of his priesthood, Athanasius, after many struggles and many crowns of suffering, rested in peace."[57] Like Moses before him, Athanasius died before he managed to bring God's people into the rest they sought. Turmoil continued to assail the church of Alexandria as Bishop Peter—Athanasius's named successor—was driven out by the riotous attacks of the Arians of the city, led by Lucius their bishop.[58]

Peace and unity finally came to the Eastern Church in 380, when Theodosius I (347–95) became sole Roman emperor. A westerner, he was a staunch supporter of Nicene orthodoxy, after nearly half a century of emperors who favored Arianism. Shortly after his elevation to the throne he declared that the orthodox Christian faith taught by the bishop of Rome was the correct faith. As Sozomen reported, "The emperor [Theodosius] soon after convenend a council of orthodox bishops, for the purpose of confirming the decrees of Nicaea and of electing a bishop to the vacant see of Constantinople."[59] Hence, in 381 Theodosius ordered all churches in the empire to be placed in the hands of clergy who affirmed the Nicene Creed. "He enacted," Sozomen recorded, "that the title of 'Catholic Church' should be exclusively confined to those who rendered equal homage to the Three Persons of the Trinity, and that those individuals who entertained opposite opinions should be treated as heretics, regarded with contempt, and delivered over to punishment."[60]

56. Ibid., 129.

57. Rufinus, *Church History* XI.3, 64.

58. Ibid.

59. Sozomen, *Church History* VII.7, *NPNF*, vol. II, 380.

60. Sozomen, *Church History* VII.4, *NPNF*, vol. II, 378.

In May of the same year, Theodosius called the first ecumenical Council of Constantinople, which was led by Gregory of Nazianzus (329–90), who was elected archbishop of Constantinople and served in that capacity until 390. The council affirmed the Nicene Creed as the standard definition of Christian faith and strongly condemned Arianism. It also added the final clause to the Nicene Creed that emphasized the full deity and full equality of the Holy Spirit. It read as follows: "And in the Holy Spirit, the Lord and Giver of life, Who proceeds from the Father, Who with the Father and the Son is together worshipped and together glorified, Who spoke through the prophets . . ."[61] The triumph of the Nicene Creed and its theology was, in no small part, the triumph of Athanasius of Alexandria, who had spent his life explaining, defending, and laboring for the Nicene theology.

61. Kelly, *Early Christian Creeds*, 298.

—— 12 ——

Conclusion

A thanasius was bishop or patriarch of Alexandria for nearly half a century—forty-six years, to be exact. His episcopacy was incredibly productive from the standpoint of his influence and leadership in church and society. His prodigious literary output bequeathed the Christian church a wonderful legacy of theological and pastoral reflection. Athanasius's exemplary service and theological acumen are all the more amazing when one recalls that more than seventeen years of his episcopate were spent in exile.

Regarding his personal character, we have found him to be a person of deep faith, stubborn and intransigent when it came to diverting from the truth (as he saw it). He seemed incapable of compromise, whereas lesser men and women all too willingly compromised theological clarity in order to save their ecclesiastical positions—if not also their lives. His willingness to speak truth to power, even to the Roman emperor, evidenced that same divine greatness that came to fruition in the Old Testament prophets. There was a passion for truth and a holy determination in him that allowed him to reach above what was then normally anticipated from a person of his race and station to rise to true greatness in terms of service and leadership. Deeply nurtured by his lifelong study of the Scriptures, Athanasius became an expert commentator and expounder of the Holy Book. His facility in biblical interpretation was evidenced as clearly in his polemical *Orations Against the Arians* as it was in his pastoral *Festal Letters* and *Letter to Marcellinus.* He was a man who loved the vistas provided by the Word of God and effectively communicated that luminous vision to others.

Someone has said that the impact of our work can sometimes be judged by the loyalty of our opposition, and to some degree that seems true of Athanasius. He had very able and dedicated opponents who seemed determined to stop at nothing to silence and remove him, and perhaps eventually cause his death. They vilified him with charges and counter-charges that ranged from the absolutely incredible (such as murder and sorcery) to plausible outbreaks of violence leading to sacrilege. Were their charges against him based in fact? We have difficulty in knowing for certain from the distance of so many years. We do know that charges of abusing his authority and countenancing violence were so widely whispered that they were even reported by the secular Roman historian Ammianus Mar-cellinus. Yet, the historical judgment of Adolf von Harnack seems more balanced than some of Athanasius's critics (be they classical or contem-porary): "If we measure him by the standards of his time, we can discern nothing ignoble or weak about him."[1] We also know that within a decade of his death, Athanasius had already earned the epithet "great"—bestowed by Gregory Nazianzen.

We have spoken of Athanasius's theological triumph over the various other theologies of the fourth century as the victory of the Nicene Creed and its theology. And that has been a convenient way of summarizing his complicated theological perspective. We have read aspects of his theology, piecemeal, as we marched through the chronology of Athanasius's life and works. While this is not the place to mount a full-scale summary of his remarkable theology,[2] it is time to ask the more foundational question: "So what?" What difference does all this really make for the twenty-first-century Christian?

Like many contemporary readers, Athanasius sought to make serious and concerted reply to Jesus's questions from the synoptic tradition: "Who do people say that I am? . . . Who do you say that I am?" (Mark 8:27, 29). This remains one of the central questions, if not *the* central question, of Christian faith. And by insisting upon the full humanity and full divinity of Jesus Christ, Athanasius urged that the Second Person of the holy Trin-ity was made soteriologically accessible to humanity through the mystery of the Incarnation. His dictum that Christ "became what we are to make us what He is" remains as an exemplary statement of the rationale for the Incarnation. Indeed, it remains difficult to reflect fruitfully upon the In-carnation of Christ without wittingly or unwittingly reflecting Athanasius's earlier discourses upon the subject.

1. Harnack, *History of Dogma*, 3:62.

2. For readable and helpful summaries of Athanasius's theological vision, see the fol-lowing works: Anatolios, *Athanasius: The Coherence of His Thought*; McGill, *Suffering: A Test of Theological Method*; Pelikan, *The Light of the World*; and Weinandy, *Athanasius: A Theological Introduction*.

Athanasius realized that the theological struggle of the fourth century, which was largely played out and described as a controversy over Arianism, was really about the fundamental nature of the Christian God. He recognized that Arius's *Thalia*—for all its supposed elegance and "singability"—was really an ode to an alien God. Where Arius's God was viewed from the standpoint of Divine power and dominion over all things, Athanasius realized that the uniqueness of the Christian understanding of God was based on Divine self-giving and bestowal of Oneself upon others. The Christian God that Athanasius has bequeathed to us is a God who dwells in communion—a Trinitarian communion of Father, Son, and Holy Spirit. This is also a God who takes expression in an incarnational communion with human beings through the sending of God's Son into the world (John 3:16). His is a God who takes upon Himself weakness and suffering to alleviate sin and suffering in the world. In order to reconcile God and humanity, this means that, in the phraseology of the Nicene Creed, the Son must also be "very God of very God" and truly human. Hence, describing the relationship between the Father and the Son became a question of paramount importance, because that description added tremendous shape and texture to our understanding of the Divine nature as well as God's redemptive involvement with the world. Hence, the soteriological and incarnational vision that he had established in his early work *On the Incarnation of the Word of God* formed the foundation of his later thought, and it remained constant throughout his life work. Even in his polemical anti-Arian writings Athanasius linked the Incarnation of the Word and the redemption of humanity with inseparable bonds.

To use the philosophical language of Alexandria, Arius's God is more of a "monad" than a "triad"; his is a case of radical monotheism, which did not allow for the full deity of the Son of God and made little or no mention of the Divine Spirit. As One created by the Father, before all time (Prov 8:22), Arius's Christ is a demigod, at best, and a creature at least. This fact completely changes the relationship between the Father and the Son, from one of mutuality and shared Divine identity to one of hierarchy, dominion and power. If the Father is greater than and different from the Son and sends the Son into the world, then it is not the same as God coming Himself; it is more like God sending someone else to do God's work in the world. This is not a depiction of the Self-sending God of the New Testament. And this completely misunderstands, in Athanasius's view, the true nature and the unique identity of the Christian God.

In Athanasius's view, his fourth-century opponents also completely misunderstood the human dilemma and its Divine solution. The human dilemma is sin and disobedience, and so humanity needs a Savior, and not merely a Teacher or an Example to follow. This Savior, as Athanasius said powerfully, must share the bodily nature that we bear in order to be an adequate substitute for us on the cross of death. In dying for us, the Son covered our sin and destroyed our death. This was God's own doing; it was a painful, suffering-filled Divine solution to the problem faced by our race and our world. It was only as the God-Man that Jesus Christ could be the saving substitute for sinful humanity. "The Word became flesh and dwelt among us" (John 1:14)—this means that in misunderstanding both God and Christ, Athanasius's fourth-century opponents also misunderstood Christian salvation. For them salvation meant leading a moral life, being committed to God as Jesus Christ was. One's salvation was both learned and earned. But for Athanasius the key to Christian salvation was that "He became what we are to make us what He is." By faith and by the work of the Holy Spirit, Christ not only covers human sin but also recovers the Divine Image (Gen 1:26) in which all humans were created. Hence, God becomes incarnate to transform Christians and allow them to become "partakers of the Divine nature" (2 Pet 1:4). Salvation is more than moral behavior; it is even more than having one's sins covered by saving faith in Christ and His cross; salvation is nothing less than having the Divine nature (image of God) restored within humans, so that we are "in Christ" and "Christ is in us," and we become "new creatures" (2 Cor 5:17) from the inside out.

Athanasius's reflections on the nature and person of the Holy Spirit were also integral to this process. These were reported in his *Letters to Serapion* and drew the Person of the Holy Spirit fruitfully into the theological conversations of the fourth-century church. In his insistence upon the full Deity, full equality, and full eternality of the Holy Spirit—along with the Father and the Son—he both prefigured and paved the way for the Trinitarian theology of the Council of Constantinople (381), which added the "Holy Spirit" clause to the Nicene Creed.

It was this Trinitarian vision of God, this incarnational, self-giving understanding of the Object of Christian faith, and the Incarnation of the God-Man, as well as this transformational understanding of Christian salvation, that Athanasius was fighting for in the fourth century. And it is my humble opinion that we should thank God for his persistence and perseverance in lauding this brilliantly biblical theological vision. By holding

forth this Trinitarian, incarnational, Self-giving, transformational understanding of Christian faith, Athanasius established a theological legacy that
was crucial in the fourth century and remains pertinent even down into our
own times. For this reason, I join Gregory Nazianzen in calling Athanasius
"great"—and I hope my readers will join him as well.

Bibliography

Ammianus Marcellinus. *The Later Roman Empire (A.D. 354–378)*. Selected and translated by Walter Hamilton. New York: Penguin, 1986.

Anatolios, Khaled. *Athanasius*. London: Routledge, 2004.

———. *Athanasius: The Coherence of His Thought*. London: Routledge, 1998.

———. *Retrieving Nicaea: The Development and Meaning of Trinitarian Doctrine*. Grand Rapids: Baker Academic, 2011.

Arnold, Duane W. H. *The Early Episcopal Career of Athanasius of Alexandria*. Notre Dame: University of Notre Dame Press, 1991.

Ayres, Lewis. *Nicaea and Its Legacy: An Approach to Fourth-Century Trinitarian Theology*. Oxford: Oxford University Press, 2004.

Barnes, Timothy D. *Athanasius and Constantius: Theology and Politics in the Constantinian Empire*. Cambridge, MA: Harvard University Press, 1993.

Behr, John. *The Formation of Christian Theology*. Vol. 2, *The Nicene Faith*. Crestwood, NY: St. Vladimir's Seminary Press, 2004.

Bell, H. Idris. *Jews and Christians in Egypt: Jewish Troubles in Alexandria and the Athanasian Controversy*. London: The British Museum, 1924.

Chesnut, Glenn F. *The First Christian Histories: Eusebius, Socrates, Sozomen, Theodoret, and Evagrius*. 2nd ed. Macon, GA: Mercer University Press, 1986.

Edwards, Mark. *Catholicity and Heresy in the Early Church*. Farnham, UK: Ashgate, 2009.

Epiphanius. *The Panarion of Epiphanius of Salamis, Books II and III; De Fide*. Translated by Frank Williams. 2nd ed. Leiden: Brill, 2013.

———. *The Panarion of St. Epiphanius, Bishop of Salamis: Selected Passages*. Translated and edited by Philip R. Amidon. New York: Oxford University Press, 1990.

Ernest, James D. *The Bible in Athanasius of Alexandria*. Leiden: Brill, 2004.

Frend, W. H. C. *The Rise of Christianity*. Philadelphia: Fortress, 1984.

Gemeinhardt, Peter, ed. *Athanasius Handbuch*. Tübingen: Mohr Siebeck, 2011.

González, Justo. *The Story of Christianity*. Vol. 1, *The Early Church to the Dawn of the Reformation*. 2nd ed. New York: HarperOne, 2010.

Gregg, Robert C., ed. *Arianism: Historical and Theological Reassessments; Papers from the Ninth International Conference on Patristic Studies, September 5–10, 1983, Oxford, England*. Cambridge, MA: Philadelphia Patristic Foundation, 1985.

———, trans. *The Life of Antony and the Letter to Marcellinus*. New York: Paulist, 1980.

Gregg, Robert C., and Dennis E. Groh. *Early Arianism: A View of Salvation*. Philadelphia: Fortress, 1981.

Grillmeier, Alois. *Christ in Christian Tradition*. Vol. 1, *From the Apostolic Age to Chalcedon (451)*. Translated by John Bowden. Atlanta: John Knox, 1975.

Gwatkin, Henry Melvill. *Studies of Arianism: Chiefly Referring to the Character and Chronology of the Reaction which Followed the Council of Nicaea*. Cambridge: D. Bell, 1882.

Gwynn, David M. *Athanasius of Alexandria: Bishop, Theologian, Ascetic, Father*. Oxford: Oxford University Press, 2012.

———. *The Eusebians: The Polemic of Athanasius of Alexandria and the Construction of the "Arian Controversy"*. Oxford: Oxford University Press, 2007.

Hall, Stuart G. *Doctrine and Practice in the Early Church*. Grand Rapids: Eerdmans, 1991.

Hanson, R. P. C. *The Search for the Christian Doctrine of God: The Arian Controversy, 318–381*. Grand Rapids: Baker Academic, 2005.

Harnack, Adolf von. *The History of Dogma*. Vol. 3. Edinburgh: Williams and Norgate, 1898. Kindle edition.

Hess, Hamilton. *The Canons of the Council of Sardica, A.D. 343: A Landmark in the Early Development of Canon Law*. Oxford: Oxford University Press, 1950.

Kannengiesser, Charles. *Arius and Athanasius: Two Alexandrian Theologians*. Aldershot, UK: Variorum, 1991.

Kelly, J. N. D. *Early Christian Creeds*. 3rd ed. New York: D. McKay, 1972.

———. *Early Christian Doctrines*. Rev. ed. San Francisco: Harper, 1978.

Kidd, B. J. *A History of the Church to A.D. 461*. 3 vols. Oxford: Claredon, 1922.

Kopecek, Thomas A. *A History of Neo-Arianism*. Cambridge, MA: Philadelphia Patristic Foundation, 1979.

Leithart, Peter. *Athanasius*. Grand Rapids: Baker Academic, 2011.

Lössl, Josef. *The Early Church: History and Memory*. London: T. & T. Clark, 2010.

Luibhéid, Colm. "The Arianism of Eusebius of Caesarea." *Irish Theological Quarterly* 43 (1976) 3–23.

———. *Eusebius of Caesarea and the Arian Crisis*. Dublin: Irish Academic Press, 1981.

MacCulloch, Diarmaid. *Christianity: The First Three Thousand Years*. New York: Penguin, 2008.

McGill, Arthur C. *Suffering: A Test of Theological Method*. Philadelphia: Westminster, 1982.

Molloy, Michael. *Champion of Truth: The Life of Saint Athanasius*. New York: Alba House, 2003.

Newman, John Henry. *The Arians of the Fourth Century*. New ed. Introduction and notes by Rowan Williams. Notre Dame: University of Notre Dame Press, 2001.

Nordberg, Henric. *Athanasius and the Emperor*. Commentationes humanarum litterarum. Helsinki: n.p., 1963.

Norris, Richard A., trans. and ed. *The Christological Controversy*. Philadelphia: Fortress, 1980.

Payne, Robert. *The Holy Fire: The Story of the Early Centuries of the Christian Church in the Near East*. Crestwood, NY: St. Vladimir's Seminary Press, 1980.

Pelikan, Jaroslav. *The Christian Tradition: A History of the Development of Doctrine*. Vol. 1, *The Emergence of the Catholic Tradition (100–600)*. Chicago: University of Chicago Press, 1971.

———. *The Light of the World: A Basic Image in Early Christian Thought*. New York: Harper, 1964.

Pettersen, Alvyn. *Athanasius*. Harrisburg, PA: Morehouse, 1995.

Philostorgius. *Philostorgius: Church History*. Translated by Philip R. Amidon. Atlanta: Society of Biblical Literature, 2007.

Plutarch. *The Age of Alexander: Nine Greek Lives*. Translated and annotated by Ian Scott-Kilvert. Harmondsworth: Penguin, 1973.

Prestige, G. L. *Fathers and Heretics: Six Studies in Dogmatic Faith with Prologue and Epilogue*. London: SPCK, 1984.

Quasten, Johannes. *Patrology*. 4 vols. Westminster, MD: Newman, 1950–86.

Ruether, Rosemary Radford. *Gregory of Nazianzus, Rhetor and Philosopher*. Oxford: Claredon, 1969.

Rufinus of Aquileia. *The Church History of Rufinus of Aquileia, Books 10 and 11*. Translated by Philip R. Amidon. New York: Oxford University Press, 1997.

Rusch, William G., trans. and ed. *The Trinitarian Controversy*. Sources of Early Christian Thought. Philadelphia: Fortress, 1980.

Russell, Norman. *The Doctrine of Deification in the Greek Patristic Tradition*. Oxford: Oxford University Press, 2009.

Schaff, Philip, and Henry Wace, eds. *A Select Library of Nicene and Post-Nicene Fathers of the Christian Church*. Series 2. 14 vols. Reprint, Grand Rapids: Eerdmans, 1978–79.

Shapland, C. R. B., trans. *The Letters of Saint Athanasius Concerning the Holy Spirit*. New York: Philosophical Library, 1951.

Stead, G. C. "Athanasius' Earliest Written Work." *Journal of Theological Studies* 39 (1988) 76–91.

———. "The Thalia of Arius and the Testimony of Athanasius." *Journal of Theological Studies*, n.s., 29 (1978) 20–52.

Stevenson, J., ed. *Creeds, Councils and Controversies: Documents Illustrative of the History of the Church A.D. 337–461*. London: SPCK, 1972.

———, ed. *A New Eusebius: Documents Illustrative of the History of the Church to A.D. 337*. London: SPCK, 1957.

Vaggione, Richard Paul. *Eunomius of Cyzicus and the Nicene Revolution*. Oxford: Oxford University Press, 2000.

Wallace-Hadrill, D. S. *Eusebius of Caesarea*. London: A. R. Mowbray, 1960.

Weinandy, Thomas G. *Athanasius: A Theological Introduction*. Aldershot, UK: Ashgate, 2007.

Wickham, Lionel R., ed. *Hilary of Poitiers: Conflicts of Conscience and Law in the Fourth-Century Church*. Liverpool: Liverpool University Press, 1997.

Wiles, Maurice. *Archetypical Heresy: Arianism Through the Centuries*. Oxford: Oxford University Press, 1996.

Williams, Rowan. "Arius and the Meletian Schism." *Journal of Theological Studies* 37 (1986) 35–52.

———. *Arius: Heresy and Tradition*. Rev. ed. Grand Rapids: Eedrmans, 2001.

———. "The Logic of Arius." *Journal of Theological Studies* 34 (1983) 56–81.

Young, Frances M., and Andrew Teal. *From Nicaea to Chalcedon: A Guide to the Literature and Its Background*. 2nd ed. Grand Rapids: Baker Academic, 2010.

Index